THE BIG 50

NEW YORK GIANTS

The Men and Moments That Made
the New York Giants

Patricia Traina

TRIUMPH
BOOKS

Library of Congress Cataloging-in-Publication Data available upon request

This book is available in quantity at special discounts for your group or organization. For further information, contact:

Triumph Books LLC
814 North Franklin Street
Chicago, Illinois 60610
(312) 337-0747
www.triumphbooks.com

Printed in U.S.A.
ISBN: 978-1-62937-621-9

Design by Andy Hansen
All photos courtesy of AP Images unless otherwise indicated.

*To my dad, Al, for introducing
me to Giants football.*

[Contents]

[Foreword]

I had the privilege, for 35 years, of working for three of the most historic franchises in the National Football League: the Baltimore Colts, the Cleveland Browns, and the New York Football Giants.

I'm grateful for every moment I spent in the employ of these franchises, but I have to admit, I saved the best for last.

The first thing that struck me when I joined the Giants organization in 1994 was the awe I felt working for a family that had founded the franchise in 1925. Since those early years, that family's "family" has grown to include players, coaches, and employees that have brought 95 years of honor to the NFL, the most successful of all professional sports leagues.

Long before George Young, who became the first of four general managers this team has employed since 1979 (the others being myself, Jerry Reese, and Dave Gettleman), the seeds of leadership and professionalism were planted by Tim Mara, the father of Wellington and Jack Mara.

Under the Mara family's guidance, the Giants quickly ascended to the top level of the National Football League, battling for championships in their first five decades of existence with class and integrity. That commitment to excellence continued in the 1990s when the Tisch family was welcomed into the fold.

When I became the general manager, I would often tell our newer staff members—many of whom were in their first NFL jobs—that, "As you advance in your NFL careers, and perhaps even move to other organizations to fulfill your ambitions, you will never work for another club like the New York Giants."

I've had the privilege of working with just a few of the Hall of Fame owners, players, and coaches who have walked these halls of tradition. But for me, the most potent element of this franchise is the sense if you work here, you *are* part of a family. That's why regardless of what decisions I had to make as general manager, my first thought always went to whether what I was about to do would bring honor to the Mara and Tisch families.

Over the years, there have been scores of players who epitomized the very essence of what it means to be a Giant. They are tough, smart, professional, and dedicated young men who have put their unique stamp on the organization by giving all they have. In doing so, they have helped to create the memories and events this book covers.

Wellington Mara had a doctrine which he stood by time and again when it came to the extended family that his father first founded in 1925 and which today has grown to thousands of members: "Once a Giant, always a Giant."

That is why when I was inducted into the club's Ring of Honor in 2016, I said in my acceptance speech, "I want to thank the Good Lord for making me a New York Giant."

—Ernie Accorsi
Giants assistant general manager, 1994–97
Giants general manager, 1998–2006

[Author's Note]

I wasn't supposed to be interested in football.

That's the message I was given in high school when I asked the faculty advisor of our newspaper if I could cover the football team.

Not knowing any better at the time, I went along with the teacher's recommendation to cover the arts, despite my protests that I couldn't paint my way into a corner nor act with any conviction.

But I refused to give up my dream of being a sportswriter. In my spare time, I would spend hours filling a notebook with articles that I researched using the newspapers at home. Then, when I got my first computer, I used to fill up many 5¼-inch floppy disks with my musings, disks that I wish still existed, as it would be fun to go back and see what a teenaged me had to say.

It took several more years before I would get a break and come close to fulfilling my dream of being a pro football writer. One of my earliest assignments was for a now-defunct fan newspaper, *Giants Extra* for whom I wrote a weekly column called "The Sideline Spectator."

While I didn't get any money, I did gain experience and learned about being a responsible reporter. While my dad tried to teach me the game, it wasn't until an old-school journalist by the name of Howard Livingston (no, not the same Howard Livingston who played fullback for the Giants franchise from 1944 to 47) taught me how much more there was to the game than regurgitating what one saw on television and read in the papers.

Doc Livingston, a literature professor at Pace University who was able to combine his love of teaching with the ability to cover Giants training camps, taught me the importance of learning about the history behind the game. That history, he reasoned, would provide the foundation for future articles and analysis, and would hopefully lend itself to a unique, even-keeled, and objective style of reporting that has been slowly fading in the industry.

The philosophies of my dad and Doc Livingston have helped me achieve a career as a paid freelance football writer. To this day, I approach each assignment with a commitment to doing additional research so that I can present the facts as accurately as possible and let my readers draw their conclusions.

That is the very same approach I have taken with this book. After I finished writing each chapter, I asked myself if I had done enough to bring the men and moments of the Giants organization to life, and if I had done them the justice their stories deserve?

I struggled initially on what to include and what to omit, as the Giants franchise is one about which volumes can be written. I also struggled with prioritizing the importance of the events and chapters devoted to the individuals selected for this book because, in my mind, *everyone* made some impact that shaped the Giants organization into what it is today, and many events set the stage for others.

In the end, I attempted to blend a mix of old and new, while also lending my insight on the subjects, gleaned from having covered many of the franchise's men and moments over the last 20-plus seasons and seeking from the men involved new stories and angles that weren't as widely reported.

It's my hope that I have created an engaging book that resonates with Giants fans of all ages and which shows my appreciation for the maturation of one of the flagship franchises of the National Football League, one which promises its loyal fan base many more memorable men and moments to come.

THE BIG 50

NEW YORK GIANTS

1

THE BIRTH OF THE GIANTS

Imagine being granted a charter to own a professional sports franchise for the low, low price of $500.

That investment—approximately $7,500 by today's inflation rates—was made by Timothy James Mara, a thriving bookmaker from New York. In return for his money, Mara was granted ownership of the New York Football Giants, today one of the oldest NFL franchises with an estimated 2018 worth of more than $3.3 billion, according to *Forbes*.

Born July 29, 1887, in New York's Lower East Side into an Irish-American household, Mara quickly earned a reputation for being a hard-working, loyal, and honest man with a friendly personality.

He dropped out of school at the age of 13 after the death of his father and sought to earn his keep to help support his widowed mother by taking on jobs as an usher in a theater, as a concession vendor at Madison Square Garden, and as a newspaper-delivery person.

It was through his work with newspapers that Mara found a doorway into the bookmaking business, which at the time was legal. Mara first began as a runner for bookies, in which he would earn 5 percent of the bets he collected. When he turned 18, he branched out into his own business.

Ironically, Mara wasn't the first choice to head a potential New York-based football franchise. NFL President Joe Carr initially approached Billy Gibson, a boxing promoter and manager whose clientele consisted of one-time lightweight champion Benny Leonard, heavyweight champion Gene Tunney, and featherweight Louis Kaplan.

In addition to his business dealings in boxing, Gibson had been one of the owners of the New York Brickley Giants (named for Charles Brickley, a coach on the team).

However, that franchise, which took its nickname from the baseball Giants (today's San Francisco Giants), struggled to take root. Founded in 1919, Brickley's Giants didn't take the field until 1921, playing in just two games that season (both shutout losses to the Buffalo All-Americans and the Cleveland Tigers.

With the franchise having floundered and the team's ownership having endured significant financial losses, it's little wonder that Gibson was reluctant to venture into another chance at owning an NFL franchise.

When Carr offered him that opportunity, Gibson declined. However, he suggested that Carr reach out to Mara to see if perhaps he might be interested in the offer.

Mara, meanwhile, had been contemplating investing in Tunney's boxing career. After meeting with Carr, Mara was said to have jumped at the opportunity to invest in a football franchise, reportedly exclaiming, "Any franchise in New York ought to be worth $500."

(Mara's initial investment was, according to some versions of the franchise's history, actually believed to be closer to $2,500, the extra $2,000 to cover league fees and guarantees.)

And so came the birth of the New York Football Giants, which, other than for its nickname, was a completely separate entity from the defunct Brickley Giants.

Bursting with excitement to hit the ground running in his quest to give the New York area a pro football team of which it would not only be proud but also embrace, there was just one problem.

Mara didn't have a football background and didn't have the first idea of how to run a franchise.

However, two participants in Mara's meeting with Carr—Gibson and Dr. Harry March—did have a football background. As a result, Mara hired both to be the team's president and secretary, respectively.

One of March's first moves was to hire Bob Folwell, whose previous position had been as the head coach at the United States Naval Academy, to become the new franchise's head coach. A one-time halfback who played his college ball at Penn during the 1904–07 seasons, Folwell had an impressive head coaching background in the college ranks, which also included stops at Lafayette, Washington & Jefferson, and Penn.

Meanwhile, Mara rented the Polo Grounds to serve as the team's home stadium, while March put together an aggressive personnel strategy aimed at acquiring the best talent he could find.

Among those he recruited were fullback Jack McBride, a first-team All-Pro; offensive lineman Joseph "Doc" Alexander; Bill Rooney; Joe Williams; Matt Brennan; and Hinkey Haines.

The marquee player of the group, however, was the legendary Jim Thorpe. Thorpe and the Giants agreed that he would play on a part-time basis, at least until he got back in shape, but unfortunately, his Giants career was short-lived.

Despite what looked like solid talent on paper, the Giants struggled to draw a crowd, their primary competition being college football. It certainly didn't help that they were shut out in their debut game on October 11, against the Providence Steam Rollers, 14–0, a loss that cast doubt over the pro game's quality.

With Thorpe's contributions waning, any early interest the public might have had begun to wane quickly.

Although the Giants kept fighting to establish its niche in the hearts of sports fans—they wrapped up their first season with an impressive 8–4 record, tied, with two other clubs (the Detroit Panthers and Green Bay Packers) for the most wins in the 20-team NFL—the inability to draw crowds resulted in Mara losing approximately $40,000 in that first season.

Not one to be deterred by a bump in the road, Mara and March attempted to recruit one of the biggest names in the game, halfback Harold "Red" Grange, to save the floundering Giants. Unfortunately, Grange had already committed to playing with the Chicago Bears.

Established in 1925 by Tim Mara, the Giants are one of three NFL franchises (Cleveland Browns and Green Bay Packers being the others) to keep the same team nickname and city throughout its history. (Giants artifact from the Legacy Club in MetLife Stadium)

Still desperate to draw a crowd, and believing that Grange would do the trick, March arranged for the Giants to host the Bears and Grange at the Polo Grounds on December 6, 1925.

The idea worked, netting Mara a reported $143,000 in profit as more than 65,000 people purchased tickets to see Grange.

The Giants went on to lose that game 19–7, as Grange recorded a 35-yard touchdown return on an interception while also contributing 53 rushing yards on 11 carries, catching a 23-yard pass, and completing two of three pass attempts for 32 yards.

Although Mara and his Giants appeared to be trending upward, their attempt to take root wouldn't come without its challenges.

The following year, Grange and his agent, C.C. Pyle, petitioned the NFL for a second franchise after successfully acquiring an option on Yankee Stadium. This didn't sit well with Mara, whose position, like his NFL contemporaries was that a franchise was worthless if it didn't include a certain degree of territorial rights.

THE SUN ALWAYS SHINES ON THE GIANTS

Throughout the Giants history at various stadiums they've called home, there has been one constant the team has insisted on having: their bench being on the sunny side of the field.

The reason dates back to the franchise's infancy, when a nine-year-old Wellington Mara used to take his seat to watch games from the team's bench.

During one of the franchise's earliest games, young Wellington had a head cold on a day in which the weather wasn't particularly favorable, which caused his mother, Lizette, who used to watch the action from the stands, to worry.

After that game, Lizette Mara, who had noticed that the Giants team bench was on the shady side of the field, convinced her husband, Tim, to move the bench to the sunny side, where it would be warmer for the players, coaches, and her two sons, Jack and Wellington.

As for Wellington Mara, he remained a fixture on the sideline until 1951, before finally deciding it was time for him to move upstairs to watch the games.

Although Mara moved upstairs, the Giants bench continued to reside on the sunny side of the field in their home stadiums throughout the years.

Grange and Pyle, who had tried unsuccessfully to acquire a share of ownership in the Chicago Bears, formed a new nine-team league to compete with the NFL, the original American Football League (AFL). Grange went on to star for the New York Yankees franchise of the AFL.

They also tried to hurt Mara and the Giants by pilfering their personnel for the new league.

To thwart those attempts, Mara increased the salaries of his remaining players by $50 per game and signed many of them to full-season contracts despite a projected estimated loss of around $60,000.

In the end, both the Giants and AFL lost money, the AFL folding after one season. The Giants recorded three straight winning campaigns in their first three seasons, including an 11–1–1 record in 1927 for their first-ever league championship.

As a show of good faith following the AFL's folding, Mara convinced the rest of the NFL to accept the Yankees into the league, but only if Mara were allowed to control the schedule of home and away games for each club to avoid either infringing on each other's potential to maximize its revenue.

Eventually, Mara acquired ownership of the Yankees and the Detroit Wolverines, the latter of whose star player was quarterback Benny Friedman, a player Mara coveted for the Giants.

By 1930, Mara, who had been learning about football on the fly after initially saying he didn't know much about running a football team, decided to give his two sons, Jack and Wellington, more administrative responsibilities.

Before doing so, Tim Mara, who died in 1959, had established what he believed would be the winning formula for the franchise to sustain its success.

"Getting a winner, or building a winner, isn't easy," he once said. "It requires experience in the front office, long-range planning, shrewd promotion, careful appraisal of costs, and luck."

It would be that very same formula the Giants would deploy throughout their nearly century-long history.

2

THE DUKE

"I'll tell you what you can expect from an Irishman named Wellington whose father was a bookmaker. You can expect that anything he says or writes may be repeated, aloud, in your own home, in front of your children. You can believe that he was taught to love and respect all mankind but to fear no man. And you can believe that his two abiding ambitions are that he passes on to his family the true richness of the inheritance he received from his father, the bookmaker, the knowledge and love and fear of God; and second, to give you [the fans]... a Super Bowl winner."

—Wellington T. Mara, circa 1971

Such was the response of Wellington Timothy Mara, the youngest son of Giants founder Tim Mara, to a snarky journalist who questioned the team's decision to move its games from New York to New Jersey.

Mara's rebuttal, delivered during one of the numerous benefit luncheons at which he was a regular participant, wasn't just a series of carefully crafted words. They came from the heart and embodied all that Mara practiced throughout his 89 years of life.

They also represented the values that he instilled in his 11 children, including his oldest, John, the team's current president and CEO.

Mara was indeed a rare breed—a businessman who believed that another person's word and handshake were just as good if not better than a signed contract, and who treated his employees and his customers—the Giants season ticket holders—like family.

Unlike most businesspeople, who were only in the game for the profits, Mara often looked beyond short-term gains to the bigger picture. Thanks to his influence over the years, the NFL would go on to experience revenue sharing and other programs aimed at strengthening its roots.

Wellington Mara's earliest exposure to the Giants began in 1925 when he served as a ball boy for the team in its first season. Five years later, his father gave Wellington, then 14, and his older brother, Jack increased responsibility in running the franchise.

While Jack took care of the business side of the house, Wellington, along with his mother, Lizette, took care of the people side of operations, including the players and the customers.

As Wellington grew older, he took on more and more responsibility. He started as an assistant to his father in 1937. After his graduation from Fordham University he took on bigger roles, including becoming the team's secretary in 1940. In 1965, after his brother's death, Mara became the team president, fully responsible for, among other things, player personnel.

* * *

In the Giants' early years, there was no internet where people could instantly pull up scouting reports or game film on players. Scouting trips, if done at all, weren't nearly as comprehensive as they are today.

Wellington Mara's approach to scouting involved immersing himself in volumes upon volumes of out-of-town newspapers and creating notes and files on both professional and college players he thought would fit the Giants franchise.

In 1932, Wellington suggested his father add college prospects to replace some of the aging talent already on the roster. The elder Mara, who wasn't as well-versed in football as his son, followed Wellington's advice by adding prospects such as quarterback Harry Newman form the University of Michigan and halfback Ken Strong.

In 1936, the NFL held its first-ever player selection meeting, more commonly known as the draft. The draft had been put in place in part to help assure teams of the rights to the services of the players selected; as such, those players who were drafted could not stir up bidding wars for their services.

Within the Giants archives are magazines and rudimentary draft guides that still to this day bear pencil markings made by Wellington Mara identifying those players who drew his interest, such as running back/fullback Alphonse "Tuffy" Leemans, a future Hall of Famer chosen in the second round of the 1936 draft out of George Washington.

Wellington Mara's earliest video camera, used to help the coaches with shooting film during the team's earliest years. (Artifact shown is from the Pro Football Hall of Fame.)

Mara held responsibility for nearly all corners of the franchise's operations. In 1974, due to his growing league obligations taking up larger chunks of his time, he named former star player Andy Robustelli as the team's director of operations.

As much as the man nicknamed "The Duke"—the nickname today is emblazoned onto every official NFL game ball—was all about nurturing his beloved Giants, it was also Mara's selflessness in two critical areas that helped make the NFL into the billion-dollar industry it is today.

The first self-sacrifice Mara made was in 1961, when then-Commissioner Pete Rozelle approached the NFL franchise owners about pooling their television revenues so they could be distributed equally across the league.

Rozelle believed that creating a more balanced financial setting would allow for teams in smaller markets to have an equal chance of success as those teams in larger television markets.

ONE OF THE GUYS

Wellington Mara might have been the boss, but he saw himself as just another one of the guys.

"I spent all my time with the players and coaches. The players used to call me 'Duke' because of my name," Mara said years ago.

"I watched game movies and sat in on team meetings and at that time knew every assignment on the team, offense and defense. I don't have time to do that anymore. And I'm not that close to the players either. They call me 'Mr. Mara' now."

"Mr. Mara" might have been what they called the patriarch out of respect, but for many players, they viewed this kindly old gentleman as so much more.

Take, for instance, former offensive lineman Rich Seubert, an undrafted rookie free agent out of Western Illinois who was hand-selected by then-offensive line coach Jim "Mouse" McNally for an unprecedented meeting with the team's patriarch during a spring 2001 practice.

Seubert chuckled when he remembered that first meeting, recalling his reluctance to engage in conversation with the boss because he didn't know if he would even make the team. So he quickly shook hands with Mara, thanked him for the opportunity, and then hustled back to practice.

When Seubert suffered a horrific compound fracture in his leg during a 2003 game that would cost him two years of his career, imagine his surprise when none other than Wellington Mara became a fixture at his bedside almost every day of Seubert's nearly three-week hospitalization stay.

Seubert recalled just lying there, not saying much to the Hall of Fame owner. But Seubert's silence didn't discourage Mara, who carried the conversation mostly by himself by telling Seubert about what was going

Mara, whose Giants played in the largest media market at the time, didn't think twice about giving his blessing, which resulted in other owners following his lead.

"One of the things that he always preached was that the league is only as strong as its weakest franchise," said John Mara, his oldest son, and the current team president and CEO.

on back in East Rutherford so that he would still be in the loop.

Mara also made sure to provide Seubert's wife, Jodi, with whatever she needed while her husband was hospitalized.

"We were grateful for that, and it was just his company at the hospital in the mornings talking about the Giants week was pretty special," Seubert said.

In looking back, Seubert said he wishes he hadn't been so reluctant to open up around the Giants patriarch and that he had gotten to know him better.

"As an undrafted rookie, the first couple of years, you're afraid to talk to anyone—let alone the owner of the team—because you weren't sure if you are going to be there the next day," Seubert said.

As Seubert's tenure grew with the Giants, he soon came to realize just what the phrase, "Once a Giant, always a Giant" meant.

"The running joke around here," John Mara said, referring to his father's practice of treating every employee like family, "is that employees leave feet first."

But that practice of treating staff and players like family is just part of why Wellington Mara was so revered by all who knew him.

"The Mara family has meant the world to me, and the Giants are the only team I played for, and it was an awesome family to play for," Seubert said.

So great in fact that after moving to California following his retirement after the 2010 season, Wisconsin-born-and-bred Seubert eventually returned to New Jersey because, as he put it, he "missed" his extended Giants family.

"It really is a family," he insisted. "I'll always be a Giant, and my family will always be Giants fans. We're among the biggest fans. It was an honor and a privilege to play for this franchise and Mr. Mara, and I'm glad I got to experience it with the greatest city in front of the greatest fan base."

"That was the motivation behind agreeing to share dollars in revenues equally, and I think that philosophy has certainly paid off for the NFL," Mara added. "It has proven to be the right way to run a professional sports league because everybody is on pretty solid economic footing based on the sharing of television revenues, the largest source of income for all the teams."

Wellington Mara's second act of selflessness occurred in 1966, when the NFL and rival American Football League (AFL) began contemplating a merger.

Mara's Giants were in direct competition geographically with five of the AFL franchises, whose younger, more dynamic rosters seemed ready to make Mara's Giants, a franchise that had seen several of its marquee names retire in the 1960s, an afterthought.

The decision to ultimately merge with the American Football League had its risks. Mara, who believed that the NFL would outlast the rival league, knew that eventually his Giants would rebuild and become competitive again. However, he had his concerns about the other NFL franchises being able to withstand more years of competition by the upstart AFL.

With Mara once again leading the way, the groundwork was put in place for the 1970 NFL-AFL merger.

Even after the merger, Mara's contributions to the growth of the league didn't cease. From 1984 to 2005, he served as president of the National Football Conference. He was also a member of the Hall of Fame and realignment committees and would serve as co-chairman of the long-range planning committee and on the NFL Management Council's executive committee.

Mara was also part of a select group of senior owners who led the NFL Commissioner Search Committee when Rozelle announced his retirement. That committee ultimately recommended Paul Tagliabue, who had previously served as a lawyer for the NFL, as Rozelle's successor.

Of all the contributions made by the bookmaker's son, it was his loyalty—sometimes, some might argue, to a fault—and his insistence of treating his players, staff, and customers as an extended family, that set him apart from his contemporaries.

"He would spend so much of his time responding to letters from fans," John Mara recalled. "What he used to say to me is that if a person cares enough about your team to sit down and compose a letter, they deserve a response, so I've tried to carry on that philosophy."

From little gestures such as providing staff with holiday hams and turkeys to the bigger acts of kindness such as assisting those who suffered major illness or tragedy, Mara's legacy is still felt within the halls of the Quest Diagnostics Training Center, the team's East Rutherford, New Jersey headquarters.

3

I.T.

"L.T."

Say those initials to the scores of quarterbacks who faced the legendary Lawrence Taylor from 1981 to 1993, and don't be surprised if any of them curl up into a ball.

Taylor would become the centerpiece in the Giants 3-4 defense that Bill Parcells, who returned to Ray Perkins' staff after the 1980 season as the Giants defensive coordinator, turned into a force.

Thanks to the New Orleans Saints, who in 1981 declined a trade with the Dallas Cowboys and instead used the No. 1 overall pick on University of South Carolina running back George Rogers, the Giants were able to get the wildly talented defensive lineman turned linebacker out of the University of North Carolina with the No. 2 overall pick in that year's draft.

While L.T. was, well, tailor-made for Giants football, the feeling wasn't mutual, at least not at first.

During his first visit to the Giants team facilities, Taylor, a Dallas Cowboys fan as a youth who favored No. 56 in honor of Cowboys linebacker Thomas "Hollywood" Henderson, was unimpressed by his new team's facilities, housed in the middle of a swampland.

"I couldn't believe how ugly everything looked and smelled," Taylor wrote in his 1987 autobiography *L.T.: Living on the Edge*.

"The stadium itself... was this big blob of cement rising out of a swamp with a lot of roads running around it. Later on, when I finally signed my first contract, I remember looking out the window of the car as I drove away from the stadium thinking, 'I have to be here for six years; somebody's got to be kidding!'"

Meanwhile, some of Taylor's new teammates didn't know quite what to make of this rookie sensation about whom everyone was raving.

"When Lawrence was about to be drafted, we were like, 'Why?'" defensive captain and fellow linebacker Harry Carson remembered.

"We were already a pretty good group of linebackers, and we didn't necessarily feel that we needed another linebacker; we felt like we needed offense."

But, Carson said, all it took was one practice for any questions about why the team wanted Taylor and not an offensive player to be answered.

"We went through our first practice session, and when we saw him in drills, it became pretty clear why they drafted him. You could see it right off the bat how fast he was, how agile he was, how he was able to rush the quarterback, and devise spontaneous moves.

"So yeah, we saw he was a tremendous talent, and quite frankly, Lawrence elevated our play. I mean, we were good, but he just made us so much better."

George Martin, who, like Carson, was a team captain when Taylor arrived on the scene, pointed out that in every social circle, a newbie doesn't necessarily earn his stripes right away.

But Taylor, Martin said, was an exception.

"Lawrence came in for his first day of practice and started on the third string. By lunchtime, he was a starter—that's the truth. I mean, he was a phenom from the very first snap of the ball. This is a guy who played with what they call reckless abandon—he sacrificed his body, and he had one objective, and that was to go out and terrorize the opponent."

Carson, Martin, and some other veterans took the lead in making Taylor feel like part of the family. As the rookie became more comfortable in his new surroundings, opponents would soon realize that the old conventional ways of neutralizing the Giants defense would have to be revamped.

* * *

The mere presence of No. 56 on the field created many sleepless nights for the coaches charged with figuring out how to slow him down, and endless nightmares for the offensive linemen tasked to block him.

Thanks to Taylor, some new methods were devised to slow him down that to this day are still part of the game. Washington head coach Joe Gibbs is credited with designing the two-tight end offense and the H-back position to slow down Taylor.

Another legendary head coach, Bill Walsh of the 49ers, came up with a strategy in which his best offensive line pass blocker, guard John Ayers, would try to block Taylor on passing plays, while the tight end would be asked to anticipate and wait for Taylor's downhill charge on running plays.

No matter what opponents tried to do to Taylor, he somehow managed to steal the show in the defensive meeting room every Monday when the coaches and players reviewed the film from the previous game.

THE ORIGINAL SACK MASTER

In 1981, Lawrence Taylor's consistent harassment of quarterbacks wasn't just inspirational to the legions of fans who would excitedly chant "L.T.! L.T.!" whenever he enforced his will against opponents.

Those "sacks" as they came to be known, would become an official league statistic starting in 1982.

As football enthusiasts know, a sack, by its proper definition, is when a defensive player tackles the quarterback at or behind the line of scrimmage.

But Taylor, credited with 132.5 sacks during his Giants career (second-most in franchise history behind Michael Strahan's 141.5 sacks, though Taylor would have just passed Strahan had his 9.5 uncredited sacks from his rookie season counted) had his own definition.

In *The Blind Side: Evolution of a Game* by Michael Lewis, Taylor once defined a sack as follows:

"A sack is when you run up behind somebody who's not watching, he doesn't see you, and you really put your helmet into him. The ball goes fluttering everywhere, and the coach comes out and asks the quarterback, 'Are you all right?' That's a sack."

Taylor, who had a creative way with words, would go on to say that simply wrapping up the quarterback in a tackle for the sack wasn't good enough as far as he was concerned.

"I don't like to just wrap the quarterback. I really try to make him see seven fingers when they hold up three. I'll drive my helmet into him, or, if I can, I'll bring my arm up over my head and try to axe the sonuvabitch in two. So long as the guy is holding the ball, I intend to hurt him. If I hit the guy right, I'll hit a nerve, and he'll feel electrocuted, he'll forget for a few seconds that he's on a football field."

Ouch!

"Monday was pure magic," remembered former defensive back Beasley Reece, who formed a close bond with Taylor that still exists to this day.

"You'd be sitting there watching film of what L.T. did, and you'd realize the superhuman nature of this guy's ability.

"It was unreal. He threw tight ends around like they were rag dolls. And then he threw tackles—guys that outweighed him by about 50 pounds—out of the way so he could get to the quarterback."

Reece chuckled over one such memory in which Taylor put his freakish athleticism on display during a Thanksgiving Day game against the Detroit Lions in 1982. That day, Taylor, playing with an injured knee, intercepted quarterback Gary Danielson's pass and ran it back 97 yards for the game- winning touchdown.

"This is a 250-, 260-pound linebacker, and I was just a skinny little defensive back who's supposed to be fast, and I took off at the same time as he did," Reece said. "I'm telling you, I never gained an inch on him. I mean, he could fly—as big as he was, he could run, like the wind. And I remember escorting him into the end zone."

Taylor consistently played at a high level, but one of his best seasons was in 1986 when he was named the league's MVP, the first defensive player since 1971 to earn the honors. Taylor finished that season with a career-high 20.5 sacks as he helped lead the Giants to their first-ever Super Bowl championship.

* * *

"There used to be a thing I used to call 'the asshole quotient.' The bigger the asshole you are, the better the player you had to be…. Think of the great players that you've seen around the league who have been just complete jerks. At the end of the day, what was the sum total of their career and their effect on their teams?"

Giants fans may recognize those words as having come from general manager Dave Gettleman at the 2019 NFL Scouting Combine after getting a question about talented players who tended to create unwanted distractions in the locker room.

But there's little doubt that those words also fit what the Giants had with Taylor, who lived his life his way and who sometimes created headaches for the Giants.

Hall of Fame linebacker Lawrence Taylor—better known as "L.T."—not only changed the Giants franchise, he revolutionized the position. (Copyright New York Football Giants)

One of the biggest headaches Taylor created came when he signed a contract with Donald J. Trump's New Jersey Generals to commence in 1988.

The Giants, not wanting to lose their star player to any team, let alone to the rival USFL league, came through with a new contract that would end any business flirtation he had with Trump and keep him in Giants' blue.

Taylor, by his own admissions in his autobiography, dabbled in drugs and alcohol. He wrote that he arranged for teammates to provide him with clean urine samples to pass off as his own.

Linebacker Lawrence Taylor, 1981–1993.
(Giants artifact from the Legacy Club in MetLife Stadium)

In 1987, he was suspended 30 days after testing positive for cocaine; in 1988, he was suspended for failing yet another drug test.

He also staged some contract-related holdouts that irked Giants management.

And in the strike-shortened season of 1987, Taylor was one of the first to cross the picket line, a move that, had it been made by any other player, probably would have resulted in him becoming an outcast among his peers.

No matter what Taylor did off the field, he showed up on game day, more than willing to sacrifice his body.

One of Taylor's most heroic performances came in 1988. Despite dealing with a torn pectoral muscle that necessitated him wearing a harness, he put on a Superman-like effort, recording three sacks, two forced fumbles, and a pass breakup in addition to seven tackles in a 13–12 Giants victory over the New Orleans Saints.

The following year, Taylor suffered what turned out to be a broken bone in his right ankle in the Giants' 34–24 loss to the 49ers at San Francisco. Initially declared out by Parcells leading up to the following week's game against the Eagles, the head coach eventually "upgraded" Taylor's status to "doubtful."

The Giants ended up losing that game 24–17, but Taylor, injury be damned, was out there for his teammates and coaches.

* * *

L.T. was a sack machine, a quarterback's worst nightmare, a guy who liked to live his life on the edge.

But he also had a softer, more sentimental side that, while he kept it suppressed when he was on the field, was still very much a part of who he is as a man.

"The real L.T. is not the tough, mean-guy monster that a lot of fans believed," Reece said. "The real L.T. is a fun, loving guy. I believe if you go back and look at every tackle he ever made, none of them were mean- spirited or violent. When [Washington quarterback] Joe Theismann broke his leg (during a *Monday Night Football* game), L.T. was the one who was freaking out, calling for the doctors and pacing around worrying.

"I think L.T. just got that reputation of being a monster because he was just so big that it looked like he was punishing people. But he really was the most incredible and gifted athlete I've ever stood close to and was incredible to watch," Reece added.

In 1991, the Giants underwent some drastic changes, including the sale of half the team to the Tisch family and the resignation of head coach Bill Parcells.

Also part of that upheaval was the realization that "Superman" was starting to morph into a mere mortal.

Taylor, who had made the Pro Bowl 10 straight seasons, recorded just seven sacks in 14 games, his lowest total since 1982, when the league first began tracking sacks.

The following year, he ruptured his Achilles tendon in a November 8 win over Green Bay, an injury that very well could have spelled the end of his Hall of Fame career. Taylor, however, insisted on leaving the game on his terms.

In 1993, Taylor returned for the start of the season, and would finish his career on the road against the 49ers in the divisional round of the NFC playoffs. In his postgame press conference, not long after the last of the "L.T.! L.T.!" chants faded from the stands at Candlestick Park, Taylor announced his retirement.

"I'm calling it quits," he said, fighting back the tears as he stood on the podium as an active player for one final time.

"I've done everything I can do. I've been to Super Bowls. I've been to playoffs. I've done things that other people haven't been able to do in this game before. I'm happy for the 13 years I put in. But it's time for me to go."

Fittingly, no Giants player would ever wear No. 56 again. In 1999, Taylor was a first-ballot Pro Football Hall of Fame selection. He would also earn a place on the NFL's 75th Anniversary All-Time Team, while forever holding a place in the hearts of Giants fans.

4

SUPER BOWL XXI

The final score, 39–20, is etched on the first of four Vince Lombardi trophies that proudly greet visitors to the Giants' East Rutherford, New Jersey, headquarters.

But that final score didn't even begin to tell the story of how the Giants' first-ever World Championship came about.

The Giants, off a 14–2 record—a franchise record for most wins in a 16-game season which, as of 2019 still stood—would go on to face the Denver Broncos, the holder of an 11–5 regular-season record, in front of a capacity crowd assembled at the Rose Bowl in Pasadena, California.

Giants quarterback Phil Simms, the team's first-round draft pick in 1979, put on a record-setting performance for pass completions (based on at least 15 attempts) by completing 22 of 25 passes (88 percent) for 268 yards, and three touchdowns.

As spectacular as Simms' performance was—and his completion percentage is a record that, as of Super Bowl LIV, still stands—the Giants defense, perhaps a little irked over how national reporters and fans were fawning over Broncos quarterback John Elway, would steal the show.

On the surface, Elway's numbers in that game—22 of 37 for 304 yards, one touchdown, and one interception—aren't horrible.

But what the Giants defense did to Elway and his band of merry men after Denver took a 10–7 lead early in the game, was by far the masterpiece.

"We knew—Lawrence [Taylor], Carl [Banks], George Martin, Jimmy Burt, and I—that we had to push the pocket and get in Elway's face," defensive tackle Leonard Marshall recalled. "We knew that we could not allow him to escape the pocket or be able to get outside the pocket and throw the ball up in the air and hope that one of the guys run up underneath it.

"So, we wanted to harass the hell out of him. We wanted him to be thinking about who's coming. Is it 70 [Marshall]? Is it 56 [Taylor]? Is it 58

[Banks]? Is it 75 [Martin]? I mean, we wanted that guy's head on a swivel looking at us more than looking downfield."

Elway, a stubborn player in his own right, would do his best not to let the Giants see him sweat, particularly on the Broncos' first possession of the second quarter when he marched his team from their 20-yard line to the Giants' 1-yard line.

That's when the Broncos woke the sleeping Giants, and boy, did Denver pay the price.

"Our backs were sort of against the wall, and everybody was looking to make a play," Carson remembered. "The Broncos were prolific and running the ball, but also you had John Elway, who was a deadly passer and who was also not afraid to run the ball. So what we had to do is make sure that we knew exactly where the ball was going."

The Giants defense tracked the ball with laser-like precision. On first-and-goal, Elway tried to run it in himself only to be met with a big bear hug by Taylor, who stopped him for a loss of one yard.

On second-and-goal from the 2-yard line, fullback Gerald Willhite tried to power his way into the end zone, only to be greeted by Carson, who stopped the runner for no gain.

On third-and-goal, running back Sammy Winder, the Broncos' leading rusher that season, tried to cross the plane with no luck, as another Giants linebacker, Carl Banks, who finished with a team-leading 10 tackles in that game, wrapped Winder up for a loss of four yards.

"We were very fortunate to have different guys make plays," Carson said. "We were all jacked up, and you know, taking on their best, and we were able to repel their charge and come away without scoring a touchdown."

Banks remembered Carson and Taylor being "pissed off" that the Broncos had managed to penetrate that deeply into Giants' territory.

"We were pretty prideful defense, and we were pretty ticked off that they were there," Banks recalled. "I don't remember if it was Harry or Lawrence, but one of them said, 'These guys are not going to score a touchdown; we are not going to let them score a touchdown.'

"So the fact that we were already upset that they were down there and that one of our captains tells us we're not letting them score a touchdown, that set the stage."

THE ONE THAT GOT AWAY

For all of Phil McConkey's contributions in the Giants Super Bowl XXI victory—he even found and returned a lost gun lying on the field—there is one play in particular that, to this day, still sticks in the receiver's craw.

It was the second play of the second quarter, a third-and-3 from the Giants 41-yard line, which in the official gamebook is recorded as "Simms pass over middle incomplete to McConkey, falls @ DB45."

Besides being one of Simms' three incomplete passes on the day, McConkey said it still gnaws at him that he didn't make the catch.

"We're on our 40-yard line, and I'm in the slot. And you talk about changing things up—normally in a situation like that, the defense thinks 'Okay, I'm covering McConkey in the slot. He's going to go six yards and curl up, and they're just going to do a quick pass and pick up the first down,'" McConkey said.

But the Giants changed their plans when they saw how the Broncos lined up and had McConkey run a post pattern.

"I came in motion—came up to about six yards. The defense expected me to stop and turn around to try to pick up the first down. I stutter-stepped the defensive back at six or seven yards, and he squatted on me, which means he's coming up because he thinks I'm going to stop there, and then I take off," McConkey said.

At this point in the story, McConkey recalled how, thanks to the changeup, the defender is so out of position that it was almost laughable.

That is until the defender did something unexpected—and unsportsmanlike.

"He sticks out his right leg and catches my leg enough to where I stumble and go to the ground," he recalled. "Now remember, the safeties were split, so there was space the size of the Grand Canyon down the middle of the field.

"Simms threw the ball, and it went incomplete. I was outraged because it should have been a penalty, and it should have been a 60-yard touchdown.

"That sticks with me more than the three successful plays I had," he confessed. "I still like wake up sometimes at night wondering could I have done something more to avoid him tripping me, which is illegal, by the way."

Fortunately for the Giants, the missed tripping call didn't hurt them but given just how much McConkey wanted to be perfect on every play, it's understandable why he'd be upset even if the play had no effect on the outcome.

On that third-down play," Banks continued, "I line up, and I just said to myself, 'This guy's not gonna block me, whether the ball's coming to me or not.' I beat him at the line of scrimmage and tracked the ball down in the backfield."

The Giants defense was just getting warmed up.

On their ensuing possession, which began at their 15, Elway and the Broncos went backward. Marshall sacked Elway on the very first play of that drive for a loss of two—one of Marshall's two sacks that day.

Elway then missed tight end Clarence Kay on a pass over the middle, which brought up third-and-12.

With the Broncos having no choice but to pass, Elway tried to buy time in the pocket only to be met by Martin, who dropped him for a loss of 13 yards and the safety, which narrowed the Broncos' lead to 10–9 at the half.

In the third quarter, the Giants offense started to take over the game, scoring on each of its three possessions.

Simms got things started with a 13-yard touchdown pass to tight end Mark Bavaro to give the Giants a lead which they'd never relinquish.

That drive, which looked as though it would die when the Giants made it to their 46-yard-line only to fall one yard short of receiving a fresh set of downs, was extended thanks to a gamble by head coach Bill Parcells.

On a fourth-and-1 from the Giants' 46-yard line, backup quarterback Jeff Rutledge discretely slipped onto the field, took the snap from center, and pushed his way forward two yards to pick up the first down.

Kicker Raul Allegre converted a 21-yard field goal, the second of the Giants' three scores in the third quarter.

Running back Joe Morris added a one-yard rushing touchdown after a flea-flicker from Simms to McConkey fell one yard short of pay dirt, the score giving the Giants a 26–10 lead.

Most teams might have been feeling good about their chances for a victory at that point, but not Parcells' Giants—and certainly not the defense, which did not let up.

Marshall sacked Elway on the final play of the third quarter for a loss of 11 yards. On the first play of the fourth quarter, cornerback Elvis Patterson picked off Elway's second-and-25 pass intended for receiver Steve Watson and returned it seven yards.

That interception set up one of the most iconic touchdowns of that game, a six-yard touchdown pass from Simms originally intended for Bavaro. The ball hit the big tight end's hands, volleyed into the air, and then landed in the anxious arms of McConkey, an undrafted free agent from the U.S. Naval Academy who endeared himself to his coaches, teammates, and Giants fans with his gritty style of play.

After the Broncos got a 28-yard field goal from kicker Rich Karlis, the Giants basically put the game on ice with a two-yard touchdown run from Ottis Anderson, a player they had acquired via an in-season trade that year.

The Broncos would get a garbage-time touchdown on a 47-yard pass from Elway to receiver Vance Johnson over the middle to make it 39–20.

However, it was too little too late, as the underdog Giants had snatched the victory from the Broncos thanks to a ferocious defensive effort that finished with four sacks and an interception, as well as a record-setting performance from the "other" golden-haired quarterback—Simms—named the game's MVP.

In the postgame locker room, a story made its way around that fittingly was the perfect postscript to a night to remember.

Precisely six months before that glorious night in Pasadena, Parcells, who knew how to challenge his players, issued what, in retrospect, was an all-time classic following a training camp practice.

"This team is not talented enough to just show up and go out there," he said at the time.

Maybe not at that time, but when push came to shove, the players rose to the occasion and saved their best for last.

5

THE GREATEST GAME EVER PLAYED

It was the type of NFL Championship Game that had everything a diehard football fan could want—intrigue, glamor, wall-to-wall action, national attention, and a historical setting (Yankee Stadium).

Well, *almost* everything.

If you happened to be a New York Giants fan, the 1958 Championship Game, more commonly known as "The Greatest Game Ever Played," saw Big Blue end up on the losing side of a 23–17 overtime contest against the Baltimore Colts.

So what was it about this game that made it so "great" given how it ended?

The 1958 Championship Game was arguably the most significant catalyst for propelling professional football to new popularity heights for several reasons.

It was the first-ever pro football game to be televised to a national audience (except for the New York area, where it was blacked out). It was also the first-ever pro football playoff game to go into overtime.

Some historians also believe this was that game that helped push pro football to become the nation's most popular sport—even if the game was rife with errors and controversy.

From a technical standpoint, the game itself resembled more of an exhibition game than a contest between the NFL's two best teams.

The Colts, a 3½ point favorite over the Giants, blew a 14–3 halftime lead. Their kicker, Steve Myhra, missed a 31-yard field goal, only to be granted a do-over thanks to a penalty, the do-over ending up blocked by the Giants.

And between the two teams, there were eight fumbles, six of which were lost, and one interception, that thrown by the Colts legendary quarterback Johnny Unitas.

* * *

Entering the game, the Giants had a 10–3 season record (including a win against Cleveland in the Divisional round) under head coach Jim Lee Howell, and a five-game winning streak.

On December 14, the Giants after their 13–10 win over the Cleveland Browns, with whom they had finished the 1958 season in a tie for the divisional lead at 9–3, would break the tie with the Browns the following week in a 10–0 shutout to win the division crown.

Meanwhile, the Colts of the NFL (not to be confused with the Baltimore Colts of the AAFC/NFL which, per Pro Football Reference,

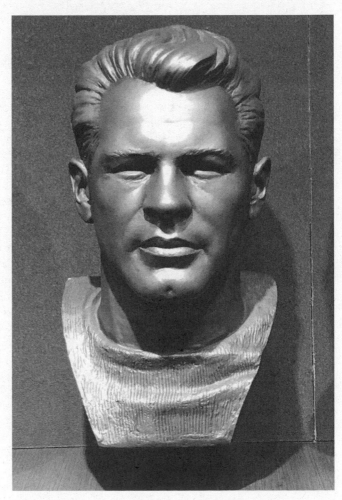

Halfback Frank Gifford, 1952–1960, 1962–64.
(Giants artifact from the Legacy Club in MetLife Stadium)

existed from 1947 to 1950), were coached by the legendary Weeb Ewbank to a 9–3 season that year, their six-game winning streak to start the 1958 season snapped by none other than the Giants, who beat them 24–21 at Yankee Stadium.

It was a loss that stuck in the Colts' craw, according to defensive tackle Art Donovan, who years later in an interview with Tom Barnidge for NFL.com, didn't mince his words.

"In the last minute of the game as the Giants let the clock run out, they were standing across the line of scrimmage, laughing at us. I said,

THE KICK

Had it not been for kicker Pat Summerall, "The Greatest Game Ever Played" might not have materialized.

The kick came on December 14, 1958, on a snowy and bitterly cold day at Yankee Stadium, the site of that season's regular-season finale between the Giants and the Cleveland Browns.

Going into that game, the Browns had a one-game lead over the Giants. With a win, the Browns would eliminate the Giants from postseason consideration.

However, if the Giants, who had beaten the Browns earlier in the year 21–17, won that game, they would tie the Browns for the best season record in the Eastern Conference and force a tiebreaker.

With the weather conditions less than ideal, the Giants and Browns were tied 10–10 in the fourth quarter. With time ticking down, Giants head coach Jim Lee Howell decided to send out Summerall to attempt a 49-yard field goal that, if he converted, would give the Giants the lead and put them in good shape to seal the win.

Summerall, who had missed a field goal attempt placed at the 25-yard line earlier in the game, not only had to kick on a snow-covered turf, he also had to attempt his game-winning kick in low visibility conditions.

With Charlie Conerly holding and Ray Wietecha snapping the ball, Summerall, a straight-ahead kicker, managed to split the uprights to give the Giants a 13–10 win and to force the tiebreaker with Cleveland the following week.

The Giants went on to win the tiebreaker 10–0, thus earning a spot in the league championship the following week in what would become "The Greatest Game Ever Played."

'You rotten bastards,' and I picked up some stones on the field and started throwing them at them. Man, I wanted another shot at them."

Donovan wasn't the only one who wanted revenge against the Giants. In that same interview with Barnidge, defensive end Gino Marchetti revealed the Giants gave the Colts some prime choice bulletin board material that fueled their desire to beat the snot out of New York.

"The Giants were cocky. I remember reading that [Giants quarterback] Charlie Conerly had said after our first game that the Giants 'out gutted' us. That article was on our bulletin board weeks before the Championship Game."

As fate would have it, Donovan and Marchetti and the rest of their teammates would indeed get another shot at the Giants, though this time on a much bigger stage.

* * *

As scores of football fans enjoyed the first-ever broadcast of an NFL playoff game, they certainly got their money's worth.

Nursing a 17–14 fourth-quarter lead, all the Giants needed to do on their final possession of the game was to run out the clock.

The Giants turned to halfback Frank Gifford to help them seal the deal.

On his first two runs, Gifford recorded six yards. But then on third down, with the Giants needing four yards, Gifford came up one yard short on what was perhaps the most controversial call that season.

In his book, *The Glory Game*, Gifford recalled changing the play in the huddle to a sweep called "Brown Right, Over 49 Sweep," a play in which he was to take the ball wide around the right side of the formation and then cut it back hard upfield to pick up the yardage needed.

At first, everything went according to plan. Gifford took the ball, spotted a hole, planted his foot, and turned up the field for the first-down marker.

But after Gifford gained about three of the four yards needed, Marchetti broke free from Giants right tackle Jack Stroud's block and headed directly toward Gifford.

Gifford, determined not to be denied that all-important fourth yard, scratched and clawed his way to get himself into a position to fall forward as Marchetti was pulling him down.

Mission accomplished, he thought.

He was wrong.

Marchetti ended up suffering an ankle injury on the tackle, which stopped the clock. Then, as Gifford recalled, referee Ron Gibbs did something unusual amid the chaos of Marchetti's injury.

"Gibbs had picked up the ball at the end of my run. He held on to it, and he didn't put it back down until all the chaos had subsided, and Gino had been removed from the field. Then they brought out the chains. And it was a couple inches short."

Gifford, clearly unhappy with the spot, let Gibbs know about it, but his argument went nowhere.

With the officials not willing to reconsider, Gifford and his teammates did what they thought was the next best thing: They tried to convince head coach Jim Lee Howell to go for it on fourth down.

But just as Gifford's argument with referee Gibbs went nowhere, so too did his plea with Howell, who ordered the team to punt from their 43-yard line.

The Colts had new life.

Unitas, as he had done in the fourth quarter of the game, marched his team right down the field from his 14-yard line, picking up four first downs on the drive to set up a 20-yard game-tying field goal by Myhra.

With time having expired and the game ending in a tie, both teams seemed uncertain what to do. The officials instructed both benches to send their captains back to midfield for a coin toss for what would become the first-ever overtime period to be played in the postseason.

The Giants won the coin toss and elected to receive. However, their first drive of the sudden-death period was doomed almost from the start.

Don Maynard lost track of the opening kickoff in the lights, and muffed the kickoff, though he did recover it on his 20-yard line.

The Giants offense didn't have much luck either, going three-and-out.

As Unitas, the legendary Colts quarterback, drove the Colts closer to pay dirt, another mini-crisis developed when NBC's broadcast feed cut out, leaving hundreds of thousands of television viewers with blank screens just as the game was entering a critical juncture.

Desperate to get the game back on the air for viewers without missing a single play, officials from NBC begged the game's officials to call a TV timeout, which was granted. Fortunately, NBC's technicians managed to restore the feed just in time for what would be the thrilling conclusion to a wild day.

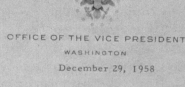

OFFICE OF THE VICE PRESIDENT

WASHINGTON

December 29, 1958

Personal

Dear Frank:

I have just turned off the television after seeing the fabulous playoff game. While I am not supposed to take sides in such a contest, I must admit that I was pulling for the Giants probably because of my friendship and admiration for you and Don Heinrich.

I know you must be disappointed as to the result. But certainly you can be proud of the superb performance you gave. I also saw the game last week with the Browns and I will have to agree with George Marshall when he rates you the best all-around back in pro-football.

In any event, it was a great season for the Giants, for football and for you personally.

My wife, Pat (USC '37), joins me in sending our best wishes for the New Year.

Sincerely,

Richard Nixon

Mr. Frank Gifford
New York Football Giants
100 West 42nd Street
New York, New York

A congratulatory letter written by Richard Nixon to Giants halfback Frank Gifford following the 1958 Championship Game. (Giants artifact from the Legacy Club in MetLife Stadium)

That conclusion saw Colts fullback Alan Ameche make like a battering ram on a play called "16 slant." The Giants defense, according to Gifford, anticipated the play would flow to the left side of the offensive formation, where the Colts had had success running the ball.

Instead, Ameche lowered his head and drove forward behind the right guard.

Ameche made it into the end zone for the one-yard, game-winning touchdown at 8:15 into the sudden-death period, with not a single Giant defender managing to impede his forward progress.

The score gave the Colts a 23–17 overtime win and their first-ever NFL championship, capping what had indeed been a great game filled with just about every plot twist and turn imaginable.

As for the controversial call, Gifford would receive years later some closure on the matter thanks to a letter written to him by Ron Gibbs' son, Joseph.

"Dad told me a few days before he died, 'You know, Joe, maybe Frank was right... maybe he did make that first down.... We shouldn't have ever picked up that ball before the measurement," Joseph Gibbs wrote.

Although Gifford, who had also lost two fumbles in that game, was vindicated, it was, of course, too late.

"It had been an emotional roller coaster, and now it left an unbelievable empty feeling," Gifford wrote in his book. "You'd done the best you could—we all had—and it hadn't been good enough. There was nothing more to be said. It was time to move on."

Eventually, the players did move on, but not before their respective roles in "The Greatest Game Ever Played" attracted scores of new fans, making the National Football League one of the nation's most favorite sporting events.

6

THE SPOILERS
OF PERFECTION

They're called the New York Giants, but as far as their critics were concerned, the New England Patriots, the holders of an 18–0 record coming into Super Bowl XLII, were the real giants.

In a modern-day version of "David versus Goliath," the Giants, who just a few weeks earlier had given the Patriots a run for their money in the 2007 regular-season finale, were not only looking to spoil the Patriots' quest to join the 1972 Miami Dolphins as the only NFL team to go undefeated, New York was also confident they could do so.

But as the accolades continued to shower down on the Patriots and portray the Giants as merely a speed bump in New England's quest, the Giants decided to have a little fun with the whole thing, starting with the moment they left Giants Stadium for Phoenix, Arizona, the site of the Super Bowl.

When the Giants' chartered flight touched down at Phoenix Sky Harbor International Airport, members of the team filed out solemnly, the majority of them either dressed in all black or sporting a black accessory.

As cameras captured the NFC champions' arrival, there was a hint of snark among the assembled media, who suggested that the Giants were dressed appropriately for their upcoming funeral.

The Giants? The idea was said to have come from linebacker and defensive co-captain Antonio Pierce, who later explained the concept was to show unity on what was without question the team's biggest business trip that season.

But Pierce, who also had a mischievous side to him and who always seemed to know about what was said about the team, most certainly had an ulterior motive behind the color choice.

At his media session at the Sheraton Wild Horse Pass hotel in Chandler, Arizona, Pierce, one of a handful of players chosen to address the media after the team's arrival, was asked if he was going to a funeral given his attire.

"Maybe I am," he cracked, his grin spreading from ear to ear.

Then turning serious—or so it seemed at the time—Pierce said, "I don't know anything about [a funeral]. I've got a football game to play Sunday. The Lombardi Trophy is here, and we plan on taking it back to New York and playing a hell of a game."

Defensive end (and fellow defensive captain) Michael Strahan was even more direct.

"We were going to a funeral," he said in an interview for NFL Films' *America's Game: 2007 New York Giants Super Bowl XLL Championship* documentary. "Either we were going to a funeral for the Giants, or we were going to a funeral for the Patriots."

If the plan was to make it a funeral for the Patriots' perfect season, the Giants would have to find a way to slay their Goliath. So with only two possible outcomes for that quest—either the end of the Giants' dream to win their first Super Bowl championship since 1990 or the cessation of the Patriots' perfect season, the color choice worked on so many levels.

That included some bad luck, which, for the Giants, everything that could have gone wrong that week did.

For starters, cornerback Aaron Ross boarded the plane for the long ride battling a stomach virus that necessitated figuring out a way to keep Ross' germs from hitting the ventilation system and potentially infecting others on board the aircraft.

Receiver Plaxico Burress, already dealing with torn ligaments in his right ankle, a torn ligament in his left pinky, and separated shoulder suffered in the NFC title game in Green Bay, would suffer another injury in the days just before the big game when he slipped in the shower and sprained his knee.

And receiver David Tyree, who would come up with one of the greatest receptions of all-time in that game, was beginning to make head coach Tom Coughlin nervous when during Friday's practice before the game, Tyree couldn't catch a cold, let alone a pass.

But as they had proven before, this Giants team was resiliency personified, something they'd again prove in a matter of days in front of a worldwide audience.

* * *

The Giants' objective to stop the Patriots offense can be best summarized in seven words: Stop the run and pressure the passer.

Easy enough, right? Well, not according to the Giants' detractors, who were quick to point out that not only were the Patriots perfect record-wise, they also had the league's best passing offense (295.7 yards per game), and the fifth-lowest sack total (21) surrendered that season.

The Giants, however, were so confident in what they were planning that Burress shared with the media his final score prediction for the game: a 23–17 Giants win.

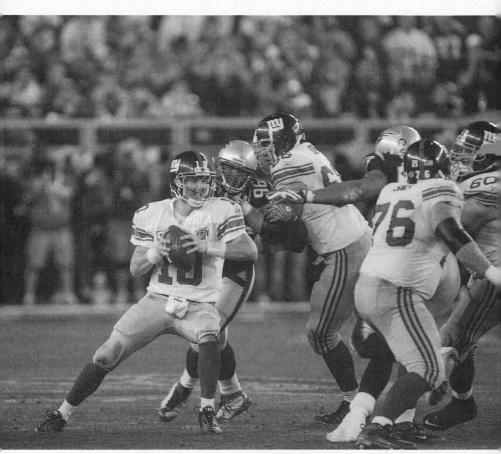

Quarterback Eli Manning looks to get away from the Patriots' pass rush in Super Bowl XLII. (Copyright New York Football Giants)

"We're only gonna score 17 points?" Patriots quarterback Tom Brady asked with a grin when told of Burress' prediction. "Yeah, okay."

Pretty soon, Brady wasn't laughing.

After winning the coin toss, the Giants ran a 16-play, 63-yard opening drive that ate 9:59 off the clock before capping it with a 32-yard field goal by kicker Lawrence Tynes.

That drive was the longest in Super Bowl history, breaking the previous mark set by the Giants in Super Bowl XXV.

If the Giants hoped that Brady would be off his mark after such a long delay, they were mistaken. Brady and the Patriots answered with a much "quicker" scoring drive lasting 5:04 and consisting of 12 plays and 56 yards, the drive aided when the Giants were flagged for defensive pass interference on third down to give the Patriots new life.

With the ball on the Giants' 1-yard line, running back Laurence Maroney, held to just 36 rushing yards on 14 carries in that game, gave his team a 7–3 lead with the first play of the second quarter.

That score would be the last time either side would put points on the board until the fourth quarter.

Not that there weren't close calls, particularly for the Giants. With just under two minutes left in the first half, the Patriots started to get into a rhythm only to have it disrupted on a first-and-10 from the Giants 44-yard line when defensive end Justin Tuck sacked Brady and forced a fumble. Fellow defensive end Osi Umenyiora, alertly fell on the ball at the Patriots' 49-yard line, squashing any threat of the Patriots scoring before the half.

After a scoreless third quarter, the Giants took a 10–7 lead on a five-yard pass from Eli Manning to Tyree on a play the Giants hoped would fool the Patriots into thinking they were going to run it in.

Tyree, more known for his special teams play, was probably the last man the Patriots thought might get the ball, yet there he was making the play he had worked on in practice.

Manning also might have played a part in fooling the Patriots when he pointed to the safety, which some thought was him telling Tyree who to block. They then ran play-action off the run, and Manning was able to connect with Tyree for the score.

The Giants' lead, however, would be short-lived. With 2:25 left, Brady hit receiver Randy Moss, who beat cornerback Corey Webster, on a six-yard touchdown pass to make it 14–10, the final points the Patriots would score in that game.

With less than three minutes to play and the Giants set to go on offense, Strahan had a message for his teammates.

"Seventeen, fourteen is the final, fellas," Strahan told them. "Okay? One touchdown and we are world champions. Believe it and it will happen."

Manning, whose nickname is "Easy E," given his laid-back demeanor, didn't have to be told twice.

He was secretly licking his chops over the opportunity, given how the game had played out. In an interview for the *America's Game: 2007 New York Giants Super Bowl XLII Championship* documentary, Manning said if he had to be trailing late in the game, he preferred it be by four points instead of three because that one-point difference meant a team had to be aggressive—and Manning wanted to go for the jugular.

Things started promising enough. Manning connected with receiver Amani Toomer on an 11-yard pass, but in a snap, it looked as though their drive seemed destined for the graveyard.

That is until Jacobs, their big, bruising running back, pounded his way through the middle of the Patriots defense on fourth-and-1 to keep the Giants' drive alive.

Armed with a fresh set of downs, the Giants would soon stage one of the most memorable plays in Super Bowl history. On second-and-5 from his 44-yard line, Manning tried to connect again with Tyree on a deep pass along the Giants sideline only to see the ball nearly be picked off by Asante Samuel.

With time ticking down and no choice, there was little doubt from anyone watching the game, let alone playing in it, that the Giants were going to need to pass the ball if they were to have any chance of accomplishing the impossible.

That's exactly what they did in putting together a play for the ages.

On the play, a third-and-5, Manning, a quarterback not known for his mobility, found himself under heavy pressure after a jailbreak by the Patriots.

As he was being chased and pulled at, Manning, for a split second, thought about shoveling the ball to right guard Chris Snee, who was the closest Giant.

But Manning, a gunslinger by nature, put to use some training he and the offense had run in practice.

In those drills, the backup quarterbacks, Jared Lorenzen and Anthony Wright, were, as part of the scout team, tasked with charging through the offensive line and trying to knock the ball from Manning's grasp.

Lorenzen, who more closely resembled a defensive tackle size-wise, posed the biggest challenge for Manning because, as Manning recalled, Lorenzen wanted more than just a strip of the ball.

THE PLAY THAT ALMOST WASN'T

While football historians immortalize David Tyree's helmet catch, the game-winning touchdown reception by Plaxico Burress had maybe a touch more drama behind it than anyone initially realized.

For one, Burress wasn't even a sure thing to play in the Super Bowl.

That Tuesday morning before the game, Burress, who already was dealing with a season-long ankle issue, had slipped in his hotel room's shower, injuring his knee.

That injury hampered Burress throughout the week, making him a game-time decision. But Burress was determined to go out there and endure the rigors of a three-hour football game.

Although he would catch just two passes for 27 yards, it was his second reception that helped cement one of the greatest upsets in sports history.

The Giants, who had first-and-10 at the Patriots 13-yard line with less than two minutes to go, anticipated an all-out blitz. So they called "62 Café," a play designed to block the all-out blitz while getting their receivers in single coverage.

Adding to the Giants' good fortune was a tidbit they had picked up on film about 5'9" Patriots cornerback Ellis Hobbs, who had coverage against 6'5" Burress on that game-changing play. Hobbs sometimes came down hard on slant routes, so the Giants figured that if they could fake him to the inside, they would have a good chance of beating him to the outside.

Sure enough, Burress managed to fake Hobbs to the inside as Eli Manning pump-faked to get Hobbs to bite. That allowed Burress to get to the corner virtually uncovered. Manning read the coverage and lobbed a fade to his No. 1 receiver, who kept his feet in bounds to help ruin the Patriots' quest for a perfect season.

"Lorenzen took it to the next level, and it was like he was the d-tackle trying to get a sack," Manning said.

It's not known how often Manning held onto the ball during the season-long practices in which that drill was run. Still, Manning credited that drill work, and especially Lorenzen, who tragically passed away in 2019, for his contributions to one of the biggest wins in Manning's career.

"All the work I had with Jared Lorenzen, I think that was a big help in getting out of that pocket," Manning would later say.

With Manning still on his feet and making the throw down the field, there was just one problem.

He had no idea to whom he was throwing other than it was someone in a white jersey.

What Manning did on that play—throwing the ball up for grabs in the middle of the field with no plan—wasn't exactly something Coughlin endorsed. "Nothing good ever comes of that," the head coach would say.

Except this time would be different, as Tyree, perhaps the last person anyone expected to be in a position to make a catch at that moment, did make the catch which, to this day, is widely regarded as one of the most spectacular catches in Super Bowl history.

That catch saw Tyree, with defensive back Rodney Harrison draped all over him as he fell to the ground, pin the ball against his helmet with one hand until he was able to free his second hand to keep it from touching the ground.

That catch kept a critical Giants drive alive.

With first-and-10 at the Patriots' 24-yard line, Manning, who should have been sacked on the play before, was finally brought down by linebacker Adalius Thomas for a one-yard loss.

No matter though, as the Giants' "Comeback King," who in the 2007 postseason had already engineered fourth-quarter, game-winning drives in the divisional round and the conference title game, did it again when he hit rookie receiver Steve Smith on third-and-11 for 12 yards.

On the next play, Manning saw Burress slip behind the coverage.

Manning pump-faked to get the defender, Ellis Hobbs, to bite and then waited for Burress to cross the plane, the quarterback tossing a fade toward Burress' back shoulder for the 13-yard score to give the Giants a 17–14 lead.

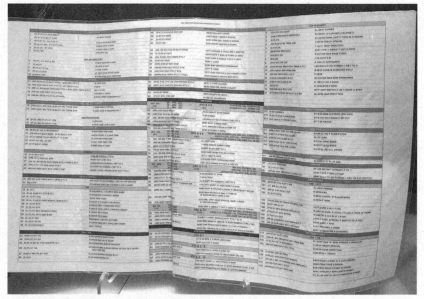

One side of head coach Tom Coughlin's play card from Super Bowl XLII.
(Giants artifact from the Legacy Club in MetLife Stadium)

Before the confetti could fall, there was still one more piece of business to take care of. The Giants scoring drive had left the Patriots with 29 seconds to mount a comeback—an eternity for Brady.

Except Brady's prowess was no match for the Giants defense, which finished the game with nine quarterback hits including five sacks among Brady's 48 pass attempts.

On their final drive, Brady missed receiver Jabar Gaffney on a deep pass to the right side. Then on second down, Giants rookie defensive tackle Jay Alford recorded the Giants' fifth sack of the game, dropping the quarterback for a 10-yard loss.

On third down, Brady, who earlier in the game had success exploiting a matchup between receiver Randy Moss and cornerback Corey Webster, went back to that well. But Webster wasn't having it this time, as he broke up the deep pass.

With 10 seconds left, Brady tried one more Hail Mary, again intended for Moss. This time, safety Gibril Wilson knocked it away, ending the Patriots' hopes for a super comeback and a perfect season.

There was so much said about the Giants' victory and what it meant to a franchise that, after starting 0-2, wasn't even supposed to be in the playoffs, let alone challenge the mighty Goliath.

While analysts spoke glowingly about how "David" had proven everyone wrong, Strahan had a much different, yet more fitting response.

"We didn't do it to prove you wrong," he insisted. "We did it to prove to ourselves we could do it."

7

GEORGE YOUNG

NFL Commissioner Pete Rozelle had been in office for nearly two decades, so putting out the fires that developed within the league was nothing new.

But if there was one emerging fire that was on the verge creating a significant nightmare for Rozelle and the league, it was the growing discord that existed in East Rutherford between Giants team owners Wellington Mara and his nephew, Tim.

Whereas Wellington Mara and his brother Jack, Tim's father, had a harmonious relationship, the business and management philosophical differences between uncle and nephew were tearing the franchise apart.

It wasn't until "The Fumble" of 1978, a play that epitomized a stretch of miserable seasons in which the Giants failed to qualify for the postseason (their last appearance coming in a 1963 loss to the Chicago Bears) that things came to a head.

How bad was it? Tim, a man not afraid to voice his opinions, and Wellington, a more reserved and quiet man set in his ways, not only avoided being in the same building together whenever possible, but they also ceased speaking.

After "The Fumble" resulted in the team's terminating offensive coordinator Bob Gibson and moving on from head coach John McVay, Andy Robustelli, the former Giants great whom Wellington had hired as the director of operations in 1973, resigned.

With a chance to start over, both Mara men couldn't reach a consensus on how to proceed.

Wellington had wanted to hire a head coach—Washington's George Allen was said to be in his crosshairs—before finding a new director of operations, since the elder Mara had the final say on football decisions anyway.

Tim, on the other hand, disagreed with his uncle.

The biggest problem was that both men couldn't agree on who to hire to run the football operations after Robustelli resigned. And the one candidate they did seem to agree on—Jan Van Duser, the NFL's director of operations—declined to be interviewed for the Giants' position.

With the tensions continuing to rise within the organization, Rozelle knew he had to do something—and fast. He sent both Maras a list of candidates to head their football operations.

On that list was George Young, a bespectacled football executive who spent 15 years as a high school teacher in the Baltimore school system. A college defensive lineman at Bucknell, Young was a 26th-round draft pick in 1952 by the Dallas Texans, but his career as a player ended before it had a chance to begin when he was one of the last players cut in training camp that year.

He then got his start working as a member of the front office when he was hired to assist the legendary Don Shula with the Baltimore Colts in 1968 after impressing Shula with his work done on a free-lance scouting assignment. Young would ultimately join Shula in Miami as the Dolphins' director of pro scouting before coming to the Giants.

With Rozelle's strong endorsement of Young, both Maras, after speaking with Young, agreed to offer him the job.

Young, however, had one condition that had to be satisfied, and that was he wanted the final say on all football-related matters, a role that Wellington Mara had held for years.

Said to initially be reluctant to agree to Young's condition, the elder Mara eventually put his trust in Young, who, on Valentines' Day 1979, was signed to a five-year contract to become the team's first-ever general manager with full football decision-making authority.

"We were not able to get all of Don Shula," Wellington Mara said after the announcement of Young's hiring. "I'm glad to get his right arm."

Young, on an initial meeting, struck one as a standoffish and somewhat unkempt grouch.

In reality, he was anything but.

Ernie Accorsi, who spent the 1970–74 seasons with Young in Baltimore, and who later served as the Giants assistant general manager under Young during the 1994–97 seasons, remembered Young as a man who appeared disheveled but who was actually meticulously organized.

"If you walked into his office, there were piles and stacks of papers and records and files all over the place," Accorsi recalled.

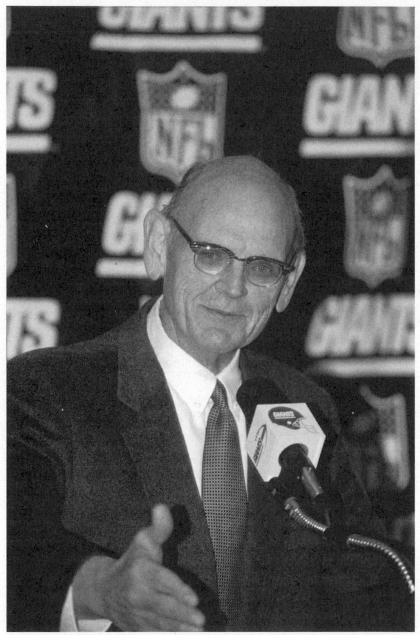

George Young, named the Giants general manager on February 14, 1979, became the first general manager in franchise history to be given full authority over all football decisions. (Copyright New York Football Giants)

"I mean, it was not a clean desk, but he had such an organized mind. So if you walked in there and asked him, 'Do you have a negotiation file on Player X?' He'd reach under 43 files and pull it right out—he knew right where it was."

Accorsi also marveled at how Young, win or lose, kept his cool during games.

"George was poised. You might hear a groan here and there, but he didn't complain about the officiating, and he didn't criticize players. He just sat there. One day I asked him, 'How do you just sit there and don't say a word?' So he said to me, 'Would it make any difference if I complained about the officiating?'"

Even when Young's contract negotiations with players didn't pan out, Accorsi remembered a man who shrugged his shoulders and was on to the next option.

"He was so practical and realistic on how he looked at things and poised on how he looked at things and philosophical," Accorsi said. "If we lost a guy, he was like, 'We'll find somebody else.'"

Less than two weeks after he was hired, Young brought Ray Perkins, who had served a one-year stint as the offensive coordinator for the San Diego Chargers, to be the Giants' new head coach. And later that offseason, Young's first draft pick for the Giants was a young quarterback out of tiny Morehead State University in Morehead, Kentucky, by the name of Phil Simms.

Given his background in personnel, Young rebuilt the Giants literally from the bottom up via the draft.

From 1979 to 1995, 119 of his draft picks made the final roster as either a starter or reserve, and appeared in a minimum of 10 games with the team. In addition to Simms, some of his more notable draft picks included Hall of Fame linebacker Lawrence Taylor; tight end Mark Bavaro; linebackers Carl Banks, Pepper Johnson, and Gary Reasons; running back Joe Morris; offensive linemen Billy Ard, William Roberts, Jumbo Elliott, and Karl Nelson; defensive backs Terry Kinard, Mark Collins, and Perry Williams; defensive lineman Leonard Marshall, and receiver Lionel Manuel.

When Perkins left the Giants after the 1982 season to succeed the legendary Paul "Bear" Bryant as head coach at the University of

THE GOOD GUY

George Young did so much more for the Giants besides repairing a shattered franchise.

Because of Young and the people he helped groom who worked for him, the Giants have been able to enjoy continuity and a degree of stability. The Giants next three general managers—Ernie Accorsi, Jerry Reese, and current general manager Dave Gettleman—all have ties to Young. Accorsi was his assistant, Reese was a scouting director under him, and Gettleman worked for Accorsi.

In addition to his impact on the franchise, Young was a beloved figure among the beat writers who covered the team daily and who cherished the time the "grouch" would take to kibitz on and off the record.

That spirit of Young's memory still lives on today in the annual George Young Good Guy Award, named after Young in 2001. The award, presented by the Giants chapter of the Pro Football Writers of America, is given at the end of each season to the player who exhibited outstanding cooperation in helping the media do its job during the season.

Alabama, Young named Bill Parcells, previously the team's defensive coordinator, as the new head coach.

With Young having made good use of the draft to rebuild the one-time depleted Giants roster, New York went on to earn eight playoff berths, including winning Super Bowl championship titles in the 1986 and 1990 seasons.

Along the way, Young was named as the NFL Executive of the Year five times (1984, 1986, 1990, 1993, and 1997). And in January 2020, he was elected to the Pro Football Hall of Fame.

For as good as the 1980s were to Young, the opposite mostly held true for the next decade.

One of Young's most significant mistakes in his career occurred about midway through 1991. Parcells suddenly resigned in May of that year, citing health concerns for his sudden departure.

Young, who at times was said to have had a rocky relationship with Parcells, would admit years later that he wasn't happy that the head coach had walked away.

Before Parcells had resigned, Young allowed defensive coordinator Bill Belichick, whose demeanor, Young felt, wasn't a good match for the New York market, to take the head coaching job with the Browns.

Young was believed to have been interested in promoting wide receivers coach Tom Coughlin after Parcells resigned, but Coughlin left the Giants after 1990 to become the head coach at Boston College.

With Parcells' timing having thrown so much out of whack, Young named running backs coach Ray Handley—his "worst mistake," as Young would later describe the move—as Parcells' successor.

The move was disastrous. Handley would go on to win 14 games over his two seasons, but he better became known for his contentious relationship with the media and with some of his players.

After finishing with a 6–10 mark in 1992, Handley was fired by Young, who hired Dan Reeves as the new head coach.

Besides Young's mistake with Handley, he also struggled to adapt to two significant changes to the roster-building process: free agency (introduced in 1993) and the salary cap (introduced a year later).

Young had trouble retaining his own players, primarily because he struggled to understand their market values. Those players he was able to keep were ones on which he often overspent, many times leaving the Giants in proverbial cap hell.

Between his inability to handle free agency and the salary cap and his sudden struggles in the first round of the draft, which failed to yield productive players as his picks from the prior decade had become, Young appeared to have lost his touch.

If all that wasn't enough to drag Young down, in 1994, he was told by his doctor to drop some weight from his 6'3" frame. He lost over 150 pounds, suddenly appearing very gaunt.

Because his illness had taken a toll on his stamina, he hired Accorsi to help Harry Hulmes and Rick Donahue, two of Young's right-hand men, who had handle some of the more stressful daily tasks such as player contracts.

Young, whose health continued to decline, left his post as Giants general manager after the 1997 season, turning the reins over to Accorsi.

Young then accepted a newly created position in the league office as a senior vice president of football operations, a post he held until just before his death on December 8, 2001.

Before Young resigned from his Giants' post, he had one final moment that he would cherish in his remaining days.

After the Giants defeated the Washington Redskins to clinch the NFC East division title in 1997, Young waited until the stadium had emptied. He then walked onto the field and sat down on the Giants bench, where he stared at the empty seats as his eyes filled with tears.

"I've had a wonderful job here," said Young, whose 19 years of service with the Giants put him fifth in terms of longevity by a New York team executive, passed only by Ed Barrow (25 years) and Brian Cashman (22 years) of the Yankees, Lester Patrick of the Rangers (21 years), and Bill Torrey of the Islanders (21 years).

"We've had our ups and downs," Young added, "but I've never had a bad day."

8

THE END OF THE 18-YEAR CHAMPIONSHIP DROUGHT

In the modern-day NFL, it's a struggle to build a dynasty capable of winning championships year after year.

Certainly before the 1993 advent of free agency, in its current form, one might think it would have been a little easier to dominate the league. Yet for the Giants, who had won three championship titles (1927, 1934, and 1938) in their first 14 years of existence, they would undergo an 18-year championship drought that ended in 1956, a year in which the Giants finished 8-3-1 and beat the Chicago Bears 47-7 in the Championship game.

The Giants' return to glory was often credited to third-year head coach Jim Lee Howell, though a lot of credit must be given to Howell's top two coordinators, Vince Lombardi (offense) and Tom Landry (defense), whose innovation helped position the Giants for better days.

When the two teams—the Bears with the league's best offense and the Giants with the best defense—ended up against one another in the 1956 Championship game, the schedule makers probably couldn't have dreamed up a better scenario.

The game took place Sunday, December 30, 1956, at Yankee Stadium, capping the Giants' first season at the historic "House That Ruth Built" after their having spent the first 31 seasons of their existence at the Polo Grounds.

Prior to the 1956 Championship game, the two teams had met 35 times (including postseason) since the founding of the NFL, with the Bears leading the series 20-13-2. The 1956 Championship Game was also the fifth time the two clubs met in the playoffs, with the Bears, installed as a three-point favorite for that year's championship game, holding a 3-1 postseason advantage over the Giants.

The Giants objective was to slow down the Bears' three-pronged offensive attack of fullback Rick Casares and passers Ed Brown and Harlan Hill. Tasked with leading that charge was a defense consisting of Rosey Grier, Andy Robustelli, Dick Modzelewski, and Sam Huff.

By the time kickoff rolled around on that December date with destiny, the Yankee Stadium turf had frozen over thanks to some earlier precipitation in below-freezing temperatures. The field conditions were so bad that the Giants were unable to go through their final pregame warmup.

It turned out that they didn't need to, nor did Howell, who typically offered a pregame pep talk before each game, say anything to his players, whom he knew wanted to win the game "more than anything."

The Bears, determined to live up to the fictional "big and bad" descriptors that have been attached to the species in fairy tales, would be bad, all right—bad as in they were no match for the Giants, who took all of five minutes after kickoff to bury the Monsters of the Midway.

"THE GIFFER"

There are many heroes from the Giants 1956 season, but probably none as celebrated as Frank Gifford, the league's Most Valuable Player that season, and the Giants team leader in both rushing (819) and receiving (603).

Gifford, named to the 1950s All-Decade Team as a halfback, was one of the last professional football players to excel on both sides of the ball. He began his Giants career as a defensive back before finally adding halfback and flanker to his contributions.

In the 1956 championship win over the Chicago Bears, he scored the Giants' final touchdown on a 14-yard pass from Charlie Conerly, finishing that day with 131 receiving yards on four receptions, an unprecedented total for a halfback.

Gifford, whose Giants career spanned the 1952–60 and 1962–64 seasons—he briefly retired during the 1961 season after a violent hit by Eagles linebacker Chuck Bednarik that left him with a concussion—was a four-time All-NFL selection and was voted to eight Pro Bowls. He also appeared in five Championship Games with the franchise.

His regular-season career totals include 3,609 rushing yards on 840 carries, 367 receptions for 5,434 yards, and 14 touchdown passes on the halfback option, his touchdown pass total among the most thrown by any non-quarterback in league history. Gifford also currently holds the Giants franchise record for most career touchdowns (78).

The Giants set the tone on the opening kickoff when Gene Filipski returned the ball 54 yards. The Giants would then jump out to a 13-0 first-quarter lead when running back Mel Triplett got his team on the board with a 17-yard touchdown rush capped by kicker Ben Agajanian's PAT.

Agajanian would add field goals of 17 and 43 yards, the latter his longest conversion of that season, to make it 13-0.

In the second quarter, the Giants continued to pile it on, making it 20-0 on Alex Webster's three-yard rush.

The Bears finally got on the scoreboard on a nine-yard touchdown run by Casares to make it 20-7, but that was simply a drop in the bucket compared to the scoring clinic the Giants put on that afternoon.

Interestingly, some believe the Bears' choice of footwear played a significant part in their crushing defeat. The Giants, who in 1934 had discovered the advantage of wearing basketball shoes on frozen turf, had once again used that equipment for this particular game.

According to a report in the December 31, 1956, edition of the Chicago Tribune, the Bears used a sneaker with a different type of sole, one with rubber cleats that weren't as sticky as that of the basketball shoes used by the Giants.

At halftime, Chicago switched their shoes to gain better traction on the icy field. However, it was too late as the Giants continued to pile it on.

New York, up 34-7 at the half, got second-half scores by Kyle Rote (nine yards) and Frank Gifford (14 yards), both on passes by quarterback Charlie Conerly.

Even the Giants special teams got into the scoring fun. Just before halftime, Ray Beck blocked a punt deep in Chicago territory, the ball being recovered in the end zone for the touchdown by Henry Moore.

With the Giants enjoying a comfortable lead, Howell pulled many of his starters in the fourth quarter.

By the time the game ended, the Giants had destroyed the Bears 47-7, with Conerly finishing 7 of 10 for 195 yards and two touchdowns, a 152.1 passer rating—and his best postseason showing as a Giant.

Meanwhile, in the other locker room, the Bears had come full circle. After destroying the Washington Redskins 73-0 in the 1940 playoffs for their biggest playoff victory, Chicago was now on the other side of the fence, having suffered their worst playoff loss in franchise history.

9

JERSEY'S NATIVE SON

In 1983, Bill Parcells thought he was ready to be an NFL head coach. Then reality set it.

Born August 22, 1941, in Englewood, New Jersey, Parcells originally joined Ray Perkins' Giants staff in 1979 as the team's linebackers coach. He'd last only one season, moving to New England the following year to be their linebackers coach before returning to the Giants in 1981 to be Perkins' linebackers coach and defensive coordinator.

He didn't disappoint. The Giants defense finished 1981 with the third-best unit (yards allowed and points against), and the seventh-best unit in 1982 (yards allowed) and eighth-best unit (points against) as Giants reshaped their defensive image into a competitive, disciplined team.

In 1983, the Giants defense, and in particular the linebackers who considered Parcells another one of the guys, learned they'd have to share him with the rest of the team when the New Jersey native was named the new head coach following the resignation of Perkins.

At first, the defensive players weren't happy. Parcells, they said, was one of them, an honorary member. But sometimes when you care enough about one of yours as the Giants members of the defense did about Parcells, you have to let go.

"Once he became the head coach, we realized we had to take a different approach because if we continued to refer to him as 'our guy, our position coach,' we were concerned that the other guys wouldn't necessarily have the respect for him," linebacker Harry Carson said.

"So, we adjusted to him as the head man, and we were able to sort of work together to get certain things done."

It wasn't easy. Parcells had been "one of the guys" as the Giants' linebackers coach and, later, defensive coordinator, and despite his success in those roles, his first year as head coach was a disaster.

Besides the 3–12–1 record, Parcells lost both of his parents that season, leaving general manager George Young to wonder if the weight of everything overwhelmed Parcells. Young was also intrigued by veteran

Giants head coach Bill Parcells (center) keeps a close watch on his team while flanked by defensive coordinator Bill Belichick (right) and linebacker Gary Reasons.
(Copyright New York Football Giants)

college coach (and good friend) Howard Schnellenberger, whom he considered as a potential replacement for Parcells.

Ultimately, Young decided against making a change. But Parcells' near demise caused him to reevaluate his approach to his still-new role as a head coach and make some key changes.

One of the first changes he made was to detach himself from any personal feelings he might have had for his defensive players, and, in particular, his linebackers.

Parcells always had an eye for talent, but he and Young didn't always see eye-to-eye regarding personnel. But after the 1983 season, they did agree to move on from linebackers Brian Kelley and Brad Van Pelt, one half of the famed "Crunch Bunch" that also consisted of Carson and Lawrence Taylor.

The Giants would add linebackers Carl Banks and Gary Reasons, the team's first-and fourth-round picks in the 1984 draft and two players who would become staples, along with Carson and Taylor, in that great Giants defense of the 1980s.

Parcells also went from being a mild-mannered, sweetheart of a guy to a wise-cracking, sometimes cantankerous man who was far less forgiving of mistakes players made to beat themselves.

Rather than become a ranting lunatic—though some of his former players might argue that at times he was—Parcells figured out how far he could push each of his players—and then tried to push them even further.

Defensive end George Martin, a defensive captain and one of Parcells' guys, shared a story from the coach's early days with the team, illustrating just how masterful Parcells was at pushing buttons.

It all started when a highly touted rookie defensive lineman, whom Martin declined to name, kept jumping offside during a practice. Martin and his teammates figured that Parcells would rip the young rookie a new one, yet surprisingly, Parcells said nothing.

The second time the rookie jumped offside, the players again braced for an anticipated thunderous response by Parcells.

Again, nothing.

The third time it happened, Parcells finally called a time out and brought his players together. The players, already starting to feel bad for the rookie whom they anticipated was going to get a verbal flogging in front of the entire team, were instead stunned by what transpired.

"Parcells gathers us together," Martin said, "and says, 'Guys, this is the kind of shit that we will no longer tolerate in this organization. These are the kind of mistakes that get you beat, and I, for one, will never, ever be accepting of that kind of performance.

"'And if it ever happens again, I'm going to hold you, George Martin, responsible.'"

Martin can laugh about the incident now, but back then, he certainly wasn't laughing.

"I was an innocent bystander who hadn't done anything wrong, and the guys were like, 'Why is he bringing you into this?'" Martin recalled. "After practice, I stormed off—I was so pissed you could see smoke

"TUNA!"

With all apologies to the fictional Jim Halpert of *The Office* fame, Bill Parcells is the one and only "Tuna."

But how did Parcells, who used to anoint his players with creative monikers like "Sluggo" (nose tackle Jim Burt), "Bebo" (offensive lineman Brad Benson), and "Biff" (guard Bill Ard) get his nickname?

Was it because Parcells, like Halpert, got caught by an annoying co-worker bringing a tuna sandwich to work one day instead of the usual ham and cheese?

There are multiple stories about where the "Tuna" nickname got its origins, starting with Parcells' own account in 1997 when he claimed the nickname came about during his first coaching stint with the New England Patriots in 1980 as the team's linebackers coach.

"There was an old commercial from StarKist with Charlie the StarKist Tuna. So, my players were trying to con me on something one time, and I said, 'You must think I'm Charlie the Tuna,' you know, a sucker. And that's kind of how it started," he said.

Ten years earlier, during the days leading up to Super Bowl XXI, Parcells told a slightly different tale of his fishy nickname's origin, claiming he got it because he did indeed eat tuna fish every day.

Then there are other fisherman's tales that claim Parcells got the name after some bad nights at the card table or because he had a stout type of build resembling a tuna fish.

Wherever the nickname came from, people can no doubt agree that it is a perfect fit for this one-of-a-kind Jersey guy.

coming out of the earholes in my helmet. When I got to the locker room, Parcells comes after me and says, 'Hey Martin, get over here.'"

Still fuming, Martin gathered himself and met with Parcells, who asked him if he knew why he had been singled out.

"I told him I had no idea," Martin said. "He then tells me, 'You are one of my guys. You're a team captain. You're a leader. People look up to you. If you think that that kind of performance is acceptable, they're gonna follow your lead. They also know that you are a sacred cow around here. So if I come down on you, they'll realize that nobody is above my wrath.'"

Bill Parcells: defensive coordinator/ linebackers, 1981–82; head coach, 1983–1990.
(Giants artifact from the Legacy Club in MetLife Stadium)

That was the brilliance of Parcells and his button-pushing tactics. And as a happy postscript to that story, Martin said that the rookie in question never jumped offside in practice again.

The other side of Parcells' brilliance was that for as much as he dished it out, he also was man enough to take it, especially from the players he challenged.

Banks learned that during a particularly embarrassing incident that happened during a game against the Los Angeles Rams in his rookie season. That week, the Giants had played a sloppy, penalty-filled game that, with each yellow flag, was raising Parcells' blood pressure to new levels.

Parcells became so irritated with his team's lack of attention to detail that he vowed to cut the next player who committed a penalty.

That happened to be Banks, whose penalty came on a kickoff when he engaged in a shoving match with his opponent.

"I came off the field to the sideline, and he told me to sit my you-know-what down and that I was cut," Banks said.

"I came back, and I lashed out back at him, and he was like, 'What did you say?' I said what I said again, and he just turned around and went back to coaching the game. When I showed up for work that Monday, I didn't know whether I had a job or not."

Banks did indeed have a job after giving Parcells what he was looking for—no, not a verbal retort to the coach's in-game button-pushing, but a Hall of Fame quality performance week in and week out.

* * *

As a head coach, Parcells finished with a 183–138–1 overall record, becoming the first head coach in league history to coach four different teams (the Giants, Patriots, Jets, and Cowboys) in the playoffs, and a two-time NFL Coach of the Year award winner (1986 and 1994).

If there was one common thread in Parcells' career, it was his knack for turning descending teams into contenders, the first time of which he did in 1984 with the Giants.

That season, the Giants fell to 3–3 after their first six games, including back-to-back losses by large margins to the Rams (33–12) and the 49ers (31–10).

On October 14, 1984, the Giants, needing a win, visited the 3–3 Atlanta Falcons. The Giants not only beat the Falcons, 19–7, the Giants defense went from allowing opponents an average of 23.7 points in their first six games, to 15.9 points per game in their last 10 contests.

The Giants would also qualify for the playoffs for the first of three seasons in a row under Parcells, who, in the first two postseason appearances, saw the Giants lose in the division rounds, but who, in the 1986 season, won its first Super Bowl championship (XXI).

Parcells would go on to lead the Giants to the playoffs in two more seasons, once in 1989, when they lost the divisional round, and then in 1990, when they were victorious in Super Bowl XXV. In eight seasons as the Giants head coach, he finished with an 85–52–1 record, including postseason.

In 1991, after the last of the confetti from Super Bowl XXV had been swept up, times were changing for the Giants and Parcells.

The Giants underwent a significant organizational change when co-owner Tim Mara sold his half of the club to Preston Robert Tisch.

Meanwhile, Parcells, then 51 years old, began having health issues that ultimately led to him resigning his head coaching position with the Giants on May 15, 1991.

Less than a month later, Parcells underwent successful single-bypass heart surgery and opted to spend the next two seasons in the less stressful broadcasting arena before returning to coaching with the Patriots from 1993 to '96 before jumping over to the Jets in 1997–99.

Parcells' final stint as an NFL head coach came in 2003–06 with the Dallas Cowboys. Along the way, he also served as a front office executive for the Jets and Dolphins. When Canton came calling, one of the most successful head coaches in the modern NFL era entered the Pro Football Hall of Fame as a Giant.

10

AHEAD OF THEIR TIME

They are both members of the Pro Football Hall of Fame, one a defensive back who still holds the Giants franchise the NFL mark in career interceptions (74), and the other a standout offensive lineman was widely regarded as one of the best at his position.

They—defensive back Emlen Tunnell and offensive tackle Roosevelt "Rosey" Brown—were also among the first African American players to join the Giants, two men who became close in spite of an eight-year age difference because they ended up rooming together on the road.

On the field, Tunnell and Brown—each of whom remained with the Giants after their respective playing careers ended—both took the NFL by storm because of their elite athletic abilities and high moral character which made them athletes who were ahead of their time.

* * *

Emlen Tunnell, 6'1", 190 pounds, was known as "The Gremlin," a moniker that rhymed perfectly with his given first name and which captured his tendency to create problems for opposing offenses.

Born March 29, 1924, in Bryn Mawr, Pennsylvania, Tunnell grew up in a single-family household in Garrett Hill, his parents having divorced when he was a young child.

He received an athletic scholarship from the University of Toledo, but in 1942, he suffered a broken neck.

Tunnell eventually recovered from his injury, but once cleared medically, he switched to basketball. However, with the nation at war, Tunnell tried to enlist for active duty with the Army and Navy only to be rejected due to his injury.

Not to be deterred, Tunnell enlisted in the U.S. Coast Guard. During his duty, Tunnell performed acts of heroism in saving shipmates from a fire and a near-drowning to posthumously earn the Silver Lifesaving Medal in March 2011.

Following his duty, Tunnell returned to school, this time at the Following his duty, Tunnell returned to school, this time at the University of Iowa. In 1948 Tunnell, looking to earn money for himself and his family, decided to pursue a pro football career. He hitched a ride with a driver of a banana truck passing through his hometown which dropped him off near the Lincoln Tunnel. From there, Tunnell made his way to the Giants' executive offices to seek a tryout.

Impressed by Tunnell's determination and his athleticism, the Giants signed him to a one-year contract worth $5,000 with a $500 signing bonus, making him the first African American player in franchise history.

Initially, Tunnell played both sides of the ball. After showing more natural ability as a defensive back, the decision was made to move him exclusively to defense, a decision that Tunnell initially didn't endorse, but which he later accepted.

As a defensive back, he became a key spoke in Steve Owens' "Umbrella defense," a 4-1-6 alignment that on passing downs usually saw the two defensive ends drop back into coverage with the four defensive backs.

Tunnell, whose other nickname was "Mr. Defense," was the deep safety in that defense. He would go on to appear in 130 regular-season games with 112 starts for the Giants, recording 74 of his career 79 interceptions and 1,240 of his 1,282 yards from interceptions for New York.

Tunnell also contributed as a kickoff and punt return specialist, recording 2,206 punt return yards on 257 returns (8.6 average) and 1,215 kickoff-return yards on 46 returns (26.4 average) with the Giants in regular-season play.

In 1952, Tunnell had one of his most productive seasons, racking up 924 all-purpose yards from his kickoff, punt, and interception returns. That total surpassed the 894 rushing yards accumulated by Dan Towler of the Rams, who led the league in rushing that season.

Tunnell would become part of a defensive backfield that helped defeat the Chicago Bears, 47–7, in the 1956 championship game, the last Giants' team championship until the 1986 postseason (Super Bowl XXI).

While his on-field contributions were certainly enough to earn him legendary status within the franchise, how Tunnell conducted himself off the field was just as admired.

In his *New York Times* obituary, there was a story of how Tunnell, in his final season with the Giants in 1958, was honored by the organization.

While grateful for all the gifts he had received that day, the most endearing to him was a small cash gift of $28 he received from a group of about two dozen homeless people to whom Tunnell had, through the years, donated whatever spare change he had in his pockets.

Tunnell, who was traded to the Green Bay Packers to close out his career, later rejoined the Giants as a scout and as the franchise's first African American assistant coach.

He was, in fact, responsible for scouting future Giants defensive back Carl Lockhart, whom he nicknamed "Spider" because of how Lockhart was all over the field covering receivers like a spider closing in on its prey.

Tunnell, an iron man who played in 158 consecutive games, became the first African American to be inducted into the Pro Football Hall of Fame.

Emlen Tunnell's Silver Lifesaving Medal, awarded posthumously on March 9, 2011. Tunnell saved his Coast Guard shipmate Alfred Givens after he fell overboard into 32-degree waters. (Artifact shown is from the Pro Football Hall of Fame)

Before his death, the four-time first-team All-Pro and nine-time Pro Bowler once opined that he could probably continue making tackles at age 50 because while "your body may go, your heart doesn't."

In a sad twist of irony, his death on July 23, 1975, at the age of 51, came from a heart attack suffered in his Pace University dormitory room, where he had been staying during the team's summer training camp.

"Emlen changed the theory of defensive safeties," Giants head coach Jim Lee Howell once told the *New York Times*.

"He would have been too big for the job earlier, and they'd have made him a lineman. But he had such strength, such speed, and such quickness that I'm convinced he was the best safety ever to play."

* * *

Roosevelt "Rosey" Brown truly was born to be a Giant.

Chris Mara, now the Giants senior vice president of player personnel, remembered being awestruck by Brown.

"I was a young boy when I used to go to Yankee Stadium every Saturday to watch all the players, and he was a freakish-looking athlete, both physically and the way he moved around," Mara recalled.

"I remember seeing this giant of a man back then, and I would be in awe because he was so much bigger and more athletic than everybody else on the field."

Brown was born on October 20, 1932, in Charlottesville, Virginia. As a young boy, his build and intelligence often belied his age. When he was six years old and about to start school, he took a test which he aced so well that he skipped first and second grade and went straight into the third grade.

Despite his size, Brown didn't play football until high school, and only because the head coach at Jefferson High School was intrigued by Brown's physical stature.

Brown's mother gave her permission for her son to play football, but his father, who wouldn't find out about it until a year later, objected because Rosey's older brother had suffered an injury playing the game that was attributed to his eventual death.

After graduating from high school at 15, Brown received a scholarship to attend Morgan State in Baltimore, Maryland, from which he graduated at 19. Having grown to 6'3" and 255 pounds, Brown first came to the Giants' attention when team co-owner Wellington Mara noticed an article in *The Pittsburgh Courier's* sports page in which Brown was among those named to the paper's all-star football team.

Brown was the Giants' pick in the 27th round in the 1953 draft, the 318th overall selection. He signed a one-year contract with the team for $3,000 (no signing bonus).

An impressive and imposing figure with a 29-inch waist and a physique that would make a Greek Adonis envious, Brown initially didn't appear to have special football traits—that is until head coach Steve Owen and line coach Ed Kolman decided to train him to play on the offensive line.

At first, Brown second-guessed his decision to play football when, during training camp, he squared off against Arnie Weinmeister and Al DeRogatis, both of whom hit Brown so hard that he had to take a physical inventory to ensure he hadn't lost any body parts.

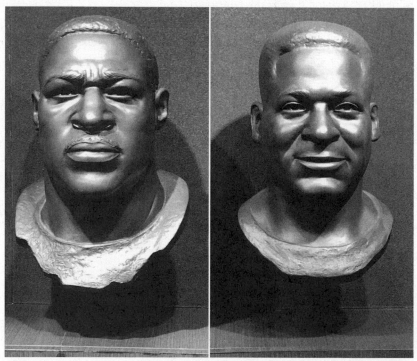

Offensive lineman Roosevelt "Rosey" Brown Jr, 1953–1965 (left) and defensive back Emlen "The Gremlin" Tunnell, 1948–1958 (right). (Giants artifacts from the Legacy Club in MetLife Stadium)

But Brown stayed with it and the gamble that the Giants took in training him to play offensive tackle paid off. Brown, who was quick, strong, and who played with power, redefined the left tackle position by becoming one of the first offensive tackles to pull (a role previously filled by smaller, more athletic guards) and fire out to the second and third levels downfield as an on-the-move blocker.

"I get my satisfaction from doing the job," he told the *New York Times* in 1964. "When one of our backs breaks away for a big gain, I feel good because I knocked somebody down on the other side, which made the play go. That's my satisfaction. I don't think it takes too much to run with the ball if someone makes the blocks."

To watch Brown mow down multiple linemen down the field was like watching a choreographed dance. In the NFL Network's *Top 10 Greatest Giants of All-Time* video, Giants Hall of Fame running back Frank Gifford credited Brown for his success and said that were it not for Brown's blocking, the running back might not have had his Hall of Fame–worthy career.

"There are no great running backs without great offensive linemen," said Gifford.

Throughout his Hall of Fame career, Brown, named to eight All-NFL teams and nine Pro Bowls, delivered many fine performances. His best might have come in the 1956 NFL Championship Game against the Chicago Bears, a game in which Brown handled the vaunted Bears defense to earn "Lineman of the Game" honors.

In 1975, Brown became only the second player to be elected to the Pro Football Hall of Fame on the merits of his offensive line play alone.

"Yeah, I would say it was very rare," Chris Mara said of Brown's athletic ability as an offensive lineman. "I mean, between him and Emlen, they were both freakish athletes who were way ahead of their time."

Like his friend Tunnell, Brown, voted to the NFL's 75th Anniversary Team in 2000, was the very picture of durability, having missed four games due to injury over his 13-year NFL career. In March 1966, he was hospitalized with phlebitis but attempted to play for a 14th season that summer only to conclude that it was time to retire.

Also, like Tunnell, Brown found work with the Giants organization after his playing career ended. He was initially hired as the team's assistant offensive line coach and then was promoted to offensive line coach in 1969. In his later years, Brown went into scouting and made a significant impact on Chris Mara, an up-and-coming scout.

"I think Rosey's specialty as a scout was the offensive and defensive line play," Mara said. "Obviously, as a former offensive lineman, he knew all the techniques. And I know we were in a different era, but his knowledge of offensive line play was terrific, and that carried on with the defensive linemen. So it was great knowledge for me to listen to him talk about it and to learn about the little different things that offensive and defensive linemen did."

Brown would spend nearly 50 years in the Giants' employ before dying in June 2004 from a heart attack.

GENERAL TOM

By the end of the 2003 season, the Giants were a mess.

How bad was it? Besides limping to a 4–12 record that included eight straight losses to end the season, the Giants finished that year with a then-franchise-record 127 penalties for 1,090 penalty yards, as well as a minus-16 turnover differential, tied with Buffalo for the worst in the NFL.

The Giants needed a change at head coach, and co-owner Wellington Mara, who addressed the team as they were packing up their belongings for the long off-season ahead, promised his players that he would find the very best head coach he could.

Mara, his son John, his business partner Bob Tisch, and general manager Ernie Accorsi put together a small head coaching candidate pool. Among those candidates were then-Rams defensive coordinator Lovie Smith, Romeo Crennel and Charlie Weis (both coordinators on Bill Belichick's Patriots staff), and Tom Coughlin, the Giants receivers coach under Bill Parcells, who was also once the head coach at Boston College and of the expansion Jacksonville Jaguars.

Mara and Accorsi, who did most of the initial legwork to meet with the various coaching candidates, met with Coughlin at the Newark-Liberty International Airport Marriott in what turned out to be an interview like none other.

"Before we could even ask a question, Tom went into a long monologue about all the problems that our organization had," Mara said.

"You know, how we were weak in this area, how we can add to this area, and what needed substantial changes. Ernie and I both thought about 20 minutes into this meeting that this was not going to be the right guy for us, and this guy was going to be impossible to deal with."

So what changed their minds?

For starters, Accorsi said that Coughlin ultimately stopped talking and allowed both he and Mara to get in some thoughts and ask some questions.

But for Mara, he still had some concerns about Coughlin's reputation as head coach at Jacksonville, where he was branded a "hard-ass," given his obsession with little nuances that most coaches don't give a second thought about.

When he was hired to head the Jaguars, Coughlin, according to a story in the *New York Times*, left no stone unturned, fussing over details such as how long it would take the Jaguars to get from their bench into the locker room at halftime, and how far back seats in the coaches' meeting room would be from the video screens.

And his rules—there was any number of rules that left his players scratching their heads over the purpose. These included showing up for a meeting at least five minutes early in what would later become known as "Coughlin Time," strict dress codes while on road trips, mandatory practice attire, how to sit in meeting rooms, and other rules that some thought were over the top.

Not even the unexpected and unavoidable incidents were easily forgiven by Coughlin. In a September 20, 1999, *Sports Illustrated* article, it was reported that Coughlin fined Jaguars cornerback Dave Thomas $1,500 when Thomas skipped a mandatory meet-and-greet banquet on an off-day because he stayed home with his two-year-old, fever- stricken son.

Coughlin also fined Tavian Banks and Cordell Taylor $500 apiece when both arrived late for a team meeting after being involved in a car accident on a rain-slicked bridge.

Despite this history, Mara wasn't quite ready to give up on Coughlin as a candidate. He reached out to some of Coughlin's former players for some feedback, one of whom was tight end Pete Mitchell, who had been college teammates with Mara's brother-in-law and who had not only played for Coughlin at Jacksonville but who also played for the Giants.

"I had a long, honest conversation with Pete about Tom," Mara recalled. "Pete said he couldn't have imagined playing for anybody else, that Tom was a great coach to play for. Yes, he was tough, but he was also fair. He got the most out of his players, and if he had to do it all over again, he'd play for Tom and not think twice about it.

"That had a huge effect on me," Mara added. "It erased any doubts that I had at that time about whether Tom was going to be too strict, too tough, and too stubborn to be successful here. We ultimately came to

THE REVOLUTION MYTH

Tom Coughlin and Jim Fassel's respective coaching styles couldn't have been any more different.

"Fassel was more of a player's coach and lacked in some of the discipline and the rules and things like that," said punter Jeff Feagles, who played for both head coaches. "So now you've got a new sheriff in town, and that's what rocked the boat, because you had guys who were just not used to that."

While some were turned off by Coughlin's military-like style—most famously defensive end Michael Strahan (who, by the end of his career, came to appreciate Coughlin), and running back Tiki Barber (who struggled to embrace Coughlin's management style)—several players claim there was never a full-scale revolt against the head coach, despite what might have been reported.

"I had no problems with [Coughlin's rules] because I'm a rule follower," said Feagles. "At that point in my career when Tom came in, I was basically in my 15th season, so I had been down that road with new coaches and had not made it that long in my career if I hadn't done things the right way."

"He expected the most out of us, and let's be honest—for the offensive linemen, that was all the stuff you did already—being on time, working hard, and expecting more out of ourselves," added guard Rich Seubert, who also played for both Fassel and Coughlin.

"Coach Coughlin's mentality was you work for what you got, you never give up, and mind over matter. I mean, the five-minute rule? It's not hard to set your clock five minutes ahead of time."

Defensive end Osi Umenyiora, another player who experienced both coaching styles, agreed that playing under Coughlin's rules wasn't hard.

"I had one training camp under Fassel, but you know, my college years were hell—we're down there in Alabama in the heat practicing two, three times a day in full pads. It was intense, so I didn't know any better," Umenyiora said.

"I was like, 'Okay, we're here, we're making a lot of money, so if Coach wants you to show up five minutes early, then do it.' I didn't take any offense to him, but I could see how other people who had played a while in the league or had been in a different system maybe didn't see the need for him to behave in that sort of manner. But I didn't mind that at all."

Nor did a lot of guys on the team, who adapted some of Coughlin's rules, such as showing up for meetings five minutes early, even long after their playing careers ended.

the conclusion that this was the right guy at the right time because we needed somebody who would bring some discipline to us, but who also knew how to win and knew how to get the most out of players."

Despite team ownership's concerns being assuaged about the then-57-year-old Coughlin, the Giants players still had to buy into the program this very focused and confident man was set to offer.

While Coughlin's rules drove many players crazy—and, for some, broke thanks to the fines they received—his purpose and attention to detail were exactly what the discipline-starved Giants lacked.

On January 6, 2004, Coughlin was named the 17th head coach of the New York Football Giants, and two days later, when he met the media for the first time, just as he had done in his meeting with Accorsi and Mara, Coughlin took control.

Standing at a podium, dressed in a navy-blue suit bearing a small American flag lapel pin, Coughlin's speech sounded much like a cross between a general getting ready to lead his troops into battle and a politician.

"We must restore our belief in the process by which we will win," Coughlin said. "We must replace despair with hope and return the energy and the passion to New York Giant football," he said, before continuing to mention things like "the basic axioms" behind a successful franchise; how he believed that the players craved discipline and structure; and how he was determined to eliminate the "cancer of injuries."

It was a speech that was so stirring that Giants vice president/communications Pat Hanlon, yelled out, "Let's go play ball! What are we waiting on?"

Coughlin smiled and replied, "Can we start right now?"

* * *

While Coughlin was determined to hit the ground running, his tenure with the team got off to a rocky start.

In his first season, he ran afoul of the NFLPA when his off-season program was found to have violated CBA guidelines.

The infractions, as reported to the NFLPA, including a scheduled classroom session before teams were allowed to start their off-season program; a weight training session that exceeded the maximum time limit; and the mandating of players to eat at least one meal at the team's facility.

The Giants were stripped of two OTAs as a result of their infractions.

Then there were the fines. In the summer of 2005, he fined three players—one of whom was a rookie who hadn't even earned his first NFL paycheck—$9,000 each for arriving 15 minutes past an 11:00 PM training camp curfew—this after they were delayed due to traffic and construction detours.

Had Coughlin been consistently winning right out of the chute, perhaps his ways might have been better tolerated.

Such was not the case. In 2004, his first season with the Giants, his team fell to 6-10 after a 5-2 start. The following year, he led the Giants to an 11-5 record, only to end up being humiliated in a 23-0 shutout loss to the Panthers in the NFC Wild Card round.

The 2006 campaign was even tougher to swallow. After starting 6-2, the Giants would limp to an 8-8 finish and another postseason loss in the Wild Card round, this time to the Philadelphia Eagles.

With the frustration beginning to grow over Coughlin's rigidness, some of the more senior players began to lock horns with the stubborn Coughlin.

The rumor mill, meanwhile, began churning as to whether the Giants might dump the "out of touch" Coughlin.

Ultimately, the Mara and Tisch families decided against making a change. John Mara, concerned about a full-blown mutiny developing in the locker room, met with Coughlin and suggested that he start showing more of a human side.

So too did Coughlin's own family, who implored him to show the players the same side of his personality that he showed his family and his grandchildren.

Charles Way, a former Giant player who was the team's director of player development at the time, also urged Coughlin to lighten up. Way pointed out that many of the players Coughlin coached didn't have father figures in their lives and that Coughlin could maybe help fill that void if he was willing to show more of a nurturing side.

Besides softening his stance with the players, Coughlin also agreed to address another elephant in the room: the media. In his early tenure with the team, Coughlin famously sparred with the press, treating his mandatory press briefings as though he were having a wisdom tooth extraction without Novocain.

To mend any hard feelings, Coughlin invited senior members of the Giants beat to his office for one-on-one, no holds barred (and no-retaliation) conversations about how he could improve his relationship with the press corps.

Coughlin considered the feedback and began reinventing himself.

When his players reported for the start of the 2007 offseason program, Coughlin introduced a leadership council consisting of several veteran players selected based on their leadership abilities to serve as his locker room generals.

That summer, during training camp—back in those days, teams were allowed to hold practices twice per day, and with fewer restrictions regarding the use of full pads—Coughlin surprised his team when he canceled a meeting and took the players, coaches, and staff bowling.

"I wanted the players to see me in an entirely different environment," Coughlin later explained after the word of his surprise field trip got out to the media.

He even took the players' teasing of his lack of bowling skills with a smile.

"They were busting my tail for throwing a ball in the gutter, saying, 'Coach, you're awful,' and, 'You can't even keep it in the alley for 25 feet.' It was fun, and a way of letting players see you in a caring manner and letting them know you are human and passionate and concerned about them outside of football."

In the end, Coughlin's willingness to show his softer side would be the critical missing ingredient in what turned out to be a successful career in which he'd lead the Giants to two Super Bowl championship seasons (2007 and 2011).

While Coughlin proved John Mara and Ernie Accorsi to be right, in later years, the head coach struggled to win with the rosters he was given. After winning Super Bowl XLVI, the Giants finished in third place in the division four years in a row, their won-loss record slipping with each year.

Coughlin eventually decided that enough was enough and stepped away after the 2015 season after posting a 110–93 record (including playoffs) in 12 seasons as head coach.

12

SAM HUFF

There's a long-standing belief in today's NFL that defenses win championships. But back when the NFL was building a following, defensive players were often characterized as nothing more than brutes who lacked the glamor and appeal of their offensive counterparts.

That all changed, however, with the arrival of Robert Lee "Sam" Huff.

Huff was born and raised in Edna, West Virginia, the site of the No. 9 coal mining camp, where his upbringing helped, in part, instill the sense of urgency Huff would later show during his NFL career.

As a young boy, Huff knew that he didn't want to follow in his father's coal-mining footsteps.

"What I really wanted to do," Huff said in the documentary, The Violent World of Sam Huff, "was to go to school and get an education and to maybe be a high school coach or college coach or something along those lines."

The 6'1", 230-pound Huff enrolled at West Virginia University, where he was an All-American guard for the Mountaineers under head coach Art "Pappy" Lewis, a former NFL offensive lineman picked in the first round of the 1936 draft by the Giants.

Late in Huff's college career, former Giants defensive lineman turned scout Al DeRogatis paid a visit to WVU to watch All-American guard Bruce Bosley. Instead, DeRogatis was so taken by Huff's athletic prowess that he brought Huff's name to the attention of the Giants personnel department as a prospect to consider for that year's draft.

In 1956, the Giants drafted Huff in the third round to play on the offensive line, but for some reason, despite having excelled there in college, Huff's skill set was so unique that it perplexed Giants head coach Jim Lee Howell, who had trouble finding a spot for Huff.

The rookie, frustrated by how his career was unfolding, decided to leave camp but was convinced to return by offensive assistants Vince Lombardi and Ed Kolman. Huff returned and defensive assistant

Tom Landry, who had been developing the 4-3 defensive scheme that revolutionized the way defense was played, began grooming Huff to back up Ray Beck, the team's middle linebacker.

When Beck suffered an injury, Huff became the full-time starter, and the Giants never looked back. Later that season, Huff and company would help the Giants steamroll the Chicago Bears, whose offense had racked up more than 4,500 yards that season, in the 1956 NFL Championship Game to the tune of 47–7.

In that game, the Giants defense also held Bears running back Rick Casares, the league's rushing leader that season with 1,126 yards on 234 carries, to 43 yards on 14 rushing attempts. The Giants also limited end Harlon Hill to six receptions that barely made a ripple on the game and held Ed Brown to 8-of-19 passing, most of those completions coming in garbage time.

DEE-FENSE! DEE-FENSE!

In the early days of the NFL, highly skilled and gifted athletes would thrill spectators with their athletic prowess in making bone-crunching blocks, spectacular catches, picture-perfect throws, and power runs in which the running backs seemed to transform into human bulldozers.

The defensive players? For the most part, they were usually an after-thought—a group of men who weren't introduced at the start of the game, and whose annual salaries didn't often compete with their offensive counterparts.

In 1956, defensive players began to get their just due when, during a game against the Chicago Cardinals at Yankee Stadium, on November 11, 1956, the visitors were driving down the field when suddenly a small group among the 61,000-plus in attendance began to chant "Dee-fense! Dee-fense!" as encouragement to stop the Cardinals from driving down the field.

The Giants held off the Cardinals that day, 23–10, and a new iconic chant—one that would later expand to other sports—was born.

"Dee-fense! Dee-fense!" became a part of Giants' games, with the chant expanding to when their defensive heroes—among them, future Hall of Famers like linebacker Sam Huff, defensive back Emlen Tunnell, and defensive end Andy Robustelli—ran out onto the field.

As the defense was doing their thing, the Giants offense had itself a day. The Giants got touchdown runs from Mel Triplett and Alex Webster, touchdown passes from Charlie Conerly (to Frank Gifford and Kyle Rote), a special teams score from Henry Moore's recovery of a blocked kick in the end zone, and two field goals from kicker Ben Agajanian.

As the Giants defense continued its dominating ways, Huff's star power increased. He was the first NFL player to be featured on the cover of *Time* magazine and was the subject of a half-hour documentary, *The Violent World of Sam Huff*.

Thanks to his rugged good looks, Huff also became a pitchman for Marlboro cigarettes.

But it was his classic battles that further endeared Huff to a growing legion of fans.

He famously sparred with Jim Taylor of the Packers, a battle that reached a climax in the 1962 Championship Game (won 16–7 by the Packers).

And then there were the battles against Jim Brown, the Cleveland Browns running back who was one most dominating players of his era.

There weren't many things or people who could stop Brown from taking over a game, but Huff turned out to be one of them, especially when it mattered most.

In 1958, Brown had rushed for over 100 yards and scored a touchdown in both regular-season meetings with the Giants, both losing efforts.

So, after facing the Giants in the regular-season finale, Cleveland would meet the Giants again in the divisional playoff round on December 21, 1958.

In that 10–0 Giants win, Huff and his defensive buddies held Brown to eight rushing yards on seven carries and the Browns offense to 86 total yards.

For Huff, who very rarely missed a chance at making a tackle, there was one play in the NFL Championship Game played a week later against the Baltimore Colts that he would later claim haunted him for years after. That play was the one-yard, game-winning score by fullback Alan Ameche in overtime to beat the Giants 23–17.

"I can still see the picture of him running through that big hole at the goal line," Huff recalled for the *New York Times*. "We had keyed our defense to the backs instead of the tight end on that play. I had lined up between [Dick Modzelewski] and Rosey Grier in our goal-line defense, to our right of their center. And they ran the play to our left. That still haunts me."

* * *

With the Giants, Huff found a second family that, in later years, he recalled made playing the game fun.

After the 1963 season, however, he and defensive lineman George Seals were traded to the Washington Redskins for defensive lineman

Linebacker Sam Huff, 1956–1963.
(Giants artifact from the Legacy Club in MetLife Stadium.)

Andy Stynchula and halfback Dick James, the move blindsiding the then 29-year-old Huff.

"It's kind of like getting hit with a bomb," he said after learning of the trade, for which he blamed then head coach Allie Sherman. "It's so unexpected; I still haven't gotten over the shock."

Huff's world was turned so upside down that at one point, he contemplated retiring.

After reflecting, Huff decided to continue his career with Washington. In a 1966 game against his old team in which Washington destroyed the Giants 72–41 (the 113 points making it the highest-scoring game in NFL history), Huff extracted some revenge against Sherman.

With Washington already ahead 69–41 and with only seven seconds left in the game, Washington called a timeout and then sent kicker Charlie Gogolak (Giants kicker Pete Gogolak's brother) to attempt the 29-yard field goal.

Gogolak made the kick to boost Washington's point total to 72. Later, Huff admitted that he was the one who called the timeout because "Charlie needed to practice."

* * *

Huff didn't fear much during his lifetime, but the one thing he did admit to fearing was that despite an impressive NFL career, he might not win the approval of the Pro Football Hall of Fame voters.

In a *New York Times* interview done before his 1982 enshrinement, Huff made his surprising confession.

"There was no basis to believe that I deserved to be in the Hall of Fame, except if middle linebackers like Ray Nitschke, Joe Schmidt, and Bill George were in it, I felt I should be, too," he said. "They were always being compared to me when we were contemporaries, and they were in. And then Dick Butkus got in, and he came after me. That's when I started to be afraid that I might not ever make it."

His fears proved to unfounded. On August 7, 1982, Huff was presented for enshrinement by Landry, the coach who not only had the foresight to convert Huff to a middle linebacker but who also designed that 4-3 defensive scheme that took advantage of Huff's instincts and talents that made him so great.

Huff finished his NFL career having appeared in 168 games. He recorded 30 interceptions for 381 yards and two touchdowns and recovered 17 fumbles, two of which he returned for scores.

In 2010, Huff would be among the 30-man inaugural class inducted into the Giants Ring of Honor.

13

THE FUMBLE

"**W**hat the hell just happened?"

Such was the reaction of the Giants Stadium crowd who, on November 19, 1978, sat in stunned silence as they watched quarterback Joe Pisarcik line up with less than 30 seconds left in a game the Giants were about to win against the Philadelphia Eagles.

Instead of kneeling to kill the clock, Pisarcik took the snap and tried to hand the ball off to fullback Larry Csonka. The handoff was muffed, and Eagles defensive back Herman Edwards scooped up and returned the loose pigskin for a 26-yard game-winning touchdown.

In the blink of an eye, the Giants, trying to end to a playoff drought dating back to 1964, were dealt a serious blow to their postseason hopes thanks to one of the most infamous plays in the game of football.

That play is known as "The Fumble" in Giants lore, or "The Miracle at the Meadowlands" in Eagles history.

Whatever name people prefer—and there were many colorful names used by irate Giants fans that aren't suitable for print—"The Fumble" became the symbol for all that had gone wrong for the once-mighty Giants.

The fan base was so furious that after "The Fumble," some staged a ticket-burning protest outside of Giants Stadium. Yet another group orchestrated the rental of a small aircraft to fly a short but sternly written message over Giants Stadium intended for the Mara family that screamed, "15 Years of Lousy Football... We've Had Enough."

While Pisarcik was directly involved in the execution—or lack thereof—of the play, offensive coordinator Bob Gibson was the architect.

Gibson's place in Giants history was believed to have been on shaky ground even before that fateful call. Earlier in the season, reports began to emerge that there was growing discontent between the players and the assistant coaches working under then-head coach John McVay.

McVay, who succeeded Bill Arnsparger following his dismissal midway through the 1976 season, was well-liked and respected by the players, but the same couldn't be said about some of his assistant coaches.

The most significant source of the players' discontent was Gibson, who took a "my way or the highway" approach. When it came to Pisarcik, it didn't help that Gibson didn't see eye-to-eye with the quarterback in the two seasons they worked together.

Despite their differences, Gibson's decision to call the play that led to "The Fumble" was believed to have been done so more out of concern for Pisarcik.

On an earlier play, Pisarcik took the snap from center Jim Clack and dropped to the ground. However, Eagles inside linebacker Bill Bergey broke the unwritten rule of sportsmanship that called for not rushing at the opponent if the quarterback took a knee and ended up pushing Clack back and into Pisarcik.

A mini scuffle ensued but was quickly broken up before the penalty flags could start flying.

Gibson, an old-school coach who was not a fan of taking a knee to end the game—the practice more commonly known as the "victory formation"—did not want to risk having Pisarcik get hurt by an overzealous Eagles defense or see his players baited into a scuffle that could benefit the Eagles. That thinking is believed to be at the core of his decision to call a traditional power running play to run out the clock.

When Gibson made his call—Brown Right, Near Wing, 65 Slant—members of the Giants' offense were said to be so stunned that they lingered in the huddle because they were trying to talk Pisarcik out of running the play.

Meanwhile, McVay would later admit to having missed Gibson's call because his headset wasn't functioning. Had it been working, McVay later said he would have overruled his offensive coordinator's decision.

Back in the huddle, Csonka pleaded with Pisarcik not to give him the ball. But Pisarcik, a second-year NFL quarterback who, a few weeks earlier, had landed in hot water with Gibson when he changed a play call, was reluctant to go against his marching orders.

So Pisarcik, likely knowing full well that his coach had made a risky call, went to the line hoping for the best. With time about to expire and the Eagles out of timeouts, the play, now immortalized by NFL Films, unfolded to the disbelief of the more than 70,000 strong in attendance.

Once the Giants lined up, Pisarcik, on film, can be seen looking back at Csonka, lined up to the left side of the formation, perhaps trying to verify with Csonka that he would indeed take the handoff despite having asked not to get the ball in the huddle.

Clack appeared to snap the ball a split second early, possibly concerned with the play clock winding down.

Instead of the belly of the ball hitting Pisarcik in his hands, the quarterback can be seen coming away from center with hands closer to the nose of the ball.

Pisarcik turned to his right side, as Csonka, on his left side, started forward. As Pisarcik pirouetted while trying not to lose the ball, the play's timing had been compromised.

By the time the handoff was attempted, Csonka can be seen on tape having run past the mesh point where the handoff should have occurred.

Pisarcik, rather than scramble or better yet fall on the ball given the compromised timing, tried to salvage the play by attempting to tuck it into Csonka's gut. Unfortunately, he hit him on his right hip as the ball bounced out of Pisarcik's hands and to the ground.

Pisarcik then tried to smother the ball to retain possession, but it squirted away from him. Meanwhile, Giants running back Doug Kotar, the other player nearest to the ball, was unaware of what had happened as he was moving forward. In contrast, Edwards, who was rushing toward the Giants backfield, was in the perfect spot for a scoop and score, while tight end Gary Shirk tried in vain to catch him from behind.

"That was the beautiful part," Edwards said after about the play. "It came to me on the first bounce."

The score not only gave the Eagles the win to keep their playoff hopes alive, it also avenged Edwards, who earlier in the game had been beaten on one of Pisarcik's two touchdown passes.

The spectators' shock of having witnessed the play was quickly replaced by outrage. Those fans who had stayed to see the Giants wrap up the game and keep their playoff hopes alive, showered the players and coaches with boos and expletives as they left the field.

The day after the Giants made national headlines for having blown the game, Wellington Mara and director of football operations Andy Robustelli fired Gibson.

"It was not Bob's fault that the quarterback fumbled," Robustelli told reporters about the decision. "Unfortunately, it was a play that the quarterback might have doubted. The players have to believe in what the coaches tell them."

McVay meanwhile, made little attempt to hide the fact that the decision to fire Gibson was not his, calling it "an administrative decision."

The head coach, who was in a contract year, was allowed to finish out the season, but he was not renewed.

As for the Eagles, the "Miracle at the Meadowlands" was the spark that sent them to the playoffs. Two seasons later, they would make their first Super Bowl appearance.

The Giants? As is usually the case when someone is struggling, sometimes it takes hitting rock bottom before reality sets in.

The following season, the Giants began making some major franchise-changing decisions, starting with the hiring of George Young as their general manager and the selection of quarterback Phil Simms in the first round of the 1979 draft.

It would take a lot more to rebuild the franchise that hit rock bottom thanks to one coach's stubbornness that November afternoon, but at least it was a step in the right direction.

14

THE ELI MANNING TRADE

"IF HE COMES OUT EARLY, WE SHOULD MOVE UP TO TAKE HIM. THESE GUYS ARE RARE, YOU KNOW."

Such were the words written in all capital letters, bolded for emphasis, by general manager Ernie Accorsi in his scouting report about a baby-faced quarterback for the Ole Miss Rebels by the name of Eli Manning.

Yes, *that* Eli Manning, he of the NFL's first family of quarterbacks which included dad, Archie, who spent the bulk of his career with the New Orleans Saints; and big brother Peyton, who won Super Bowl championships with the Indianapolis Colts (where he spent the majority of his career) and the Denver Broncos.

Once the trade came together for Manning, there was no looking back for the Giants. But long before that happened, Accorsi had several hurdles he had to overcome to make his dream a reality.

The first was convincing team patriarch Wellington Mara of the benefits of drafting a young quarterback.

Wellington's son John, now the team president, remembers his father as having doubts about Accorsi's plan partially because of his loyalty to Kerry Collins, who had stabilized the quarterback position long after Phil Simms hung up his cleats.

"My father's reluctance had nothing to do with Eli, because he loved the Manning family and thought very highly of Eli as well," John said. "But my father was a very big Kerry Collins fan at the time. He had taken us to the Super Bowl, and he thought Kerry was still capable of winning a lot of games for us."

Mara added that his father was likely starting to feel his own mortality as he was getting up there in years and that starting over with a rookie quarterback would set the franchise—and his chances of seeing another championship—back.

"Ultimately, he saw the big picture and the long-term view," John said. "I kept telling him, 'Dad, you don't get that many opportunities in

By the time he retired after the 2019 season, quarterback Eli Manning, the only Giants player in franchise history to win two Super Bowl MVP awards, held nearly every franchise passing record. (Copyright New York Football Giants)

life to add a franchise quarterback. And if we can do that, we're going to be set for many years.'"

With Wellington Mara having consented, Accorsi had another obstacle to overcome.

The Giants had the fourth overall pick in the 2004 draft, and there were whispers that the San Diego Chargers, also in need of a franchise quarterback and the holders of the first overall pick in the draft, were eyeballing Manning.

But a combination of irony and fate was at work. In 1983, Accorsi, then the general manager of the Baltimore Colts, drafted quarterback John Elway. However, Elway not only didn't want to play for the Colts, but he also wanted to play for a team on the West Coast and threatened to forgo a career in football unless he was traded.

Colts owner Robert Irsay, in taking Elway's threats to boycott the Colts seriously, ended up trading Elway to the Denver Broncos without Accorsi's knowledge, leaving the Colts without their desired franchise quarterback.

Over 20 years later, Accorsi was involved with a team on the other end of the spectrum, as there were reports that Manning was said to be hoping to join the Giants.

Manning, to this day, won't comment on those reports, but during a 2016 interview with NFL Network host Rich Eisen on the *Rich Eisen Show*, his father, Archie, shared a little insight.

"It was a decision that Eli and (agent) Tom Condon kind of made, but Eli ultimately pulled the trigger on that, and that's what he, doing his due diligence, decided to do," the elder Manning said.

"I can't say it was pleasant from our end. Most people thought I orchestrated it, but I didn't. I don't tell my kids what to do or make their decisions."

Regardless of what anyone thought, the Chargers were in the driver's seat. And since Accorsi and Chargers general manager A.J. Smith barely knew one another, doing business with the Chargers was the equivalent of entering into uncharted waters for Accorsi.

Fortunately for Accorsi and the Giants, Smith was willing to talk business. However, Smith's first two proposals included Giants defensive end Osi Umenyiora.

"There was *no way* I was going to trade a pass rusher," Accorsi said. "No way. *That* was a deal-breaker."

With a chance to land Manning fading, Accorsi was prepared to draft Miami (Ohio) quarterback Ben Roethlisberger at No. 4.

When the draft began, Accorsi received an offer from the Cleveland Browns, who held the seventh overall pick in the draft, that he very nearly took.

"I JUST KNEW"

Ernie Accorsi would have been pleased to have had quarterback Ben Roethlisberger in a Giants uniform.

But he also knew in his heart that he'd be a lot happier to have Eli Manning. Manning, who, in addition to having the skillset and measurables that Accorsi was looking for, also had the perfect demeanor to fit into the NFL's largest and perhaps most demanding media market.

Accorsi's conviction stemmed from a conversation he had years ago with Milt Davis, a former NFL cornerback who had been on the 1958 Colts team and who had done some part-time scouting in his later years.

Davis gave Accorsi a piece of golden advice when it came toward evaluating quarterback.

"He said, 'All the physical attributes are very important. Strong arm, proper size, some athletic ability, quick release, you know, reading defenses—they're all important. But in the final analysis, the difference between the good ones and the great ones is can they take their team down the field with the championship on the line and into the end zone and be the reason it happened?'"

Accorsi believed that both Roethlisberger and Manning could be that kind of quarterback.

So why did he move heaven and earth to acquire Manning when he likely could have had Roethlisberger at No. 4?

"You got to feel it in your heart," Accorsi said. "Roethlisberger had an off-the-charts pro day. So did Eli, but on Eli's Pro Day, [Tulane] quarterback J.P. Losman showed up unannounced to work out. So Tom Condon [the Manning brothers' agent] comes up to me and tells me that Peyton Manning, who's there as well to watch, is furious with Losman for showing up unannounced.

"So I asked, 'Well, what about Eli?' Condon said, 'You know what? He doesn't give a damn.'

"And that's right where I just knew."

The Browns offered to swap first-round picks and send the Giants their second-round pick.

Accorsi admitted that he was tempted to take the deal because he thought there was a chance that Roethlisberger might still be there if he moved down a few spots, plus the extra draft pick was appealing.

But Accorsi's gut told him to stay put.

Good thing Accorsi listened. After the Chargers drafted Manning and the Raiders and Cardinals selected offensive tackle Robert Gallery and wide receiver Larry Fitzgerald respectively, the Giants were on the clock, when Accorsi's phone rang about seven minutes into his 15-minute-selection window.

On the line was Smith with a revised set of parameters that didn't include Umenyiora. Instead, Smith wanted quarterback Phillip Rivers, whom the Giants would draft at No. 4 overall, the Giants' third-round pick, and their first- and fifth-round selections in 2005.

Accorsi was fine with those terms, but even with the parameters now in place, he was still worried because he wasn't 100 percent sure the deal would be consummated.

Accorsi was, in fact, so nervous about the deal that he at one point wanted Chargers owner Dean Spanos to personally promise Wellington Mara that the transaction would be happen.

But time didn't allow for such an arrangement, and with Accorsi knowing there was no way the league would disallow his selection of Rivers if he made the pick and Smith reneged on the deal, he did the next best thing.

"Joel Bussert [the NFL's senior vice president of player personnel and football operations at the time] had me and A.J. both on the phone at the same time, and we both repeated the terms of the trade to him. Once everyone agreed, Joel said, 'We have a trade,' though I also wanted it in writing," Accorsi said.

"But thank God (Smith) kept his word."

When Manning, who was in New York where the draft was being held, later arrived at Giants Stadium, Wellington Mara was the first to greet the new face of the franchise.

"In my opinion, he has that quality you can't define," Accorsi had written in his original scouting report of Manning, whose athletic ability he compared to 49ers legend Joe Montana.

The draft day card that made Eli Manning the No. 1 overall pick in the 2004 NFL draft. Manning was traded by the San Diego Chargers to the Giants. (Artifact shown is from the Pro Football Hall of Fame)

"Call it magic," he added.

Or better yet, call Accorsi's conviction about Manning to make the quarterback the centerpiece of one of the biggest and gutsiest trades in the franchise's history.

15

CAPPY

Long before there was Lawrence Taylor, without question the best athlete to ever wear a Giants uniform in the modern-day era, the Giants had another "Superman" whom team owner Wellington Mara once described as the No. 1 player in the franchise's first 50 years of existence.

That player was Mel "Cappy" Hein, a center and linebacker whose 15-year career spanned the 1931–45 seasons. Hein was the very definition of an iron man, who refused to take a breather despite playing on both sides of the ball.

He also refused to let what he once described his "worst" injury—a broken nose suffered against the NFL's Brooklyn Dodgers in 1941, which forced him to wear a protective mask—take him out of a game for any longer than what was necessary for team doctors to fix him back up.

A team captain for 10 seasons, Hein, who got the nickname "Cappy" because of his captainship, was as a ferocious player on the field as he was a gentleman off it.

* * *

Hein was born on August 22, 1909, in Shasta County, California. A multisport star in high school, where he participated in football and basketball, Hein attended Washington State College (now known as Washington State University) from 1928 to 1930, where he anchored the Cougars offensive line as their center and helped lead the 1930 team to an undefeated record.

At the end of his college career, Hein, a strapping 6'3", 225-pound figure, was chosen by the Associated Press as the first-team center on the 1930 All-Pacific Coast football team, one of two players (the other being USC end Garrett Arbelbide) who received all but one vote by the selection committee.

With the NFL draft still five years away from coming into existence, Hein, like his contemporaries coming out of college, had to do his legwork to find a team willing to offer him a contract.

In 1931, he wrote to the New York Giants and the Providence Steamrollers, hoping one would invite him to their camp.

The Steamrollers were first to respond to Hein's inquiry, offering him a contract worth $125 per game, which Hein accepted.

Hein no sooner signed and mailed back his contract when he heard from the Giants, who offered him $150 per game. Wanting the better salary, Hein wired the Providence, Rhode Island postmaster to request delivery of his letter to the Steamrollers be returned to sender.

Fortunately, the Providence postmaster was able to locate and return Hein's letter, allowing Hein to destroy the signed contract.

With Hein having avoided entering into a legally binding agreement with the Steamrollers, who folded after the 1931 season, he was now free to sign with the Giants.

Now with the Giants, with whom he helped win two championship titles (in 1934 and 1938), it wouldn't be long before Hein took the NFL by storm with his toughness and grit.

Back in those early days, NFL players wore leather helmets without facemasks. During a game against the Chicago Bears, George Musso, a nose tackle and offensive guard who outweighed Hein by a good 30 pounds, threw a punch.

Hein, known for being a good sport and a competitor who rarely lost his temper on the field, asked Musso not to hit him again.

Musso, however, ignored Hein's request.

Hein, his ire rising, wasn't going to take a chance at having Musso hit him a third time.

"On the following play, I was ready," Hein said years later. "I snapped the ball with one hand and got him with an uppercut square in the face. I could tell he really felt it. He never tried it again."

Besides his toughness, Hein was a dominating talent whom opposing coaches knew they couldn't easily exploit.

There are many examples of his athletic ability throughout his career, but one that comes to mind occurred in a 1938 regular-season game against the Packers, whom the Giants would eventually meet and beat in that year's Championship Game, 23–17.

In the regular-season meeting, the Giants were nursing a 9–3 lead going into the fourth quarter. Hein, playing linebacker, picked off a pass and returned it 50 yards for the score and the 15–3 win.

Hein had such an impressive 1938 season that he was named the recipient of the Joe F. Carr Trophy, awarded back then to the league's Most Valuable Player, a rare honor for an offensive lineman.

He was also named a first-team All-NFL center, a title he earned in 1933–40, and was a five-time first-team All-Pro who was also named to four Pro Bowls.

Although Hein showed no signs of slowing down as he aged, head coach Steve Owen began thinking about lessening the load on his team's star player after they had acquired Chet Gladchuk from Boston College and Lou DeFilippo from Fordham.

"Mel, you'll be able to take it a little easier now," Owen told him.

So much for Owen's good intentions. Gladchuk moved to tackle and DeFilippo to guard, and Hein remained at center.

* * *

On December 6, 1942, a 10–0 Giants win over the Dodgers, Hein played what he intended to be his last game as a member of the Giants in front of a crowd of just under 28,000 fans.

As he had done so many times before in his Giants career, Hein's final play in the game proved to be key in preserving a win. Late in the fourth quarter, the Giants fumbled the ball to set the Dodgers up with first-and-goal at the Giants' 5-yard line.

But the Dodgers weren't about to get past the Giants, thanks in part to Hein. After moving the ball only three yards on three tries, Brooklyn decided to go for it on fourth down, handing the ball off to Merl Condit, one of the league's best rushers that season.

Condit took the handoff and attempted to round the left end to gain access to the end zone. But he never made it, having been stopped short by Hein, who had wrapped up Condit's legs.

When Hein later said his goodbyes to his teammates, Owen, and the Mara family, the eight-time All-League star accepted a position as the athletic director of Union College in upstate New York, a position that he had planned to accept about three years earlier.

"It's going to be nice teaching football and directing athletics at a school like Union," Hein said after the game. "But I know I'm going to miss getting in the ball game now and then. I'm going to feel might funny next fall when I see a lot of boys belting each other around out there on the field, but I've had my fun. I'm 33 now, and I guess I've played enough."

Well, not quite.

Because of the intense recruitment efforts to support the U.S. involvement in World War II, the Union College football program went on hiatus. With no program to run, Hein "felt the itch" to give the pro game another go-round and continued his NFL career with the Giants on weekends for another three seasons before finally calling it quits after the 1945 season.

* * *

According to the Pro Football Hall of Fame website, there are currently 16 two-way players from the pre-modern era who played one of their positions on the offensive line.

Hein, one of the Hall's charter inductees, is one. Chuck "Concrete Charlie" Bednarik, who spent his entire career (1949–62) with the Philadelphia Eagles, and who, like Hein, was a two-way player, having played center and linebacker, is another.

Some pro football historians consider Bednarik as the last of the two-way players. However, he only played two ways for part of his career, whereas Hein did so in each of his 15 NFL seasons.

When Hein retired for good after the 1945 season, he went back to his full-time status as a football coach at Union College. In 1947, he moved back to the pro ranks as an assistant coach of the Los Angeles Dons of the All-America Football Conference for two seasons before spending one season each with the New York Yankees and the Los Angeles Rams.

Hein was later hired by the University of Southern California as an assistant coach before being named by American Football League Commissioner Al Davis as the league's supervisor of officials in 1966, a position he retained following the AFL and NFL merger in 1970.

For as tough as Hein, a member of the Pro Football Hall of Fame's All-1930s Team and the NFL's 100 All-Time Team, was during a player, there was one opponent that he, unfortunately, couldn't beat.

On January 31, 1992, at the age of 82, Hein, one of the franchise's greatest players, lost his battle with stomach cancer.

16

ERNIE ACCORSI

As the glory years of the 1980s gave way to a new decade, Giants general manager George Young's health issues started to take a toll on his stamina.

Knowing that he needed additional help with the more stressful parts of his job, Young, reached out to a familiar face from his past.

That face was Ernie Accorsi, an established NFL executive in his own right who had been a general manager with the Baltimore Colts and with the Cleveland Browns before joining the Giants.

Accorsi, who started working for the Colts in 1970 as the team's public relations director (two years after Young began working for the club as a football executive), first got to know Young during a chance encounter at a Rustler Steakhouse next to the Townsend motel where Accorsi was staying.

"I went in, and George and his wife Lovey were sitting there," Accorsi recalled. "I had only met George for two minutes, but he was like, 'Come over and join us.' So, I sat with them, and after a while, Lovey said she was going home and asked me if I would take George home. I agreed, and George and I sat there for a couple of hours talking. From that day on, we became close."

It was that close relationship with Young that convinced Accorsi, who, after being fired by the Browns had re-settled in Baltimore to work for baseball's Orioles, decided to give football another try.

"I liked Baltimore, and I had no intention of going anywhere," Accorsi admitted. "If it hadn't been George calling, I would have stayed with the Orioles in Baltimore."

When Accorsi got to the Giants, things got off to a rocky start. He took on most of Young's scouting duties, but it was the contract work and dealing with the NFL salary cap that presented the biggest challenges.

"I said 'George, I don't know anything about this salary cap and this free agency business,'" Accorsi said.

"When I went to work, they put me in a cubicle by the draft room, and they were like, 'Here's the book on free agency and the salary cap.' It was like trying to learn a foreign language from a book, which was not how I learned things and is why I later hired Kevin Abrams [in 1999] to manage the salary cap."

When Accorsi was promoted to general manager after Young left the club following the 1998 season, one of the most significant moves Accorsi made was to fix the team's unstable quarterback situation.

Accorsi signed former Carolina Panthers first-round draft pick Kerry Collins, whose NFL career had fallen on hard times due to off-field issues that included a November 1998 arrest for an alleged DUI incident in Charlotte, North Carolina.

The decision to sign Collins wasn't universally well-received in the Giants locker room due to another incident, this in 1997, in which, according to the *New York Times*, he allegedly used a racial epithet in conversation with Panthers wide receiver Muhsin Muhammad.

Collins, however, not only became a model citizen for the Giants, but he also helped steer them to Super Bowl XXXV.

Another franchise-altering decision in which Accorsi was right in the thick of things was the team's search for a new head coach following the departure of Jim Fassel after the 2003 season.

Accorsi had kept a book on personnel who impressed him, and one name that stuck out was Tom Coughlin, a member of Bill Parcells' staff from 1988 to 1990 who went on to become the head coach at Boston College in 1991,and then the first coach in Jacksonville Jaguars history in 1995.

Accorsi also made other significant moves to help set up the franchise for its first Super Bowl win in the 2007 season, the year after he retired. But without question, his most historic and perhaps impactful move was the acquisition of quarterback Eli Manning in 2004 via trade with the San Diego Chargers.

"You never like to say you were fortunate going 4–12 like we did in 2003," Accorsi said, "But if we hadn't been fourth (in the draft order), I don't know that we would have been able to get Eli. We had Eli first and (quarterback) Ben Roethlisberger second. If neither of them had been there, I don't know what we would have done."

Many believe that the Manning acquisition was a mulligan in getting a franchise quarterback. In 1983, Accorsi, the Colts general manager, had drafted quarterback John Elway despite growing rumbles that Elway would abandon football for a career in baseball if the Colts drafted him.

When the Colts did select Elway, the growing threats by his camp to quit football became so much that Colts owner Robert Irsay, without consulting Accorsi, ended up trading Elway to Denver. Although Accorsi had no say in that trade, it was still a blow considering he drafted Elway.

Two decades later, Accorsi was finally able to stand beside his franchise quarterback along with Coughlin.

Eli Manning holds up his new Giants jersey as he poses with Tom Coughlin and Ernie Accorsi on Saturday, April 24, 2004, in East Rutherford, New Jersey.
(AP Images / Bill Kostroun)

The cost? Quarterback Phillip Rivers, the Giants' 2004 first-round pick, their 2004 third-round pick, and their 2005 first- and fifth-round picks.

Accorsi also added another of the many critical pieces to the Giants' 2007 season's championship team, that being receiver Plaxico Burress, though that transaction also had its share of hold-your-breath moments for the general manager.

The Giants, who have long had a practice of not directly confirming any negotiations with free agents for competitive reasons, broke with tradition in what Accorsi described as a "strategic" decision.

"Plaxico came in, and I had [running back] Tiki Barber come up and talk to him," Accorsi recalled. "My instincts told me Plaxico really wanted to be with us, but his agent was asking for the moon. I'm trying to close the deal, and the agent is looking to break the bank and won't close the deal with us. Then he tells us, 'Well, I'm taking [Burress] to Minnesota.' Meanwhile, I read that Plaxico, who I love, by the way, didn't even want to go and that he wanted to sign with us, but of course, players always listen to their agents.

"So, I said to [assistant general manager] Kevin [Abrams], 'I'm going to make an announcement that we lost him because I want him to see that, and I also want to put pressure on Minnesota.' I wanted to take away any bargaining edge they had because I'm competing with them. So that's why I issued the press release."

The tactic worked. Burress fired his agent and hired Drew Rosenhaus, a tough, but fair negotiator with whom the Giants have historically had a stable business relationship. On March 17, 2005, Burress, who was said to have requested jersey No. 17 in honor of the day he became a Giant, signed a six-year contract worth a reported $25 million.

Burress, who ended up playing in four out of the six years of his contract, would top the 1,000-yard mark in two of those years, the last being in 2007. And it was Burress who caught the game-winning touchdown in Super Bowl XLII—a simple over-the-shoulder fade thrown to the corner of the end zone—to give New York its first world championship season since 1990.

* * *

Given all he had accomplished with the Giants, Accorsi could have very well continued in his post indefinitely. But after the 2006 season, just a few months shy of his 65th birthday, he decided to walk away.

"There were two things," he said when asked why he left when he did.

"Number one, I never want to be pushed out. [Former] Orioles manager Earl Weaver once told me there were a lot of former Major League Baseball managers living down there in Florida who were bitter because they all thought they were great managers. They stayed too long and got pushed out. I always wanted to go out on my terms."

And the second reason?

"Quite honestly, I couldn't take the games anymore," he said. "It got to a point where I just couldn't watch the games. I'd get up on Sunday morning to go to Mass, which is something I'd look forward to, and then once Mass was over, I'd say to myself, 'You've got 12 hours of agony; if you lose the game, you know you've got like a week of agony,' and I just couldn't take it anymore."

The decision to retire might very well have saved Accorsi's life. A year after he retired, an EKG revealed he had two 100 percent blockages and needed a bypass procedure.

"Who knows what would have happened?" Accorsi said. "I mean, I hardly had any symptoms."

Before he left the Giants, Accorsi, who would later become a consultant for NFL teams looking to hire general managers and head coaches, had one more difficult decision he was called upon to help make for the Giants: recommending his successor.

The choice came down to Jerry Reese, who had worked his way through the organization's ranks from being college scout to the team's director of player personnel, and Dave Gettleman, the Giants' longtime pro personnel director.

"I recommended Jerry, and I knew that hurt Dave," Accorsi said. "But it was a toss-up. Afterward, Dave asked me, 'Did you recommend Jerry?' I said, 'Yes I did.' And he said, 'Why?' I said I wasn't going to split my vote and that I wanted to back one person."

But why Reese?

"It's hard to explain," Accorsi said. "I didn't want to show that I wasn't confident in either one. I can't even tell you why—instinctively, I just thought Jerry."

Although he recommended Reese, Accorsi still firmly believed that Gettleman had a future as an NFL general manager.

When Accorsi became a consultant, he recommended Gettleman several times for a general manager's job—once to the Falcons, twice to the Browns, and once to the Panthers, who hired Gettleman in 2013.

When the Panthers fired Gettleman in the summer of 2017 and Reese was relieved of his duties by the Giants later that year, the Giants wasted no time in snapping Gettleman up as their new general manager, partially due to their familiarity with Gettleman and partly due to Accorsi's recommendation.

"I not only got to make it up to Dave, but he ended up with the Giants anyway. And I was glad I got a chance to recommend Dave because he's an outstanding football man and a good person. I knew he was going to do a very good job for whoever hired him."

17

DECEMBER 29, 2007: SEEKING TO SPOIL

Like the rest of his teammates, Giants guard Chris Snee was physically beaten up from the long, emotionally draining 2007 season.

When Week 17 rolled around—with the Giants already having a playoff berth locked up that could not change regardless of what they did in the regular-season finale—Snee was secretly hoping that Tom Coughlin, his father- in-law and head coach, would consider going easy on the players.

Looking back, Snee said he should have known better.

"The minute he came in, you could see the look in his eye, and you knew it was going to come out of his mouth," he recalled.

"And when once he said, 'We're going to play to win,' I was like, 'All right; I'll just hop in the ice tub, and we'll get ready to go play this game.'"

The decision by Coughlin to play his starters for the entire game certainly drew a lot of criticism for the risk. With nothing to be gained or lost as far as playoff seeding was concerned, why would Coughlin risk of having key players suffer injuries for a game whose outcome meant nothing?

The answer is because the game meant something to Coughlin—and he wanted it to mean something to his players as well.

"Our objective is to win," Coughlin repeatedly told the media in the days leading up to that regular-season finale held on the Giants' home turf. "That's what we work for, that's what we prepare for, that's what we practice for. And it will be no different this week."

If there was dissension among the ranks, the players, to their credit, kept their mouths shut, shrugged their tired shoulders, rolled up their sleeves, and went to work.

This, after all, was a game that the Giants could make history if they somehow found a way to beat a Patriots team that, before that Week 17 meeting, had scored 551 points in building a strong case to join the 1972 Miami Dolphins as the only team to have an undefeated season.

Stopping the Patriots, who had one of the most prolific offenses of the modern era of football, wasn't going to be easy. But Giants defensive co-captain Antonio Pierce, their middle linebacker, had a different perspective about the challenge that in retrospect helped take away any intimidation his teammates might have initially felt.

"All those [numbers] didn't come against us," said Pierce.

"Those 551 points, those 15 wins—that wasn't against the New York Giants. This is just one game. It isn't our fault the guys before decided to give up all those points."

He had a point. And what better reward for the Giants players than to cut the mighty Patriots down to size?

"I wanted to play," running back Brandon Jacobs recalled. "At the time, I was dealing with some nagging injuries, but I was like, 'Man, I want to see what this undefeated stuff is all about, so I hope Coach lets us play.'"

Center Shaun O'Hara remembered how Coughlin didn't mince words when he addressed the team the Wednesday before the game.

"Coach Coughlin wanted to be the first one that talked to us in the team meeting," O'Hara said. "He wanted to set the mood for the week. So he came in and flat-out said, 'I know everybody's got thoughts about resting your players and don't get anybody hurt. Well, you tell me who's going to get hurt, and I'll sit them down right now.'"

Not a single player volunteered an opinion.

O'Hara also revealed that Coughlin's selling point to the team was the chance to become the spoiler of the Patriots' perfect season.

"It was kind of refreshing to hear him talk about that," O'Hara admitted. "We're not going to bow down. We're not scared of them— we're not scared of anybody. Let's go play. And I felt relief. He gave us the push, 'Hey, you know what? Let's be the first team to beat them. If they go 15–1 and we're the ones who to beat them, that's kind of cool.' And I think that got the juices flowing."

With the juices flowing, the Giants came out to a mostly Patriots crowd that had infiltrated Giants Stadium. The Giants then reminded those paying customers who donned Patriots jerseys that this was their house, and they weren't in the mood to step aside as the Patriots chased perfection.

Except for the fourth quarter, when New England took a 38–28 lead on Laurence Maroney's five-yard touchdown run with 4:36 left in the game, the Giants were never down by more than three points in the game. In fact, with 9:12 left in the third quarter, the Giants even had a 12-point lead.

Although the Giants came up just short of pulling off the upset, quarterback Eli Manning, on their final drive, converted all three third-down attempts, including a three-yard touchdown pass to receiver Plaxico Burress to cut the Patriots' lead to three points with 1:04 left.

The Patriots prevailed—barely—by a score of 38–35. While the Giants had lost the game, in terms of the bigger picture, they were actually winners.

"That one game right specifically made us feel like, 'That's undefeated? They just gave us everything they had, and that's undefeated?'" Jacobs said. "We're like, 'Okay, well we should have won and we're the one team they probably don't want to see again.'

"We knew that they didn't want to play us again because there was no way that they would be comfortable seeing us on the other sideline at any point ever again that year."

Rightfully so. The Giants were the only team that season to score at least 30 points against a Patriots defense that, through 15 games that season, had allowed opponents an average of 15.9 points per game.

After the game, Snee remembered stopping to chat with a few members of the Patriots with whom he was friendly.

"They weren't exactly saying, 'We hope we don't have to play you again,' but they did say, 'If we play [the Giants] again, it's going to be a tough game,'" Snee said.

Even Coughlin, who hated to lose any game, saw the bright side. "There is nothing but positives," he said during his postgame press conference. "We had everything to gain and absolutely nothing to lose. I don't know of any better way to prepare for the playoffs than to go up against a 15–0 team."

"Maybe now," Pierce quipped after the game, "people will stop talking about us being a bad 10–6 team."

While the media gushed over Patriots quarterback Tom Brady, Eli Manning had something tucked away in his pocket.

According to an ESPN report, Manning was said to have been told by his brother Peyton before the game that the Patriots defense was beatable (a claim that the younger Manning didn't directly deny).

Manning, taking whatever advice he had gotten from his brother and combining it with his own meticulous preparation, had one of his better performances.

He completed 22 of 32 pass attempts for 251 yards, four touchdowns, and one interception—not bad for a young quarterback who the prior season had drawn questions from critics about his ability to win.

"This is the momentum you look for," Coughlin told reporters. "Playing this hard with this intensity—this is what you want to take into the playoffs."

That intensity is precisely what the future Super Bowl XLII champions took into a postseason that covered every extreme imaginable.

18

THE "BALD EAGLE"

He was finished—or so the critics of Yelberton Abraham Tittle Jr, better known as "Y.A." in football circles, believed.

But Tittle, who as a college junior at LSU, took part in the famous "Ice Bowl" game between the Tigers and Arkansas in a blustery snowstorm, would quickly show his harshest critics that he had plenty of football left.

Tittle began his pro football career in 1948 with the Baltimore Colts, who at the time were part of the All-America Football Conference (AAFC).

When the Colts folded after the 1950 season, Tittle was drafted in 1951 by the San Francisco 49ers for whom he played 10 seasons.

As part of the 49ers' "Million Dollar Backfield," (which also included halfbacks Hugh "The King" McElhenny and John Henry Johnson, and fullback Joe "The Jet" Perry), Tittle was a shining star whose crowning achievements might very well have been being named the NFL Player of the Year in a 1957 United Press poll, and, before that, becoming the first NFL player to be featured on the cover of *Sports Illustrated* (November 22, 1954).

But just as real stars fade over time, so too did Tittle's star in San Francisco. Having turned the corner age-wise into his thirties, whispers about him being washed up soon reached the level of a low-volume roar.

In August 1961, the 49ers finally decided to move on from their one-time franchise quarterback, shipping the 34-year-old Tittle to the New York Giants in exchange for second-year guard Lou Cordileone, the 12th overall pick in the 1960 draft.

Tittle, who knew that there were talks of the 49ers planning to move on from him, at first wasn't happy with the trade destination. In his book *Nothing Comes Easy*, Tittle recalled 49ers head coach Herman "Red" Hickey telling him about the trade—and the player the team got in return from the Giants.

"Who the hell is Lou Cordileone?" Tittle wrote. "They didn't even bother to trade a name player for me. Tittle for a guard named Cordileone? Well, that takes me down a peg."

Besides being upset over what the 49ers received in return, Tittle was upset over being traded to the East Coast. He had hoped that if a trade did happen, that his next team would be the Los Angeles Rams, because he didn't want to leave behind his family and his off-season insurance business based on the West Coast.

The shoulder pads that quarterback Y.A. Tittle wore throughout his career with the 49ers and later the Giants. (Artifact shown is from the Pro Football Hall of Fame)

Tittle was so distraught over the trade that at one point, he even contemplated retiring. Eventually, he warmed up to the idea of joining the Giants after speaking with his wife and was soon off to report to the Giants' training camp in Salem, Oregon.

Tittle's arrival to the Giants was met with mixed reactions. Allie Sherman, who had been promoted from offensive coordinator to head coach following the retirement of Jim Lee Howell after the 1960 season, saw Tittle as insurance in case 40-year-old Charlie Conerly couldn't make it through the season and youngster Lee Grosscup wasn't ready.

Many of the players, however, saw Tittle as an outsider and initially gave him the cold shoulder. It didn't help that Tittle, in his first season with the Giants, suffered a back injury right out of the chute, that occurring in the team's first exhibition game.

"THE END OF MY DANCE"

On November 22, 1954, Y.A. Tittle, then with the 49ers "Million Dollar Backfield" and the man credited with coining the phrase "alley-oop" as a sports term to describe a high-arching pass, became the first NFL player to be featured on the cover of *Sports Illustrated*.

In 1964, Tittle appeared in perhaps one of sports' most iconic photos, a picture snapped by Morris Berman of the *Pittsburgh Post-Gazette* that captured a battered, bruised, and bloody-faced Tittle on his knees in the end zone of Pitt Stadium.

That photograph not only epitomized the Giants' season, which would see them fall from first to last place, it also preceded the end of Tittle's illustrious career.

The Giants, who finished 2–10–2 that year, lost that September 20, 1964, game to the Steelers. In that game, Tittle, the defending league MVP, had thrown an interception returned eight yards for a touchdown by Chuck Hinton in the second quarter.

But it was a brutal hit by John Baker which left the 37-year-old quarterback dazed and confused, and the ensuing act of compassion by linebacker Bill Saul who is seen towering over the crumpled Tittle with his hand gently on the quarterback's shoulder that spelled the end for the Bald Eagle.

"That was the end of my dance," Tittle said years later of what that photo captured. "A whole lifetime was over."

Tittle, who missed the 1961 regular-season opener, was back by the second game. That season, he would go on to start 11 games (including postseason), throwing for 2,337 yards, 17 touchdowns, and 16 interceptions.

Conerly, meanwhile, retired after the 1961 season, leaving the Giants to look to Grosscup, the 10th overall pick in the 1959 NFL draft. However, Grosscup's career never got off the ground, as in the eight games over two seasons he was with the Giants, he completed just 16 out of 47 passes for 231 yards, two touchdowns, and four interceptions.

With the Giants offense now in the hands of the man nicknamed the "Bald Eagle" for his receded hairline, the Giants went on to enjoy a 23–5 record over the 1962–63 regular seasons, both times qualifying for—and losing—Championship Games to Green Bay (16–7 in 1962) and Chicago (14–10 in 1963).

Over time, Tittle began to earn respect and trust from his teammates by repeatedly demonstrating just how tough he was. He also began to quiet his critics, who opined that he was washed up.

His finest moment—and he had many in his seasons with the Giants—might have been on October 28, 1962, in a 49–34 thrashing of the Washington Redskins.

In that game, Tittle threw seven touchdowns passes, becoming, at the time, the fourth man in league history, according to the Pro Football Hall of Fame website, to accomplish that feat (four more players have since tied that mark).

The recipients of Tittle's touchdowns that day included tight end Joe Walton (three), running back/receiver Joe Morrison (two),and halfback Frank Gifford and receiver Del Shofner (one each).

The touchdowns were just a small part of how good Tittle, who finished 27 of 39 for 505 yards with no interceptions thrown and a 151.4 NFL rating, was that day.

At two different points in that game, Tittle went on a roll. With his team nursing a 21–20 lead in the third quarter, he hit nine straight completions, including a 53-yard touchdown pass to Del Shofner and a 26-yarder to tight end Joe Walton as the Giants would go score 28 unanswered second-half points (21 of them in the third quarter) to wrap up the game.

In that game, Tittle also set franchise single-game records for touchdown passes thrown (seven) and for passing yards (505).

The seven touchdown passes still stands; the single-game passing yardage record was broken by Phil Simms when he threw for 513 yards against the Cincinnati Bengals on October 13, 1985.

* * *

Although he never won a title game with the Giants, Tittle did help lead them to a first-place record in three of his four seasons, part of a 32–13–3 regular-season record in New York. He also set an NFL record in 1963

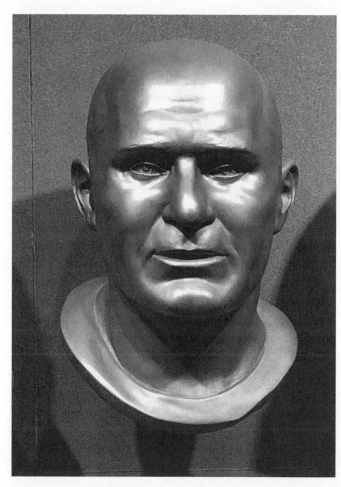

Quarterback Y.A. Tittle, 1961–64.
(Giants artifact from the Legacy Club in MetLife Stadium).

when he threw for 36 touchdowns in 13 games, a mark Colts quarterback Peyton Manning broke during the 2004 season when he threw 49 touchdowns in 16 games.

Even more surprising was the fact that the older Tittle became, the tougher he seemed to get.

In the 1963 Championship Game against the Chicago Bears, Tittle, then 37 years old, took a vicious hit from Bears right end Doug Atkins and left linebacker Joe Fortunato.

Despite the hit, which caused some instability in his left knee, Tittle still somehow managed to complete a 14-yard touchdown pass to halfback Frank Gifford.

Tittle would keep going in that game. However, with his Giants ahead 10–7, he again took a vicious hit on a first-down pass attempt to Gifford.

This time, it was Bears right linebacker Larry Morris who caught Tittle as he threw the ball. And this time, Tittle went down to the ground, his left knee failing to support his weight.

Determined to soldier through the pain, Tittle refused to come out of the game. At halftime, the Giants' doctors treated the injury and then taped his knee, hoping to stabilize it. They also determined that Tittle wouldn't make the injury any worse by continuing to play on it.

In the second half, Tittle finished 8 of 21 as the Giants were shut out in the game's final two quarters on their way to a 14–10 loss.

Tittle, who per eyewitness accounts was clearly affected by the injury, praised the Bears after the game, refusing to point the finger at his offensive line for having failed to protect him on the play on which he was injured, though he did admit that the injury forced him to change his style of play.

"I couldn't get set up after I hurt the knee," he told reporters afterward. "I had to throw off my back foot. I lost my maneuverability. I couldn't run."

Tittle retired as a Giant after 17 seasons in pro football, four of which he spent with Big Blue. When he was inducted into the Pro Football Hall of Fame in 1971, he went in as a Giant—the same team for which a decade earlier he almost refused to join—with team president Wellington Mara serving as his presenter.

Tittle was also was part of the franchise's inaugural "Ring of Honor" class in 2010 and remains the franchise record holder in single-season touchdown passes with 36, set in 1963.

He also holds the franchise record for most consecutive games with a touchdown pass thrown (15 over the 1962–64 seasons).

19

THE BRILLIANCE OF BILL BELICHICK

Long before Bill Belichick became known as the master of the Patriots way, he was the Giants' "other" Bill—the ambitious, football-obsessed young assistant who rose through the team's rank to become their defensive coordinator after the Giants promoted Bill Parcells to head coach.

Belichick was part of Ray Perkins' inaugural coaching staff in 1979, appointed as a special teams coach and defensive assistant. Yet despite having lettered in football as a center and tight end during his college career at Wesleyan University, he gravitated to the defensive side of the ball.

When Belichick had to work with the Giants linebackers, linebacker Harry Carson admitted there was some initial uncertainty among the players about Belichick's qualifications.

"Generally, when you're a coach, you probably have played the position and can, from your personal experiences, understand what a player might be thinking or how he's going to react in certain situations," Carson said.

"Because Bill had never played linebacker, I think there were times in your head where you thought, 'Well, what does he know about playing linebacker? He never played the game.'"

Carson remembered those early days going into the meeting room with Belichick and how the coach would draw up plays for the defense to practice. "We'd look at what he put up on the board, and we'd go, 'Nah, Bill, I don't think that's gonna work.'

"But then we'd go out on the field, and we'd start to run the defense as he drew it up and it would work. We also started to realize that he thought differently than a traditional linebacker. I mean, he was much more into putting players in certain positions. So he won us over because the things he did helped us to become a much better defense."

* * *

While both Belichick and Parcells were regarded as football geniuses and sticklers for detail, they could not have been more different personality-wise.

"Well, for one, Bill Parcells has a personality," defensive end George Martin said with a chuckle when asked what the biggest difference was between the two men. "Belichick has no personality. He really doesn't. He's an Xs and Os man, period. I think he wrote a book one year, and he talked about how he had to put his personal life on hold during the season.

"According to him, during the season, there is no daddy, there are no birthdays or funerals. There are no disruptions; it's all about football, and he was consumed by football, whereas Parcells, I think, understood that people are human and that there are going to be things that, believe it or not, are more important than football."

But it was that dedication and passion to football that Martin said made Belichick into the football savant he's known as today.

"That man knows football as intimately as anyone. He is just a remarkable individual when it comes down to Xs and Os," Martin said.

"We would go out with a very great game plan against an opponent, and if for some reason, that game plan or the execution wasn't working, at halftime, he would always come in with the perfect adjustment every single time. And if it was executed the way he explained it, it was sheer genius.

"I'll give you another example. When he was the special teams coach, he always had what they call 'trick plays,' but it'd be unfair to characterize those plays that way. What he had were plays that would always capitalize on the opponent's mistake. And I can tell you that 99 percent of the time, if executed the way he explained it, it was flawless."

Linebacker Carl Banks said Belichick took pride in teaching and providing the method behind his madness on his drills and strategy.

"He didn't waste a lot of time with things that didn't make sense. So if we had to hit a blocking sled, we had to do it a certain way, and that reason was explained to us," Banks said. "He often gave real-life analogies as to why we had to do things a certain way to prepare for a particular blocking scheme.

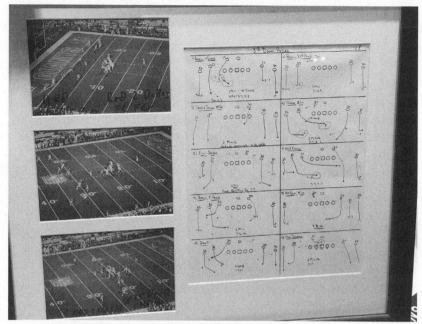

A page from defensive coordinator Bill Belichick's playbook illustrating part of the Giants' strategy used in Super Bowl XXV against the Buffalo Bills.
(Artifact shown is from the Pro Football Hall of Fame)

"The game plans he put together were for the 90 percentile of players. And if that one player found himself in an unfortunate situation, he'd say, 'Look, we can protect everything but this play, if this happens, then they caught us off guard. But this is as much [yardage] as they should make on a play like this.'

"And he also said if the other guys do their part, no one would have to worry about being exposed."

Belichick's ability to anticipate and adjust with such precision to this day still amazes his former players.

"His brilliance is in his simplicity," Banks said. "That's what people marvel at, but the one thing that you'll notice about every team he has coached is that they're fundamentally sound.

"It's very hard to find their players out of position. And if you go on to beat him on some things, so be it. But his teams don't make a lot of mistakes. And when you have everybody on the same page, it's pretty easy to game-plan."

And what about Belichick's meshing with the personalities in the Giants locker room?

"That's easy," Martin said. "It worked well because it yielded results.

You know that old saying, 'Damn the torpedoes if it results in a victory'? We had experienced the misery of losing for so many years, and there was nothing worse than that. So if you're going to have this guy with no personality come in and tell you that he has a philosophy for winning and you find out it works, well hey, we might not like the smell or the color, but we'll take that any day of the week."

Belichick delivered, all right. Still, he might very well have saved his most creative and downright genius game plan of his Giants coaching career for Super Bowl XXV to stop one of the most prolific offenses in the league at the time.

In 1990, the Buffalo Bills offense, led by quarterback Jim Kelly, finished with the league's best scoring offense, averaging 26.8 points per game.

The Bills had also scored on 66 out of 72 red-zone trips, with 48 of those scores being touchdowns.

That season, the Bills debuted their K-gun offense, which featured three receivers (including Hall of Famers Andre Reed and James Lofton) and a single running back (Hall of Famer Thurman Thomas), with Kelly having the autonomy to call his own plays out of the shotgun formation.

The K-gun also often operated sans the traditional huddle. Kelly would get his guys to the line of scrimmage and call the plays, audibling as necessary. That approach created a fast-paced tempo designed to wear out opposing defenses and limit substitution of personnel in between plays.

The Bills offense, which had scored 95 points in two playoff games, presented a "pick your poison" dilemma for Belichick and the Giants defense.

Do they try to stop Thomas, who finished that year third in rushing yardage with 1,297? Do they go after the receivers? Or do they go after Kelly, tied for fourth that year with Boomer Esiason of the Bengals with 24 touchdowns and whose offensive line had only allowed 20 sacks all season?

In the game of football, conventional wisdom dictates that if a team is successful stopping the opponent's running game, they'll give themselves a fighting chance at winning.

But if you're Bill Belichick, you don't accept conventional wisdom until you've looked at the full picture.

In studying the K-gun, Belichick realized that limiting the Bills' time of possession wasn't going to be enough. So Belichick and his staff came up with a multi-step plan designed to disarm the Bills' K-gun.

The multi-step plan was simple. The Giants would scheme to take away the Bills' crossing patterns that Kelly relied on hitting so that his receivers could run for large chunks of yardage.

The Giants also planned to flood the Bills receivers with as many defenders as possible before, during, and after the catch, with a focus on trying to knock the ball out and limiting the yards after the catch.

Belichick also wanted the defensive backs covering the receivers to be physical, which meant hitting Reed and Lofton as they came off the line of scrimmage. The defense was to also rush at Kelly on virtually every play.

As for Thomas, well, let him have his day in the sun.

Belichick's thinking was if the defense could disrupt the timing of the K-gun and the Giants offense could exercise ball control via its running game to keep the Bills offense on the sidelines, the Giants would have a good chance at a victory.

At first, Belichick's defensive game plan was met by skepticism by some of his players who were part of a strong run defense that allowed 91.2 rushing yards per game, the fourth-best mark in the league that year.

But as Carson previously said, Belichick had a way of thinking differently and coming up with ways to put the defense in the best position to make plays. And with Belichick more concerned about Kelly lighting up the scoreboard than Thomas imposing his will via the ground game, the players soon bought in.

It worked to near perfection. On their opening drive, the Bills went three-and-out, something they hadn't done since a 29–14 loss to Washington on December 30, 1990.

It was a sign of things to come. The Bills ended up converting only one of their eight third-down attempts.

While Thomas did indeed run wild—he finished with 135 yards on 15 carries and a rushing touchdown—none of Kelly's 212 passing yards resulted in a touchdown pass. The Giants ended up holding Reed and Lofton to a combined nine receptions for 123 yards, with Lofton's lone catch, which went for 61 yards, being the longest by a Bills receiver that day.

While all the buzz after that game was about Scott Norwood's missed field goal that would have won the game for the Bills, were it not for Belichick taking away the nucleus of the Bills offense and keeping their scoring to a minimum, Norwood's missed field goal might not have even mattered.

20

THE MAN IN THE MIDDLE

If it weren't for girls, one of the greatest linebackers in franchise history might never have become a part of Giants lore.

Harry Carson, who grew up in Florence, South Carolina, had a passing interest in football as a youth, but not one that was strong enough to where he aspired to play the game recreationally, let alone as a future living.

Harry Carson, who grew up in Florence, South Carolina, had a passing interest in football as a youth, but not one that was strong enough to where he aspired to play the game recreationally, let alone as a future living.

When he was in seventh grade, Carson changed his mind when he noticed the Wilson High School football players enjoying a particularly attractive perk.

"I remember standing by the fence when the game was over, and the players were exiting the field and walking through the fence to the house to change [out of their uniforms]," Carson recalled. "And there were a whole bunch of beautiful girls waiting for their boyfriends when they came out of the field house.

"So I thought to myself, 'Wow, that's what I want to do. I want to be one of those guys who has a pretty girlfriend.' So girls were the incentive for me to play football."

In his freshman year of high school, Carson decided to try out for the football team. However, he would soon learn a valuable lesson that would serve him well in later years.

That lesson took shape during one of his first practices, on a hot late- summer day when he learned that one can't just show up and look good in the uniform.

"Back then, [coaches] didn't ease you into anything. You just went full bore the first day of practice," Carson said. "I remember going through a blocking and tackling drill. When it was my turn, I had to go against an older guy who was either a junior or senior.

Hall of Famer Harry Carson was the anchor in the middle of the Giants defense from 1976 to 1988. Carson was also a Super Bowl champion (XXI), a nine-time Pro Bowler, a two-time first-team All-Pro and a four-time second-team All-Pro and has been credited with executing the first-ever "Gatorade Shower" victory celebration.
(Copyright New York Football Giants)

"When we collided, I just knew that that was not a place for me to be because I'm already exhausted from running around, so I quit."

After Carson quit the high school football team, he became the subject of mockery by the coach, who perhaps tried, through shame, to coax Carson back. But having made up his mind, Carson walked off the field and turned in his uniform.

As he was walking home, the echo of the coach's mockery echoed in his head. Carson then remembered walking past another field where members of the Florence Boys Club were practicing football and how one of their coaches, taking note of Carson's physical stature, persuaded him to give football another chance.

"One of the coaches called me over, and he said, 'Man, you should be playing football,'" Carson said, noting that the second coach hadn't been aware that Carson had just quit his high school team.

Carson agreed to show up the next day for the Florence Boys Club's practice, and this time, he did so with a new approach.

"I came back the next day and got a uniform, and I practiced. I sort of eased my way into playing," he said. "But through that [first] experience, I knew I had to prepare to play the game and not just show up thinking that I can do it like everybody else."

Carson eventually went back to his high school football team, and by the time he graduated, he had developed a bulldog mentality as a football player. So it was only fitting that he would go on to play college ball with the South Carolina State Bulldogs.

In four seasons for head coach Willie Jeffries, Carson, a defensive lineman, was the very definition of an iron man, never missing a single game.

Named a team captain in 1975, Carson and the rest of the Bulldogs recorded six shutouts and held their opponents to an NCAA record 29 points in 10 games, a mark that still stands today.

In 1976, the Giants drafted Carson in the fourth round (No. 105 overall).

"When I was drafted, I thought I was going to be a defensive lineman because that was the position I played when I was at South Carolina State," he said.

The Giants had other ideas.

"The Giants needed a run-stopping linebacker. So when I came to the Giants, I remember [defensive coordinator] Marty Schottenheimer calling me aside and telling me that he would like for me to come back and spend a few weeks with him [before training camp]. He tutored me—we were watching film, going out on the field, going through drills, and so forth."

Although the conversion from defensive lineman to linebacker took time for Carson to gain a comfort level with, he was determined to reward Schottenheimer's faith in him.

THE BIRTH OF THE GATORADE BATH

Harry Carson has often been credited as the creative genius behind the celebratory Gatorade bath.

But Carson, who made the ritual famous thanks to his creative disguises, said it was nose tackle Jim Burt who conceived the idea, and who did so as a retaliatory action as opposed to a celebratory one.

In 1984, the Giants were getting ready to play the Washington Redskins, and, as Carson recalled, head coach Bill Parcells had been particularly hard on Burt leading up to that game.

"Parcells had been riding Burt all week in practice about how [Redskins center] Jeff Bostic was going to kick his ass," Carson recalled.

"So we get into the game, and Burt is playing a great game—he's dominating Jeff Bostic. Toward the end of the game, he approached me and said, 'You know, that Parcells is a [bleep]. He was driving my ass all week, and we should get him.'

"I said, 'What do you mean *we*?' He said, 'Because you're Parcells' boy and if you do something to him, he's not going to say anything. But if I do something to him by myself, he's going to have my ass.'"

Burt's idea was to dump a bucket of Gatorade over Parcells' head toward the end of the game. Carson reluctantly agreed to go along with the idea, but it wasn't until 1986 that the Gatorade bath began to catch on.

In Week 2 of that year, the Giants hosted the San Diego Chargers, who were coming off a 50–28 rout of the Miami Dolphins.

The Giants, who went into that game as the underdogs, ended up beating the Chargers 20–7 for their first win of the 1986 season.

"As time was winding down, we were sort of overjoyed that we shut them down," Carson recalled. "So in the act of being jubilant, I got Parcells with the Gatorade, the first time I got him by himself."

"It's the New York market, and I was his project. So if I failed, it would have reflected on Marty because I was his choice."

Carson worked diligently to make his transition a smooth one. And he succeeded. Midway through his rookie season, he took over as the Giants starting middle linebacker and finished that year named to the All-NFL Rookie team.

The new position fit Carson's athletic gifts well, as he went on to lead all Giants defenders in tackles in five of his 13 seasons as a Giant.

Rather than get angry, Parcells began to expect the weekly shower, regardless of the elements.

"Now it wasn't that I wanted to do it," Carson said with a laugh. "Parcells is one of those superstitious people that if you do something once and it works, you have to keep doing it. So I kept doing it as we were winning."

Parcells would end up being doused 13 more times that season and three times during the postseason right through Super Bowl XXI.

As the ritual gained popularity—television cameras made it a point to zoom in on the Giants sideline in anticipation of the bath—Carson decided to get creative.

He began borrowing items from anyone who was on the sideline in street clothes. He'd then "hide" behind the Giants bench to change into his disguise, tiptoe toward Parcells with the bucket in hand, and douse his head coach, who, after the initial shock, would break out into a huge grin to the delight of the stadium crowds.

Carson's most creative moment came in Super Bowl XXI when he convinced a security guard to loan him a bright yellow jacket. Carson removed his jersey and pads, put the jacket on, and as the television cameras were following his every move, he doused Parcells.

As the ritual took hold, it also expanded to other personnel. Among the other well-known Giants who were doused at the end of Super Bowl XXI were defensive coordinator Bill Belichick and quarterback Phil Simms.

Even the next generation of Giants, such as Tom Coughlin, the team's no-nonsense head coach from 2004 to 2015, got a celebratory bath courtesy of fullback Madison Hedgecock after the Giants upset the 18–1 New England Patriots in Super Bowl XLII.

Although Carson's NFL career got off to a promising start, the Giants struggled to field a winning team in his first five seasons.

The Giants' struggles began to take a toll on Carson. In his book, *Point of Attack*, he wrote that he asked to be traded at least twice, including after the 1983 season, only to be rebuked because he was too valuable to the team.

He also admitted to contemplating retirement in 1980, only to be talked out of doing so by then-head coach Ray Perkins.

By the 1981 season, things began looking up for Carson and the franchise thanks to some bold moves by general manager George Young.

For the linebackers, the addition of Lawrence Taylor to a group that already included Brad Van Pelt and Brian Kelley gave the Giants a group of ferocious, hard-hitting players who dubbed themselves "The Board of De-Wreckers," or, as they're more commonly known in Giants lore, "The Crunch Bunch."

As the 1980s continued to unfold, the addition of Carl Banks and Gary Reasons to replace Kelley and Van Pelt would complete the renovation of the linebacking corps, shaping the group into one that would be instrumental in the team's first Super Bowl Championship in the1986 season.

That season, Carson finished with an impressive 118 tackles (second on the team). Perhaps his biggest game that year came on December 7, 1986, against Washington, in which he recorded 12 tackles (eight solo), and had an interception and pass defensed in a 24–14 Giants win that helped New York capture the NFC East division crown.

At the start of the 1988 season, Carson knew the year would be his last, as his body was starting to betray him with aches and pains—including severe headaches.

Before his swan song, Carson, in his book *Captain for Life*, recalled how the Giants were losing to a bad Detroit Lions team at home, causing the Giants Stadium faithful to boo profusely as the team went into the locker room for halftime.

Embarrassed and angry at what had transpired in the game's first 30 minutes, Carson lost his cool and went on an explosive verbal tirade filled with expletives. He challenged his teammates to be better than what they had shown and that if anyone didn't want to play, then they should "Stay the f—k in the locker room!"

That verbal tirade ended up being the only halftime adjustment the team needed. The Giants came out of the locker room and beat the Lions 30–10.

With the Giants also pushing for a playoff berth that year, Carson's bothersome right knee finally gave out during a mid-November road game against the Cardinals. Medical tests revealed that while Carson's knee was structurally sound, there was loose debris causing the joint to lock up.

Carson underwent surgery to have the debris removed, hoping that he could get back on the field as quickly as possible. Unfortunately, his

Linebacker Harry Carson, 1976–1988.
(Giants artifact from the Legacy Club in MetLife Stadium)

hopes were dashed when he learned by watching television that the Giants had placed him on injured reserve, which, at the time, meant he would have to miss a minimum of four games.

Before the Giants' final home game of 1988, both Carson and defensive end George Martin, who was also planning to retire after that season, were honored in front of the Giants Stadium crowd.

A week later, Carson did return from the injured reserve list for one last game as a Giant, a "road game" against the Jets, who played their home games in Giants Stadium. Carson picked up right where he had left off as the signal-caller and stepped right back into his leadership role.

However, his joy over having returned was short-lived as a 27–21 loss to the Jets ended the Giants playoff hopes—and ultimately his career.

By the time Carson was finished, he had left the game having justified Schottenheimer's faith in him to be the man in the middle.

Carson appeared in 173 NFL games with 167 starts between 1976 and 1988, recording eight career sacks, 14 fumble recoveries, and 11 interceptions.

In addition to captaining the Super Bowl XXI champion team, Carson was also was voted to nine Pro Bowls, was named first-team All-Pro in two seasons (1981 and 1984), and was voted All-NFC five times.

With nothing left to play for, Carson was ready to head into retirement. But about six weeks after the 1988 season ended, he received a phone call from Giants defensive coordinator Bill Belichick.

Belichick, as Carson recalled in his book, informed his defensive captain that the team was going to designate him as a "Plan B" free agent, a form of free agency that in 1992 was ruled by a jury to have violated antitrust laws.

As Carson was already planning to retire, the news from Belichick didn't change his mind about retiring.

Neither did an offer from John McVay, Carson's former head coach, who had resurfaced in the league as a front office executive with the San Francisco 49ers.

But one man who came close to talking Carson out of retirement was Bill Parcells, who reached out to his defensive captain after the team's minicamp in 1989.

"Because George Martin and I were leaving at the same time, Parcells felt like that would leave a tremendous void in leadership with the team," Carson said. "So, he asked if I would consider coming back.

"I thought about it for a day or two, and I said, 'No, I'm not going to come back.' I was pretty happy just ending my career as I had."

What Carson wasn't happy about—and rightfully so—was how his candidacy for the Pro Football Hall of Fame was handled, as he was snubbed by voters seven times.

Carson, in fact, twice requested that his name be removed from the ballot, only to have his requests denied.

Carson's requests to have his name removed from the ballot weren't so much about a bruised ego. Instead, he requested that his name be removed from consideration because he was concerned about how the repeated snubs were affecting those closest to him.

"When I first got like an award for playing football, it was exciting to be recognized, but I didn't play the game to be rewarded," he said.

"I played football, but I wasn't a football player. If I had been a football player, I would have wanted to be in the Hall of Fame."

In 2006, Carson, who changed his mind about his candidacy out of respect for the Giants organization, got his due, when he became the first inside linebacker to play in a 3-4 defensive scheme to be elected to the Pro Football Hall of Fame.

21

PHIL WHO?

When on May 3, 1979, NFL commissioner Pete Rozelle announced the Giants' first-round draft selection, sprinkled among the jeers and boos were exasperated Giants fans in attendance.

"Phil *who*?" That's what a lot of people wanted to know about the Giants' pick, quarterback Phil Simms, who played his college ball at tiny Morehead State, a school whose only other NFL player at the time was Giants tight end Gary Shirk.

The fans weren't alone in their confusion or initial dislike of the pick.

"Yeah, nobody liked Phil when he first came in," defensive end George Martin remembered. "Nobody liked him because nobody knew him."

Martin chuckled when he and some of his teammates first laid eyes on Simms. "We always thought he was a member of the Mara family because he looked like one. We thought perhaps he had some family connection.

"And he was a quarterback—nobody had a great deal of fondness for a quarterback!"

But there was something Martin and the rest of the Giants players soon learned about the offense's new quarterback.

He was one tough son of a gun.

* * *

The symbolism behind the start of Simms' Giants career was hard to miss.

He had shown up for his first day of work at Giants Stadium for an early May minicamp for rookies, free agents, and select veterans just as Joe Pisarcik, the incumbent, was leaving the stadium for a doctor's appointment to have his ailing knee evaluated.

Simms' debut practice was nothing special, but he was going to get as much work as possible to start his acclimation to life in the NFL.

However, head coach Ray Perkins had planned to redshirt the rookie that first year—that is until Pisarcik could no longer hold up.

In Week 5 of the 1979 season, Simms got his first NFL snaps in a loss to the New Orleans Saints. In that game, he finished eight of 19 for 115 yards, one touchdown, and two interceptions in relief of Pisarcik, who was later placed on injured reserve with an injury to his throwing shoulder on October 17.

The following week at home versus Tampa Bay, Simms, in his first NFL start, engineered a 17–14 win without throwing a touchdown pass. He then followed that performance up with a 32–16 triumph over the 49ers, the second of a five-game winning streak.

Simms finished his rookie year with a 6–5 record as a starter and NFL All-Rookie Team honors. He was also the Rookie of the Year runner up to running back Ottis Anderson of the Cardinals (who'd become Simms' teammate years later).

* * *

With his rookie season behind him, Simms looked to continue his growth as an NFL quarterback.

However, due to injuries and performance, Simms went from looking like a bonafide rising star to a bust.

In 1980, his statistics—48 percent completion rate, 15 touchdowns, and 19 interceptions—weren't very good, nor was his 3–10 record as the starter. The following year, he suffered a separated shoulder in a November 15 overtime loss to Washington after going 5–5, and was on the verge of being "Wally Pipped" by backup rookie quarterback Scott Brunner.

In 1982, Simms suffered torn ligaments in his knee during a preseason game when Jets defensive linemen Joe Klecko and Abdul Salaam smashed into him as his pass was picked off by Darrol Ray.

After the 1982 season, Perkins resigned, and Bill Parcells, the team's defensive coordinator, was promoted to head coach. In one of his first decisions, Parcells declared an open quarterback competition between Simms and Brunner, eventually naming Brunner as the winner.

However, with the Giants on the verge of falling to 2–4 in 1983 with Brunner as the starter, Parcells had seen enough and benched Brunner in the third quarter after an interception.

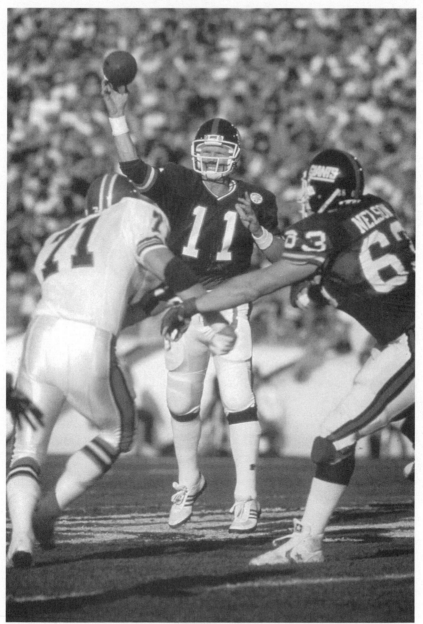

Phil Simms was nearly perfect in the Giants' 39–20 Super Bowl XXI win over the Denver Broncos. Simms completed 22 of 25 pass attempts for 268 yards and 3 touchdowns. His 88 percent completion rate is still a Super Bowl record as of Super Bowl LIV. (Copyright New York Football Giants)

Simms, now back under center, completed his first four passes for 78 yards, putting the Giants in position to score a touchdown that sliced the Eagles lead to 14–13. But on his fifth pass attempt of that game, Simms' right (throwing) hand became tangled in Eagles defender Dennis Harrison's facemask, resulting in a broken right thumb.

If there was a silver lining to Simms' strings of misfortune, it was that he underwent a significant transformation as a quarterback that off-season.

First, he dedicated himself to the weight room to increase his durability and strength.

Then there was his mental growth. On the encouragement of offensive coordinator Ron Erhardt, Simms started watching more game film to learn the nuances of the game that might have previously eluded him. He also received support from Parcells, who told Simms to go out there, sling the ball, and have some fun.

Simms' behind-the-scenes transformation was a major reason why, in 1984, he became the first Giants quarterback to throw for over 4,000 yards in a season.

Simms was also developing as a leader who probably solidified his teammates' respect when one day during a practice, he did something very few—if any—players had the guts to do.

SUPER SIMMS

In the days leading to Super Bowl XXI, a certain golden-haired quarterback emerged as the toast of the NFL.

No, not Phil Simms, whose grit and toughness helped propel the Giants to a 14–2 regular-season record. It was Denver Broncos signal-caller John Elway, whom many analysts believed would outduel the Giants.

Fate—with a big assist from the Giants defense—had other ideas.

While the Giants defense was harassing Elway and his comrades, Simms delivered a performance for the ages, completing 88 percent of his passes in that game to earn MVP honors.

That performance set a Super Bowl record for pass completion percentage based on a minimum of 15 pass attempts that, as of Super Bowl LIV, still stands.

"Coach Parcells had been riding Phil in practice," Martin remembered, "and Phil had had enough. So he told Bill where to get off, telling him to get off his back and 'Leave me the hell alone!'

"Meanwhile, we're looking at each other, and we're like, 'What did he just do?' That was a turning point right there for us; that's when we knew Phil wasn't just another quarterback."

Simms had a lot of shining moments in his career, the biggest of which was his near-perfect showing in Super Bowl XXI when he completed 22 of 25 passes for 268 yards and three touchdowns.

Before that moment, there were three games leading up to Super Bowl XXI in which Simms' leadership and skill made believers out of his harshest critics.

The first was the famous "fourth-and-17" pass play in a Week 11 road game against the Minnesota Vikings that set up the Giants game-winning field goal for the 22–20 win.

On that fourth-quarter play, Simms connected with receiver Bobby Johnson for 22 yards on a play he later revealed was one of the first plays the team had installed at the start of training camp, but one that they hadn't thrown to Johnson.

Simms would be at the helm at another critical come-from-behind win, this one against the San Francisco 49ers on the road two weeks later during a nationally televised Monday night game.

After the 49ers jumped out to a 17–0 halftime lead, Simms and the Giants came roaring back. He hit tight end Mark Bavaro over the middle on a second-and-10, the big tight end famously dragging up to seven defenders approximately 30 yards until Bavaro was finally wrestled to the ground.

Although the Giants didn't score on that drive, they would go on to score 21 unanswered points in the third quarter, two of those scores being Simms touchdown passes to running back Joe Morris and receiver Stacey Robinson.

The third notable game that year was the Giants' 17–0 home shutout of the Washington Redskins in the NFC title game.

Playing in challenging conditions featuring wind gusts of up to 25 miles per hour, Simms, (who in that game went seven of 14 for 90 yards and a touchdown) and the Giants made quick work of Washington by scoring all the points they'd need in the first half.

* * *

Like the start of his career, which was rocky, the end of Simms' career didn't exactly have the perfect storybook ending.

In 1990, he led the Giants to a 10–0 start before suffering a broken right foot on December 15, 1990, against the Buffalo Bills. Done for the rest of the year, Simms had to watch as his backup, Jeff Hostetler, led the franchise to its second Super Bowl championship later that year against the Bills.

After that Super Bowl win, Parcells resigned his position due to health concerns just as the Giants were getting ready for their spring football activities in May. Running backs coach Ray Handley was named Parcells' successor, and, as Parcells had done years earlier, Handley declared an open quarterback competition between Simms and Hostetler.

Handley ended up naming Hostetler, whose mobility he felt gave the team an advantage against certain teams, the starter for Week 1 against the 49ers, noting, "My intention is to start Jeff Hostetler in the first game. This in no way detracts what Phil has done or will do for us."

Although Simms couldn't have been happy with the decision, he took the high road.

When Hostetler injured his back in Week 13 against the Bucs, Simms regained the starting job, but only managed to win one of his four starts. Although he was named the starter in 1992, his season once again ended prematurely thanks to an arm injury suffered in Week 4.

In 1993, Simms' final season, Dan Reeves had replaced the fired Handley. As both Simms and Hostetler were set to be free agents, Reeves chose to keep Simms while Hostetler went to the Raiders.

Simms then posted his best completion percentage rate (61.8 percent) in his career, throwing for 3,038 yards and 15 touchdowns that season, all good enough to get the Giants to an 11–5 record and a postseason berth, which ended with a loss in the divisional round to the 49ers.

Simms, who also earned his second Pro Bowl berth that year, underwent off-season shoulder surgery. However, any plans for a 16th season ended when in June 1994, he was summoned to Reeves' office and was told that he could either retire or he would be cut from the team.

The decision, made by general manager George Young and agreed to by Reeves, was an emotional one for team president Wellington Mara, who publicly voiced his disagreement.

One of the reasons for Simms' dismissal was the salary cap. With Simms, due to make $2.5 million, coming off shoulder surgery, the Giants believed that they could use his salary to address other areas of need, while also turning the quarterback reins over to either Dave Brown, their first-round pick in the 1992 NFL supplemental draft, or Kent Graham, a 1992 eighth-round pick.

Although the Giants were moving on from Simms, he told reporters, "I still feel I can play."

He almost did play again—for another team. A year after his release, the Cleveland Browns, whose head coach was former Giants defensive coordinator Bill Belichick, explored having Simms to join their team as the backup to starter Vinny Testaverde.

In the end, Simms and the Browns couldn't agree to terms, and Simms would end up staying retired, having known only one professional team in his storied career.

22

STEVE OWEN

Before there was Tom Coughlin and Bill Parcells, two of the winningest and legendary head coaches in Giants franchise history, there was Steve Owen.

Owen, who like Parcells and Coughlin led the New York Giants franchise to two NFL championships, took a different path in getting to the top—a path that almost didn't include football.

Born April 21, 1898, in Cleo Spring, Oklahoma (before Oklahoma became a U.S. state on November 16, 1907), Owen initially had dreams of being a jockey.

However, his body had other ideas, as he would go on to blossom into a 5'11", 230-pound strapping young man.

Owen was recruited by Phillips University head coach Johnny Maulbetsch, who had spotted the young man lying on a grass field not far from where the football team was practicing. Maulbetsch, who himself had excelled in football at the University of Michigan, approached Owen and asked him if he had ever played football.

"No, sir," Owen said.

Maulbetsch eyed him up again and said, "Well, you're big enough to play, so why don't you come out for the team?"

Owen agreed to give it a chance, and the rest became history.

Besides excelling in football, "Stout Steve," as he was called (due to his physical stature), went on to excel in baseball, boxing, and wrestling, sometimes even wrestling professionally under the pseudonym "Jack O'Brien" in matches set up in adjoining towns.

In 1924, Owen got his first taste of pro football as a member of the Kansas City Blues, who would later change their nickname to the Cowboys. In an October 24, 1926 game against the Giants at the Polo Grounds, the Blues shut out the Giants 13–0.

Tim Mara, however, had taken note of the scrappy Owen and the work he did at offensive tackle. That winter, the Giants purchased Owen's contract for $500, and Owen instantly became a team captain on the

1927 Giants squad (a team that, for one season, also employed Owen's brother Bill, an offensive lineman). That Giants team would go on to outscore opponents 197–20 that season en route to the franchise's first NFL title.

For "Stout Steve," whose Giants playing career spanned the 1926–31 and the 1933 seasons, the 1927 season was probably his best. He earned first-team All-Pro honors and would go on to earn a place on the Pro Football Hall of Fame's All–1920s Team, having started in 66 of the 79 games he played for the Giants.

Midway through the 1931 season, Giants head coach Leroy Andrews resigned, and Mara named Owen and quarterback Benny Friedman as the head coaches.

Eventually, Owen became the sole head coach, a role he'd hold until 1953 and one that he cherished.

The Ed Thorpe Memorial Trophy, awarded to the New York Giants in 1938 for having won the league championship that season. The win was Steve Owen's final of three NFL championships as head coach of the Giants. (Artifact shown is from the Pro Football Hall of Fame)

"Teaching and coaching football has been my life for a long time," Owen would say later on. "If I can be instrumental in the development of even one boy, that satisfaction is my reward."

With Owen as the head coach, the Giants won eight divisional titles and two NFL championships, including the famous "Sneakers Game" in 1934 and the league title game in 1938.

In 1950, Owen was named "Coach of the Year" in the pro ranks, an honor which he humbly accepted.

"I appreciate it," he said when accepting the recognition. "But coaching is like being a monkey on a stick. When you are going up, you always see someone just as good going down, and vice versa."

Where Owen made his mark was in his innovation. He designed the "umbrella defense," an alignment that featured four defensive backs which represented the spokes of the umbrella, in response to game-planning against the Cleveland Brown's prolific passing offense led by the famed Otto Graham firing darts to Dante Lavelli and Mac Speedie.

Owen's umbrella defense featured a pair of future Hall of Fame players, safety Emlen Tunnell and cornerback Tom Landry, as the deep defenders.

He also had safety Otto Schnellbacher, cornerback Harmon Rowe, drop-off ends Ray Peele and Jim Duncan, and middle linebacker John Cannady in his defense.

That defense was solely responsible for handing the 1950 Browns their only two losses of that season, a 6–0 shutout on October 1 and a 17–13 triumph on October 22.

Besides the umbrella defense, Owen designed the "A-formation" on offense, an idea he first had in 1935 after seeing Chicago Bears tackle Link Lyman slide off from the customary offensive tackle position.

In his 1952 book, *My Kind of Football*, Owen explained the origin of the A-formation as follows:

> I wanted to spread without losing concentrated attacking power, and yet keep the defense scattered along a wide front so that it could not jam in on us at any point.
>
> To do this, I hit on the idea of deploying my line strong to one side, and my backs strong to the other side. So far as I know, this was an original formation.

In the A, the line shows four men to the right of center and two to the left. But in the backfield, the weight is to the left of center, with the wingback out on the left flank. The formation can be run in the other direction, with line strong to the left and backs heavy to the right. The A exaggerates the effect of a split line, to carry the spread into the backfield.

When first introduced, we did not use the man-in-motion before the snap, but that factor was soon developed for Ward Cuff. From wingback, he moved toward the slot between left

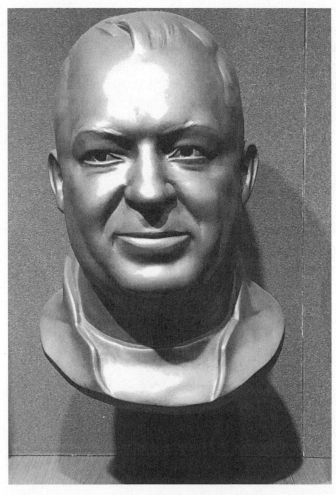

*Head coach
Steve Owen,
1930–1953.*
(Giants artifact from
the Legacy Club in
MetLife Stadium)

half [quarterback] and fullback, with the timing to arrive there
as the left half spun to make his fakes or hand offs. This reverse
alone made Cuff one of the great backs of football.

When we first experimented with the A, we had used the
standard single wing, and in practice we called my new system
A and the single wing B. After noting the possibilities the new
formation opened up, we thought it should rightly head the
alphabet as A, and we forgot about B and the other twenty-four
letters as well.

Although Owen developed the A-formation in 1935, he didn't fully
roll it out until the final game of the 1937 season, against Washington.

The following year, Owen deployed the A-formation more often as
his Giants marched straight through to a world title with a 23–17 win over
the Green Bay Packers.

Another well-known use of the A-formation came during the 1952
season in which Owen switched to that formation in a November 9 game
against the San Francisco 49ers.

New York went on to upset the 49ers 23–14 at the Polo Grounds, the
win enabling the Giants to keep pace with the Browns for first place in
the American Division.

By the time Owen left the Giants after the 1953 season, his 24th as a
coach, he had recorded a career won-loss record (including postseason)
of 155–108–17.

Owen was inducted into the Pro Football Hall of Fame in 1966.

23

THE GUARANTEE

By all accounts, Jim Fassel was a prototypical "player's coach." A man with an affable personality, Fassel also didn't hesitate to remind people that he wasn't just another Mr. Goody Two Shoes.

Perhaps the most famous example of his "I mean business" side came when Bashir Levingston, a defensive back and kickoff returner who was probably the Giants' best special teams player in 2000, was unceremoniously cut by Fassel after the player had committed a holding penalty negating a 67-yard punt return and lost a kickoff in a 31–21 loss to the Detroit Lions on November 19, 2000.

With that move, Fassel, who no doubt heard the growing chatter about how the Giants were probably the worst team in the NFL to have a winning record, sent a message to his players that no one was safe.

Just in case the surprising transaction didn't drive home that point hard enough, Fassel personally paid a visit to the special teams meeting room to curtly remind the players that they were not only easily replaceable, but if there was another sloppy screw-up like what had happened in the loss to the Lions, he was prepared to yank the offenders and replace them with starters.

With Fassel already fired up over how the Giants had lost that game and how, despite a 7–4 record, his team's potential playoffs were hanging by a thread, Fassel carried that fire into one of his daily press conferences.

In a somewhat surprising and uncharacteristic opening statement, he issued perhaps one of the most famous guarantees to come out of a New York sports figure's mouth since Joe Namath's promise of a Jets victory over the Baltimore Colts ahead of Super Bowl III.

Dressed in a black shirt, Fassel, whose job security was thought to be on shaky ground at the time, narrowed his eyes and sternly looked at the media assembled before him as he delivered an opening statement for the ages.

"I'm going to shut things down and close doors and focus on getting this team across the finish line. That's my whole goal in life right now," he said with something of a snarl in his voice. "If you've got the crosshair, if you've got the laser, you can put it right on my chest.

"I'm raising the stakes right now. This is a poker game. I'm shoving my chips to the middle of the table. I'm raising the ante—anybody who wants in, get in. Anybody who wants out, get out.

"This team is going to the playoffs. I'll make that statement—we're going to the playoffs, and I'm taking full responsibility for everything. Get off my coaches' backs. Get off the players' backs. I'm responsible for the whole thing. I'm redefining where we're going.

"I told the players it's a five-game season. I laid out the playoff scenario and told them exactly what I expected. I told them that I'm driving the train. All they've gotta do is listen and follow along."

Fassel, who would continue with a string of additional clichés that included "I'm driving the bus," "see the finish line," and "I've got to get my horse to run faster" would then spend 25 minutes answering questions, but the press conference might as well have ended right there, after he gift-wrapped perhaps the biggest headline of the season to the writers.

Years later, in a 2013 interview with *NFL AM*, Fassel admitted that his words were unrehearsed but that his intention was deliberate.

"We had played the Detroit Lions at home, and it was ugly," Fassel said on the program. "So I said, 'I've got to do something now to get this under control.'"

Fassel went on to explain that he was concerned that the media's constant harping on the faults of the team might eventually find their way to the players and create self-doubt. That's when he decided to make his bold statement to shift the focus to him.

"It was a bold guarantee," linebacker Jessie Armstead said. "It was a guarantee to say, 'Hey, you know what? What do we got to lose? Let's push everything to the table and hold nothing back.' When you get backed in a corner like we were and he made the prediction, we backed him up after that."

"It galvanized us and in a major way because I think for the first time that season, it wasn't about us as players—nobody was talking about, how badly we were playing on defense or the inefficiencies on offense," running back Tiki Barber added.

"It was, 'What the hell is wrong with the coach?' And it took all the pressure off us and put it squarely on him, which then made us want to have his back."

Following the guarantee, the Giants would not lose another game that season and would go on to become the NFC top seeded playoff team.

The Giants continued to ride on Fassel's bus through the divisional round with a 20–10 win over the Philadelphia Eagles and then a 41–0 thrashing of the Minnesota Vikings in the NFC Conference Championship.

Unfortunately for the Giants, Fassel's bus ran out of gas before the team could cap the postseason with a fourth Super Bowl championship. The Giants fell to the Baltimore Ravens 34–7 in what has been their only Super Bowl loss to date.

From an Xs and Os perspective, Barber said no matter what the Giants did on offense, the Ravens defense countered to prevent the Giants from doing the things that had gotten the team to the Super Bowl.

"Their plan was to beat us with defense and field position, and we could never bust out of it," Barber said.

"They had one of the greatest schemes ever, mainly because Sam Adams and Tony Siragusa were such big guys in the middle of that defensive line, and no one could move them out of the way.

"So all of our trapping and pulling schemes didn't work because we couldn't get one of our offensive linemen up to the second level, and (middle linebacker) Ray Lewis had the freedom to roam sideline-to-sideline on every play."

Even Giants offensive coordinator Sean Payton's halftime adjustment to run the hurry-up offense didn't work.

"The problem was the Ravens defensive staff also adjusted," Barber said. "Every time [Giants quarterback] Kerry Collins, who was in now in the shotgun as opposed to under center, would look down to take the snap, they would shift. Kerry would then look up and his pre-read processing was all screwed up.

"We couldn't make any big plays that we had been making in the second half of that season," Barber added. "We lost our identity in that game, and we lost the game."

24

THE CHAMPIONSHIP CATALYST

Sometimes it takes a good, old-fashioned kick in the ass to make wake someone up.

Such was the case of the 1985 Giants, who had finished that season 10–6, their best won-loss record in the three-year head coaching tenure of Bill Parcells, had to learn.

Thinking they were ready to make some noise in the postseason after being abruptly bounced from the tournament a year prior, that Giants team quickly got a dose of reality when they were embarrassed 21–0 by the Chicago Bears in the NFC division playoff game.

The 1985 Bears arguably had one of the all-time greatest defenses in the game, a unit that was a big reason for the team's Super Bowl XX championship season.

It was their brash and creative defensive coordinator, Buddy Ryan, who developed and implemented the "46 defense."

The goal of that defense was to throw everything at opposing offenses and dare them to try to get the ball down the field.

The concept worked like a charm. The Giants' defense, itself nothing to sneeze at, finished second that year overall behind the Bears in total average yards allowed per game (258.4 to 270).

Still, the Giants, who weren't short on confidence, believed they could stand toe-to-toe with the Bears on Chicago's frozen turf of Soldier Field.

They were wrong.

It started in the first quarter, the Giants turning the ball over on their firsts two possessions. The first turnover, which proved to be a tone-setter for how the day would go, saw Giants halfback Rob Carpenter fumble a pass from Phil Simms at his 46-yard line, the loose ball scooped up by Bears defensive end Richard Dent.

Although the Bears didn't score off that turnover, they did on the second Giants miscue, the "whiff" of a Sean Landeta punt deep in his territory. On the preceding play, Dent had dropped Simms for a 12-yard loss, setting up a fourth-and-20 at the Giants' 12-yard line.

Landeta, one of the finest punters of that time, set up to punt the ball. An unexpected gust of wind—some Chicago newspapers credited the ghost of George "Papa Bear" Halas, given the wind's impeccable timing—gave the ball enough of a push to where Landeta missed it and Bears safety Shaun Gayle scooped it up for a five-yard touchdown.

Although some like to blame that play for the Giants' loss, the truth is the Giants never recovered after that miscue.

The Giants would go three-and-out on their next three possessions, finally getting something resembling a scoring drive going on their final possession of the first half.

But their bad luck continued when they failed to score from the 2-yard line, and kicker Eric Schubert's ensuing 19-yard "chip shot" field goal attempt hit the left upright and bounced away, taking with it a chance to get on the scoreboard.

The Bears, already up 7–0 at halftime, finished off the Giants in the third quarter on a pair of touchdown passes—23 and 20 yards, respectively—by quarterback Jim McMahon to receiver Dennis McKinnon.

The Bears might have outscored the Giants that day, but the Giants had more than twice the number of bruised egos following that loss.

Nose tackle Jim Burt sat dejected on his stool. Landeta, still stunned hours later over how the wind had made him look silly, tried to explain what happened to a steady stream of reporters stopping by his locker.

Quarterback Phil Simms was at a loss for why, despite the offense having studied the Bears on tape and not being surprised by anything they had done in the game, couldn't move the ball.

Still, other players, their voices mixed with anger and sadness, believed that it was the Giants who had beaten the Giants, not the other way around.

"Anyone on that team will tell you how he will tell you that we thought we were going to beat the Bears at Soldier Field," inside linebacker and defensive co-captain Harry Carson said. "It wasn't so much that the Bears beat us; we beat ourselves."

The Giants, embarrassed over the butt-kicking the Bears had handed to them, left the field at the end of the game in stunned silence.

That silence, however, didn't last for very long, according to defensive end George Martin.

"I remember going into the locker room, and Harry Carson was extremely agitated and animated," Martin recalled.

"And for the first time—this speaks to Harry's leadership—he kicked everybody out of the locker room except for the players. I'm talking coaches, managers, owners—'Everybody get the hell out!'

"Then he had a closed-door meeting unlike any other meeting— we're talking fire and brimstone on a different level. Harry talked about the shameful performance that we had displayed, and he said in no uncertain terms that the preparation for the 1986 season began right there and then. Anybody who wasn't willing to make that commitment could get the hell out.

"His message was that there was to be no off-season—that we were going to dedicate ourselves to being as good or as competitive as the people who just kicked our butts," Martin said. "And I give Harry credit; he got 100 percent buy-in from everybody in that room."

Carson, who also credited head coach Bill Parcells for challenging the team to sharpen its focus and keep their eye on the prize for the ensuing season, said he saw a noticeable difference months later when the team reconvened for a minicamp.

"I could tell that there was a different attitude among all the players," he said. "We worked hard, and I think we came together as a group, and we became closer.

"It was one of the few times that everybody checked their egos at the door because it was so important that we win the Super Bowl. And so that was the key. That was the target on everybody's mind. And, yes, I think that losing that game to the Chicago Bears was the catalyst."

Martin agreed. Back in those days before there were NFL off-season conditioning programs as there are today, players would take several months off after a season ended and then use the longer training camps that were the norm to get themselves into playing shape.

"Harry Carson set the standard," Martin said. "He said, 'When you come into minicamp and eventually training camp, that's going to be the telltale sign of whether you're on board.'"

And what happened if someone wasn't on board?

"Harry made it known in no uncertain terms that he wouldn't tolerate people messing around, that we were going to spend our off-season working toward the 1986 season," Martin said. "Everybody came into camp in shape, focused, and realizing that we were going to have to make sacrifices and do whatever we had to do to be champions that year."

The Giants did just that. Not only did they finish the following year with a 14–2 mark (better than their 10–6 record in 1985), but they would also go on to roll over San Francisco and Washington in the postseason before dismantling Denver 39–20 for their first-ever Super Bowl championship.

25

LOMBARDI & LANDRY

If there is any doubt that coaching makes as much of an impact on a football team as does talent look no further than the New York Giants teams of 1954–58.

During those years, head coach Jim Lee Howell was fortunate to have two of the greatest coaching minds on his staff, future Hall of Famers Vince Lombardi, the offensive guru, and Tom Landry, a one-time Giants defensive back turned defensive coaching innovator.

Both men's creativity helped the Giants to a 39–22–2 record (including postseason) over that span, a period that also included two Championship game appearances in which the Giants were victorious in 1956 but who lost in 1958.

* * *

Lombardi, the oldest of five children born to Italian emigrants from Salerno, Italy, initially studied to become a priest during the first two years of his enrollment at the Cathedral College of Immaculate Conception at age 15. Two years later, he decided to pursue a different career path and transferred to St. Francis Preparatory, where he starred as a fullback on the football team.

Lombardi continued his foray into football at Fordham University (where Giants co-owner Jack Mara had been a student). At Fordham, Lombardi was a member of the school's "Seven Blocks of Granite," a team coached by Jim Crowley, a member of Notre Dame's fabled "Four Horsemen."

As the Giants reshaped their coaching staff following the departure of Steve Owen, Howell hired Lombardi to run the offense.

It didn't take long for Lombardi to make his mark not only on the franchise but on the game itself. He created a new blocking style that he called "Running to Daylight." Instead of an offensive lineman blocking a single player head-on and sending the running back through a pre-determined hole, Lombardi's scheme called for blocking a specific area (similar to zone blocking) and leaving the running back to choose which hole to exploit.

Thanks in part to Lombardi's genius, the Giants offense went from being dead last in 1953 in points scored to sixth in 1954 and then third in 1955.

Besides being an innovator, Lombardi also had an eye for talent. It was his idea to convert flanker/safety Frank Gifford into a full-time halfback.

The move was a success; in 1956, Gifford rushed for a career-high 819 yards on 159 carries with five touchdowns during the regular-season, and was named the NFL MVP by both the UPI and the NFL Newspaper Enterprise Association after helping the Giants with the 1956 Championship Game.

Years later, as a committee member of the Vince Lombardi Golf Tournament, an event to raise money for the Cancer Research Center at Georgetown University, Gifford, who before Lombardi came along also starred on defense for the Giants, remembered when he first learned of Lombardi's plan to convert him to halfback.

"He was standing at the top of a long row of steps, and he had a big grin on his face," Gifford said in a June 1975 interview with the *LaCrosse (Wisconsin) Tribune*. "That grin was typical of him. One of the first things he said to me was, 'You're my halfback.' And I never played defense after that. He built the Giants offense around me, the same way he did with (Paul) Hornung in Green Bay."

Lombardi aspired to be an NFL head coach, and it would have been a dream come true for the native New Yorker to coach the Giants once Jim Lee Howell retired.

Unfortunately for the Giants and Lombardi, Howell was uncertain as to how long he wanted to continue as head coach, and Wellington Mara was unwilling to push Howell into retirement.

That loyalty ultimately cost Mara, and the franchise, as Lombardi would leave the Giants for the Green Bay Packers, with whom he signed a five-year contract in January 1959.

Before signing on the dotted line, Lombardi, confided in Wellington Mara about the Packers offer, perhaps hoping to be talked him out of it. Mara instead gave Lombardi his blessing to take the Packers job, calling it a wonderful opportunity.

Although the Giants had hoped to get Lombardi back once Howell left his post—Wellington Mara had arranged a handshake agreement with the Packers board of directors in which the Packers agreed to let Mara speak with Lombardi once Howell stepped down—Lombardi, a man of high integrity, honored his contract. That was a relief to Dominick Olejniczak, the president of the Packers' board of directors, who told reporters before the Championship Game against the Eagles that "I'd just as soon lose both legs as lose Lombardi."

Lombardi might have honored his commitment to the Packers, but that didn't mean that he wasn't still conflicted. Gifford, in his book, *The*

Offensive coordinator Vince Lombardi, 1954–58. (Giants artifact from the Legacy Club in MetLife Stadium).

Glory Game, recalled a conversation with defensive tackle Dick "Mo" Modzelewski, who, along with defensive end Andy Robustelli, had a chance encounter with Lombardi on the streets of Green Bay.

"Any question about whether Vince truly wanted to coach the Giants was answered during one of my conversations with Mo. 'We played Green Bay in a preseason game one year,' he remembers. 'Andy Robustelli and I were walking around downtown Green Bay, and a car pulls up. It's Lombardi. 'Get the hell in!' he says. He started talking about how he wished he was coaching the Giants, and he was in tears. 'I should have been there coaching you guys,' he said. He was crying in the car."

When Howell retired following the 1960 season, the Giants, thwarted in their attempt to bring Lombardi home, promoted Allie Sherman, Lombardi's successor at offensive coordinator, to be their new head coach.

In eight seasons, Sherman went 57–44–4, including postseason, starting strong in his first three seasons by winning 33 games and bringing the Giants to three consecutive postseason appearances (all losses) before falling on hard times. Sherman's teams then suffered five straight seasons with a .500 record or worse, winning just 24 games over that period as the Giants shrunk from prominence.

Lombardi, meanwhile, led the Packers to five NFL Championship titles, including wins in the first two Super Bowls. In nine years with the Packers, he amassed a 98–30–4 record (including postseason).

* * *

Landry, the other half of the Giants coaching dynamic duo, initially wanted no part of the Giants.

Drafted by the Giants in the 18th round of the 1947 draft as a futures pick (the futures status allowed NFL teams to draft underclassmen and retain their rights until they completed college education), Landry instead signed with the New York Yankees of the All-America Football Conference (AAFC), who had selected him in the 1948 AAFC draft.

Landry's reasons for rejecting the Giants were two-fold. First, the Yankees offered more money, but perhaps equally important, they had more players with ties to Texas, Landry's home state, which made him feel more at home.

Landry's pro football career began as a punter, a role in which he excelled, and then as a backup running back behind starter Buddy Young.

However, an injury to the Yankees' defensive secondary necessitated Landry's moving to the defense where, in his first game, he was made to look silly by Cleveland Browns receiver Mac Speedie, who set an AAFC single-game record by recording over 200 receiving yards, many of those coming against Landry.

The AAFC folded after the 1949 season, with only three teams—the Colts, Browns, and 49ers—being absorbed by the NFL. Luckily for Landry, the Giants exercised their territorial rights to claim him.

In 1954, Landry was named as the Giants defensive coordinator, a role he held simultaneously while still performing as a player. Landry initially had reservations about becoming a coach, given that some of the players he'd be coaching were older and more experienced than he was.

But it wasn't too long before everyone realized what a natural Landry was as a coach.

Landry's humiliation against Speedie taught him a valuable lesson about coaching, and that was to prepare for every possible little nuance that might arise in a game. In his autobiography, Landry wrote, "I'd learned as a defensive back that it wasn't enough for me to react to the movement of the ball; by the time I saw where the ball was being thrown and tried to get there, it would be too late to stop the play."

Based on his studies, Landry created a defense that focused on reading keys. For example, if a halfback went in one direction, Landry surmised that the play would take shape as one of two possible options and would lay out those options for his teammates to stop the opponent.

Landry was, in fact, so demanding of his players on defense that he once chewed out Frank Gifford, who at the time was also contributing on defense, during a film session in which Landry pointed out that Gifford had been out of position on an interception that he returned for a touchdown.

Landry's playing career ended in 1955, but his coaching career continued to take shape. One of his most significant contributions as a defensive coordinator was the development of the 4-3-4 defensive scheme, a combination of Eagles head coach Earle "Greasy" Neale's 5-2-4 defensive scheme and Steve Owen's 6-1-4 "Umbrella" defense.

Before the 4-3-4 (four down linemen, three linebackers, and four defensive backs), pro football teams deployed a 5-3-3 alignment (five defensive linemen, three linebackers, and three defensive backs).

Landry's idea ended up being a perfect fit for the Giants' 1956 team, especially with the addition of third-round draft pick Sam Huff.

Despite Huff's tremendous athleticism and skill set, Howell, at first, struggled to find a role for Huff, who had been an offensive lineman in college.

In early October of that year, Ray Beck, the team's middle linebacker, suffered an injury. Howell and Landry converted Huff to middle linebacker to fit Landry's new 4-3-4 scheme, and the rest was history.

In Landry's scheme, the defensive front, which consisted of Rosey Grier, Andy Robustelli, and Dick Modzelewski, did the "dirty work" up front, leaving Huff to use his instincts to roam around and use his athleticism to make plays.

Landry also designed blitzes and movement by his defensive front that practically forced plays to wherever Huff was. It also opened the door for the various zone and man-to-man coverage schemes currently in use in today's game.

Not only did Huff flourish in the system, but the Giants defense also became such a powerhouse that it would help win another championship in 1956.

In 1959, Landry's last season as Giants defensive coordinator, the defense only surrendered 170 regular-season points, 49 of which came in a Week 2 game against the Eagles. The Giants lost the 1959 Championship Game to the Colts 31–17 in what would be Landry's final game with the team before being named the head coach of the expansion Dallas Rangers (later the Dallas Cowboys), the first team to be added to the NFL since the NFL-AAFC merger.

26

FIRE AND ICE: THE 2007 NFC CHAMPIONSHIP

The night of January 20, 2008, in Green Bay, Wisconsin was one of the coldest ones on record for an NFL game.

But for those who braved Mother Nature's worst—the thermometer read minus-1 degree Fahrenheit with a minus-23 degree windchill at kickoff—they were rewarded to what turned out the be one of the hottest NFL playoff games ever as the Giants topped the Green Bay Packers in the NFC Championship Game at the historic Lambeau Field.

It was in fact so cold that a steady stream of hot beverages and chicken broth available on both sidelines and heated benches, barely helped. But for the Giants, whose offensive linemen went sleeveless that night in what was perhaps a sign that they didn't fear anything—not the Packers or Mother Nature—they would end up on fire behind the night was over.

New York jumped out to a 3–0 lead in the first quarter on kicker Lawrence Tynes' 29-yard field goal on the Giants opening possession. Tynes would then make it 6–0 in the second quarter on a 37-yard conversion after the scoring drive stalled following cornerback Tramon Williams' knockdown of an Eli Manning's pass intended for receiver David Tyree.

Although the Giants had the lead, they knew settling for field goals is a risky proposition, especially in the postseason when it's the best versus the best.

And on that night, the Giants were undoubtedly up against one of the best in the game in Packers quarterback Brett Favre, who would not be denied getting his team on the scoreboard much longer.

After Koren Robinson muffed the ensuing kickoff at his 19-yard line, Williams recovered the ball on the Packers' 10 for a loss of nine yards.

No matter, as Favre needed just one play to make things right. The future Hall of Fame quarterback connected with receiver Donald Driver,

Giants wide receiver Amani Toomer tries to stay warm during the Giants-Packers 2007 NFC Championship game held at Lambeau Field. By the game's 6:42 PM ET kickoff, the mercury on the thermometer read minus-1 degree Fahrenheit with a wind chill of minus-23 degrees. (Copyright New York Football Giants)

who beat Giants cornerback Corey Webster for a 90-yard touchdown reception and the 7–6 lead.

By halftime, the Packers were up 10–6 on Mason Crosby's 36-yard field goal. But on the Giants' first drive of the third quarter, the momentum was about to flip in New York's favor when they strung together a 12-play scoring drive lasting 7:04 that cumulated in a one-yard touchdown run by Brandon Jacobs.

In reality, that drive should have never lasted that long, but thanks to three penalties by the Packers defense, the first of which came on third-and-9 when Al Harris was called for illegal contact, a penalty that wiped out his interception of a pass intended for receiver Plaxico Burress.

Three plays later, the Giants scoring drive appeared to stall again, but the Packers committed another penalty on third down, this one coming on third-and-5 when Nick Collins was flagged for roughing the passer.

On their next third-down play, the Giants again very nearly saw the drive end when on third-and-1, Brandon Jacobs picked up the first down but had the ball knocked loose. Fortunately for the Giants, tight end Kevin Boss recovered it to keep the drive alive.

The Giants must have at that point reached their limit with close calls on third-down as for the rest of that drive, they stayed out of third down. They also benefited from consecutive defensive offside penalties called against defensive tackles Corey Williams and Cullen Jenkins which put the ball at the Packers' 1-yard line to set up Jacobs' 1-yard touchdown run for the 13–10 lead.

After all that, the Giants' lead ended up being short-lived as the Packers benefited from an unnecessary roughness penalty against cornerback Sam Madison on third down.

Favre hit tight end Donald Lee for the touchdown pass and the 17–13 lead until the Giants answered with a four-yard touchdown run by Ahmad Bradshaw to make it 20–17.

Things began to heat up in the fourth quarter, starting with Giants defensive back R.W. McQuarters picking off Favre's pass intended for Robinson. Unfortunately for the Giants, McQuarters failed to hear the screaming pleas of linebacker Antonio Pierce to fall on the ball. Instead, McQuarters had the ball knocked loose by Packers running back Ryan

Grant, the ball recovered by Packers offensive tackle Mark Tauscher at the Giants'19-yard line.

Four plays later, the game was tied after Crosby's 37-yard field goal.

Suddenly the Giants' good fortune seemed to go ice-cold. Tynes, their confident kicker who never seemed to let anything bother him, missed a 43-yard field goal.

Then with 2:05 left in the game, Bradshaw had broken through traffic for a 48-yard touchdown run only to have the play nullified when right guard Chris Snee was called for holding.

The Giants, still in control and looking to run out the clock, saw the drive stall at the Packers' 18-yard line, where Tynes would get another chance to put it away. The Packers, looking to ice the kicking operation, appeared to be successful as the snap from long snapper Jay Alford was high.

BURRESS BURNS HARRIS

For as cold as it was the night of the 2007 NFC Championship Game, Packers cornerback Al Harris had to be feeling the burn by the time that game was over.

That's because Giants wide receiver Plaxico Burress, whom Harris had to cover for most of that game, was repeatedly beaten in coverage by the Giants' No. 1 wide out in what was a night for the two-time Pro Bowl cornerback to forget.

Yet despite the Giants doing everything he expected—the back-shoulder balls in particular—Harris had no answers against Burress, who caught half of Eli Manning's pass completions that day (11) for 154 yards.

According to Pro Football Focus, eight of Burress' receptions came against Harris for 123 yards and seven first downs.

Although he didn't score in that game, Burress set the tone for what was to be a long night for the Packers defense. He caught three passes on the Giants' opening drive for 36 yards, including a 19-yard slant on third-and-10 to keep the scoring drive alive.

Burress didn't stop there, burning Harris on receptions of 21 and 32 yards in the second quarter. By halftime, Burress had recorded seven receptions for 102 yards as the Giants stood toe-to-toe against the Packers in one of the most thrilling playoff games of that postseason.

Although holder Jeff Feagles managed to get the ball down, Tynes' timing had been compromised, resulting in a badly shanked kick to the left in what he later described as "one of the worst kicks of my career."

With the game tied, it was on to overtime. But any momentum the Packers might have had after the Giants' three missed opportunities in the previous quarter was short-lived when Webster made amends for having been toasted earlier in the game on the 90-yard touchdown.

Webster became the answer to the trivia question of who technically caught Favre's final pass as a Green Bay Packer when he picked off a ball intended for Driver deep in Green Bay territory.

Tynes' redemption, which came on the very next drive, was even more significant. His two earlier misses had not helped the team morale on the sideline, leaving some of his teammates to wonder if they had come this far only to lose out on the ultimate goal of playing in the Super Bowl because of all people, their kicker.

But Tynes, a strong believer in himself, borrowed a page from the cornerback school of thought which says that if you have a bad play, you forget about it and move on.

As Tynes waited on the sideline during the Giants' final drive of the game to see if he'd be needed, Coughlin urged the offense to get as close as possible to the end zone so that if they had to attempt a field goal, it would be more of a chip shot.

Unfortunately, the Giants and Manning couldn't oblige, going three-and-out after moving the ball just five yards to set up a 47-yard field goal attempt—Tynes longest attempt of the evening.

At that point, Coughlin was at a crossroads. But not Tynes, who had hoped to get another chance and who ran onto the field to get ready to attempt the kick even as the rest of his battery, punter Jeff Feagles and long snapper Jay Alford, were still on the sideline awaiting official word from Coughlin on what to do.

"I just ran out onto the field," Tynes said after the game. "He had to make a decision, and I wanted to make the decision for him."

Coughlin would later admit that his assistant coaches in the press box urged him not to try the field goal. There was even some doubt among Tynes' teammates, not so much related to Tynes' ability, but more so because thanks to the below-freezing temperatures, the ball was slick and had no "give" to the ball when one's foot struck it.

Before Tynes ran onto the field, Coughlin looked to his kicker for a sign—any sign—that would convince the head coach that trying the field goal was the right decision.

Coughlin got what he was looking for.

"'I looked right at him, and when I saw him run out there, it made a very strong impression," the head coach said after the game. "I knew he was feeling very confident. I was looking for a sign, and that was it."

This time, Tynes didn't let him down, converting the 47-yarder to send the Giants to Super Bowl XLII.

After briefly running around to celebrate his winning kick, Tynes suddenly was nowhere to be found, having made a beeline for the warmth of the postgame locker room.

"I felt good about all the kicks," said Tynes after the game. "Obviously, the operation on the second one was not what it should be, and I didn't make a good attempt at it. The last one was a good snap, good hold. It was a little bit of distance, but I had a little bit of wind."

And a lot of heart, which in the end was all that really mattered.

27

ELI
IN THE MUD

Just in case Eli Manning's gutsy performance in Super Bowl XLII—the one in which he eluded several sack attempts before connecting with receiver David Tyree for one of the most miraculous receptions in NFL history—wasn't convincing enough regarding how tough he really was, his performance in the 2011 NFC Championship Game should put any remaining doubts to rest.

On January 22, 2012, in miserable weather conditions that turned the grass field at Candlestick Park in San Francisco into a pile of mud, Manning took perhaps the worst beating of his career at the hands of a 49ers defense that had finished the 2011 campaign with the fourth-best overall ranking, the top run defense, and in having allowed opponents14.3 points per game, the second-lowest average that year behind the Steelers.

The hits administered by the 49ers defense weren't just love taps either. On one play, linebacker Patrick Willis grabbed a fistful of jersey as he flung Manning to the ground like a rag doll.

On another, linebacker Aldon Smith drove the quarterback face down into the mud like some schoolyard bully. Manning was hit so hard on that play that when he bounced back, his chin strap had shifted to over his mouth, and his helmet was crooked.

All the 49ers did to Manning that evening was hit him 12 times, including six sacks.

To put those numbers into context, Manning attempted 58 passes that day and was roughed up by the 49ers defense on 20.6 percent of those pass attempts.

By the time that game ended in a 20–17 Giants overtime win, Manning's uniform, filled with mud and grass stains that were almost like a badge of honor, had completed 32 of those 58 pass attempts for 316 yards, two touchdowns, and no interceptions.

* * *

The week before Manning and the Giants would play in the mud, the Giants, as they had done in the 2007 NFC title game, upset the Green Bay Packers at Lambeau Field, 37–20.

The 49ers, meanwhile, were coming off a narrow 36–32 victory over the New Orleans Saints. So with the Packers out of the way and the Saints sent home, the Giants, a team that went 9–7 in the regular-season and was the lowest-seeded team in that year's postseason tournament, should have been easy to handle.

Or so thought 49ers safety Donte Whitner, who after his team lost to the Giants, said, "We felt like it was ours to lose, especially after we beat the Saints. We felt like the Saints and Green Bay Packers were the two

Eli Manning's game-worn cleats from the 2011 NFC Championship Game, a 20–17 Giants overtime win vs. the San Francisco 49ers at Candlestick Park. (Giants artifact from the Legacy Club in MetLife Stadium).

best teams in the playoffs, and once they went down, we felt like it was ours to lose."

The 49ers came close to fulfilling their goal. Up 14–10 after three quarters, all they had to do was stifle the Giants for 15 more minutes, and victory would have been theirs.

Such was not the case, as the 49ers let the game literally slip through their fingers thanks in part to special teams miscues.

The big play that swung the momentum back to the Giants' side came on fourth-and-15 from the Giants 15-yard line.

Giants punter Steve Weatherford boomed a kick to the 49ers' 29-yard line where returner Kyle Williams, filling in for the injured Ted Ginn Jr, was waiting.

The ball hit the ground, and Williams failed to get out of the way of the bouncing ball, making it a live ball. Giants receiver Devin Thomas, awarded off waivers from the Carolina Panthers the prior season, was there to recover it.

Initially, it was ruled 49ers ball; however, Giants head coach Tom Coughlin challenged the play, and the replay did indeed show that the ball had grazed Williams' knee, making it a live ball and the Giants' ball after the recovery by Thomas.

With the ball spotted on the 49ers' 29-yard line, the Giants now had a short field on which to work, and put together a six-play, 29-yard scoring drive.

As had been the case throughout the game, Manning was under pressure, but he did find receiver Hakeem Nicks for a 14-yard gain on a third-and-7 despite being pursued by 49ers defensive tackle Justin Smith.

Manning's 17-yard touchdown pass to Mario Manningham on a third-and-long, couldn't have been placed any better, as Manning put the ball where only Manningham had a chance to get it, which he did for a 17–14 Giants lead.

The 49ers, who had just ten turnovers during the regular season that year, shook off Williams' earlier miscue on their ensuing drive when quarterback Alex Smith drove his team 48 yards to set up David Akers' game-tying 25-yard field goal.

After that score, the Giants and 49ers each took turns going three-and-out, that is until with 1:18 left, the Giants were finally able to get a drive going. But that drive ended up stalling on the 49ers' 46-yard line, leaving San Francisco with 19 seconds and starting field position deep in their territory, which left them no choice but to run out the clock.

With the game now in overtime, the Giants special teams would once again save the day. After the Giants' second drive of the overtime period stalled, Weatherford punted the ball, this time from his 44-yard line.

Williams fielded the ball at the 24 and ran it back five yards before being stripped of the pigskin by Giants linebacker Jacquian Williams.

Once again, Devin Thomas picked up the loose ball, this time at the 49ers' 24-yard line to give the Giants possession.

With the game conditions continuing to deteriorate, the Giants handed the ball off to running back Ahmad Bradshaw three times in a row, with Bradshaw picking up 18 yards of his 74 rushing yards for that day on those three carries.

After Manning knelt on second down for a two-yard loss to move the ball back to the 8-yard line, the Giants sent out the field goal unit.

Weatherford, the holder on field goals, was flagged for a delay of game, which moved the ball back another five yards for kicker Lawrence Tynes.

Whereas a penalty pushing the ball back would normally be a bad thing, Tynes said in this case it was a stroke of good fortune.

"It was fortunate because it took me out of a little bit of a puddle," he said.

According to Tynes, there was another big advantage the delay of game created for the Giants.

"I don't know if anyone's ever really watched the film of that first one. But thank God we got that delay of game because somebody jumped through the A or B gap. I mean that guy was going to block the field goal. So it just all worked out."

After the ball was re-spotted, Tynes, as he had done four years earlier in overtime, converted the game-winning field goal in overtime, this one a 31-yarder, to send the Giants to Super Bowl XLVI.

While there is no question that the Giants special teams were, well, special that week, Manning, who in that game engineered his seventh fourth-quarter comeback of that 2011 campaign, delivered a heroic performance under the most difficult conditions.

"The leadership he's shown all year—he's battle-tested, getting us through all these elimination games," Coughlin said of his beat-up, but victorious quarterback after the game.

"To get back up the number of times he did, it shows you the type of focus, courage, toughness, and the type of leader he is."

28

SUPER BOWL XXV

The Super Bowl's silver anniversary should have been a joyous occasion.

Unfortunately, the timing was overshadowed—understandably so—by a much more important event: the U.S. military's launch of Operation Desert Shield, the combat phase of the Gulf War.

With the NFL torn between proceeding with the Super Bowl as planned or postponing it, league officials reached out to the White House and then-president George H.W. Bush for guidance.

"You think we ought to cancel the Super Bowl because of this situation?" Bush, who enlisted in the Navy six months after the United States entered World War II, said during a White House news conference.

"One, the war is a serious business, and the nation is focused on it. But two, life goes on. And I'd say one thing. The men and women in the gulf—they want to see this game go on. They're going to get great instant replays over there."

Despite Bush's blessing to proceed with the game, no detail was spared when it came to security and crowd control, which saw metal detectors and security screenings to include pat-downs and bag searches, which weren't common back then.

Meanwhile, ABC, who held the game's broadcasting rights, decided to air news updates from Peter Jennings as warranted throughout the game, including at halftime, the scheduled halftime show broadcast on a tape delay.

In Tampa, Florida, the site of Super Bowl XXV, one was hard pressed to not find displays of patriotism literally on every corner around the city. But if there was a moment during the pregame when the show of patriotism reached a pinnacle, that had to be when Grammy Award–winning recording artist and New Jersey native Whitney Houston delivered what many consider to be the best rendition of the national anthem ever performed at a major sporting event.

Houston's version was so stirring that between the thunderous applause by the crowd and the loud chants of "USA! USA!" the crowd managed to successfully drown out the sounds of the ensuing military flyover before kickoff.

With the fans in the stadium united behind its troops, it was time to temporarily take sides in a game that would serve as a nice distraction not just for those in attendance but for the men and women stationed overseas.

* * *

Quarterback Jeff Hostetler, the Giants' third-round pick in 1984 who didn't throw his first pass until four years after being drafted, had begun to wonder if he'd ever get a chance to show that he was capable of leading an NFL offense.

After spending part of the 1988 season as the third-string quarterback (and before that getting the occasional look at other positions such as wide receiver), Hostetler got a chance to prove his worth when, after relieving an injured Phil Simms (shoulder) in a Week 12 loss against the Eagles, Hostetler got the start the following week against the Saints.

The Giants Super Bowl XXV uniform patch. (Artifact shown is from the Pro Football Hall of Fame)

After completing five of 10 pass attempts for 128 yards and one touchdown with his team trailing 9–7 at the half in that game against the Saints, Hostetler was benched by head coach Bill Parcells in favor of Jeff Rutledge.

Initially, Hostetler was so upset with the Giants that he demanded a trade. But after calming down, he signed a two-year contract extension with the Giants.

Still, with Phil Simms firmly entrenched as the starter, Hostetler again became frustrated with his role and contemplated retiring.

A season-ending broken foot suffered by Simms in Week 15 of 1990 changed everything. Hostetler was named the starting quarterback and not only led the Giants to a 2–0 record as a starter to close out the season, he also brought them to Super Bowl XXV where he showed his grit by shaking off a second-quarter, bone-crushing hit by Bills defensive end Leon Seals.

On the final play of that quarter, Hostetler and the Giants cut the Bills' lead to 12–10 at the half thanks to his 14-yard touchdown pass thrown to receiver Stephen Baker.

With 30 more minutes of Super Bowl XXV to be played, the Bills and their fans were probably feeling confident about their chances. But any confidence would soon evaporate when the momentum would take a turn in the Giants' favor.

* * *

Like the age-old question of which came first, the chicken or the egg, sports fans will probably forever debate if it's the plays made or the plays that are missed that affect the outcome of a game the most.

In Super Bowl XXV, many people will point to kicker Scott Norwood's blown 47-yard field goal attempt with eight seconds left in the game as the difference. However, for those who still want to blame Norwood for costing the Bills a championship, Buffalo had some other lesser heralded blown opportunities that cost them a chance of football immortality.

In the second quarter, future Hall of Fame receiver Andre Reed dropped a pass on third-and-1 over the middle that snuffed out a Bills scoring drive at midfield.

The Bills also had a pair of missed tackles on the Giants then record-setting opening drive to start the third quarter. During that drive, the Bills twice had the Giants in third-and-long, and both times, linebacker Daryl Talley missed a tackle, including the pivotal third-and-13 shotgun pass from Hostetler to Mark Ingram initially caught five yards past the line of scrimmage that Ingram turned into a 14-yard gain.

THE UNSUNG HERO

If there was ever a case for multiple MVP awards to be given out in a game, Super Bowl XXV was it.

Voters chose Giants running back Ottis Anderson, whose second-half rushing helped the Giants chew up the clock and keep the Bills offense off the field, as the winner of the game's most prestigious individual award.

While Anderson might have been the game MVP, had there been a postseason MVP award, a valid case could have been made to give that honor to cornerback Mark Collins.

Collins had had a strong postseason that year. In the NFC title game against the 49ers that set the stage for the Giants return to the Super Bowl, Collins, the only Giants defensive back in team history to be in the starting lineup at the same position for eight consecutive seasons, was a big reason why future Hall of Fame receiver Jerry Rice only managed 54 yards on five catches (10.8 yards per catch) with no touchdowns.

In Super Bowl XXV, Collins was even better, holding another future Hall of Fame receiver, Andre Reed, to just 62 yards on eight receptions (7.75 yards per catch) and no touchdowns.

Collins' secret? He wasn't afraid to get physical against Rice, Reed, or any other receiver he was assigned to defend.

"I don't understand why defensive backs let these fast guys run," Collins said.

"If you put a speed bump in from of a fast car, it's not going to be able to go too fast, right? So, I called myself the human speed bump. I just tried to be as physical as possible with a receiver, whether it was Jerry Rice, Andre Reed, or whoever because I knew once I get my hands on it or receiver, I pretty much got him."

Collins chuckled as he recalled sharing a beer with Joe Montana one night at a bar when the two became teammates on the Kansas City Chiefs.

"He told me, 'Jerry Rice hated you for what you did to him,' Collins said with a chuckle. "I told him I had felt the same way."

Those missed tackles by the Bills would have shut down the Giants scoring drive, but instead, running back and game MVP Ottis Anderson scored on a one-yard touchdown run over the left side to give the Giants a 17–12 lead.

The Giants, who in the first half edged the Bills in time of possession 17:56 to 12:04, put on a clinic in ball control in the second half of the game.

The 33-year-old Anderson, who rushed for 39 yards on seven carries in the first half, found his groove in the second half, adding 14 more carries for 63 yards to help the Giants set a then–Super Bowl record for time of possession, 40:33 to 19:37.

A staple of that masterful ball control game played by the Giants was their opening drive of the third quarter, a record-setting (at the time) 9:29 scoring drive that ended in Anderson's one-yard touchdown rush to make it a 17–12 game. (Ironically, the Giants would break their own record for the longest scoring drive in a Super Bowl by 30 seconds in Super Bowl XLII.)

With the Giants offense in control, the NFL's highest-scoring offense didn't get its hands on the ball again until nearly two hours of real-time had passed.

The effects on the Bills offense showed when they finally took the field. Not only did they commit two penalties on their first drive of the third quarter, but the offense also seemed out of sync.

The Bills offense wasn't the only unit to suffer due to the Giants' ball- control mastery.

Their defense was also starting to tire out after being on the field for 11:52 out of 15 minutes in the third quarter

In the fourth quarter, things didn't get any better for Buffalo. The Giants once again dominated the clock, this time holding a 10:45 to 4:15 advantage.

The Bills would score their final points of the game on the first play of the fourth quarter when running back Thurman Thomas broke two tackles on his way to a 31-yard touchdown run to make it 19–17.

Thomas very nearly had another touchdown on the Bills' final drive of the game. On third-and-1 from his team's 19-yard line, he took the handoff from Kelly and ran to the left where he had all kinds of daylight to exploit. Were it not, however, for a tackle by Giants defensive back

Everson Walls in the open field, Thomas might very well have gone all the way to the end zone.

Although Thomas had run wild against the Giants that day—he finished with 135 yards on 15 carries and one rushing touchdown—the Giants smothering of the Bills' passing attack was a key to victory.

Meanwhile, the Giants, on their first drive in the fourth quarter, ate up 7:32 off the clock and set up kicker Matt Bahr's 21-yard field goal for the 20–19 lead, ultimately the game's final score and the team's second Super Bowl championship in as many appearances.

29

PIONEER PETE

Pete Gogolak was more than just a place-kicker.

He was a pioneer whose impact on and off the field is still very much felt in today's NFL.

As a youth, Gogolak, born April 18, 1942, in Budapest, Hungary, excelled as a recreational soccer player.

Before Gogolak could decide on what to pursue as a career, the Hungarian Revolution of 1956 created uncertainty for his family, who chose to immigrate to the United States.

After settling in upstate New York, Gogolak, who attended the Ogdensburg Free Academy, soon was drawn to American football primarily due to what he perceived as a majorly attractive perk of the sport.

"The reason I played is because all the cool kids played the game," Gogolak recalled in an interview with NFL Films. "And all the girls—they were dating football players. So I said, 'Hey, I can try this game.'"

When Gogolak began watching the games on television to learn more about what would eventually become his athletic career, he noticed something unusual.

"I watched some of the professional games, guys like (Cleveland Browns kicker/offensive tackle) Lou Groza. The first time I saw him kick, I said, 'What a funny way to kick a ball.'"

Gogolak was referring to the straight-on kicking style used by professional football players at the time, a technique that more closely resembled a dancer's high-kick move.

Then there was Gogolak's kicking style, which, while not unique—there were other college players with soccer backgrounds who deployed a similar style but who never advanced to the pros—would revolutionize the position.

Gogolak, like many of today's kickers, would strike the ball with the instep of his foot, his body swiveling to add additional inertia behind the kick to give it more power and the potential for greater distance.

His kicking style initially caused some concern for his high school coach, Bill Plimpton, who feared that the youth's style might make him a target for being called offside on kickoffs given the torquing of Gogolak's body as part of the motion.

But rather than change Gogolak's style, Plimpton let the young man be. Gogolak, who was also a backup end in high school, would play his college ball at Cornell University after Syracuse University, his preferred choice, wouldn't give him a scholarship.

Gogolak set several Cornell school records, including scoring 44 consecutive point-after-touchdowns (PATs), and finished with a 98.2 percent PAT conversion rate.

Despite Gogolak's college success, he went undrafted by the NFL. However, the rival AFL was a little more receptive to his unorthodox kicking style, so Gogolak became the first soccer-style kicker to make it at the professional level when he was selected in the 12th round of the 1964 AFL draft by the Buffalo Bills.

Gogolak, who earned $11,000 in his first pro season, continued to make believers out of the skeptics who questioned his kicking style. In his tenure with the Bills, he scored 115 points in 14 games, hitting on 28 of 46 field-goal attempts and nailing all 31 PATs, setting a franchise scoring record that stood until kicker Scott Norwood, in 16 games, recorded 129 points in 1988.

Having revolutionized the kicking game, Gogolak would go on to become a central figure in the AFL-NFL merger.

Gogolak, the AFL's second-highest scorer behind Gino Cappelletti, was unhappy with the raise the Bills offered for his next contract.

In an interview with SB Nation's Buffalo Rumblings, he described the Bills' offer as "a slap in the face."

Gogolak countered by asking the Bills for a 100 percent increase in his salary, which he thought would put him where he was worth. However, the Bills balked at meeting his asking price.

Gogolak decided to play out his option year in 1965, a step that necessitated him taking a 10 percent pay cut from his year's previous salary. Although he was underpaid, in playing out his option year at the lower rate, Gogolak knew that he could shop his services around once his contract expired.

The Bills did try to retain Gogolak's services after his contract expired, but the kicker turned down their offer.

When Gogolak's contractual obligations to the Bills ended, he began drawing interest from the New York Giants of the rival NFL. Giants team president Wellington Mara had become increasingly frustrated by rookie Bob Timberlake's missing 13 straight field goals in the unpredictable northeast winds that Gogolak had seemingly mastered while with Buffalo.

Once Mara was assured that Gogolak was free of any contractual obligation from the Bills or AFL, he signed the free agent to a contract, making Gogolak the first prominent player from the AFL to jump to the NFL, and the first to change leagues since 1961 when end Willard

Kicker Pete Gogolak, widely regarded as the first NFL kicker to introduce the soccer-style kick to the game, wore this special shoe to kick. Gogolak remains the Giants' all-time leading scorer with 646 points. (Giants artifact from the Legacy Club in MetLife Stadium)

Dewveall left the Chicago Bears of the NFL for the Houston Oilers of the AFL.

Despite the legality of the transaction, the move had, in the eyes of the AFL, broken a gentleman's agreement in which team owners in each league agreed not to poach players from the other league.

With the Giants having breached the gentleman's agreement, all bets were now off as the AFL owners intended to go after NFL players.

That wasn't the only fall-out from the transaction. Behind the scenes, the AFL and NFL were negotiating a merger. According to a *Sports Illustrated* article written by Tex Schramm, the original president and general manager of the Dallas Cowboys, the "poaching" of Gogolak and the subsequent retaliation by the AFL to recruit NFL stars prolonged the finalization of the merger between the rival leagues.

Ultimately, the merger agreement was announced on June 8, 1966, with the actual merger taking place in 1970.

As for Gogolak, he would go on to have a nine-year career with the Giants. In 121 games as a Giant, he converted 126 out of 219 field-goal attempts and 268 out of 277 extra points.

He also contributed 12 punts for 491 yards, and ended up as the holder of several franchise records including most career points (646); most consecutive games scoring (61, tied with Lawrence Tynes); most PATs attempted, career (277); most PATs in a game (8, vs. Philadelphia on November 26, 1972); PATs attempted (277); most career PATs (268); most field goals attempts, career (219); and most field goals made, career (126).

Gogolak was cut by the Giants on September 5, 1975, and was replaced by George Hunt. Gogolak, named as a *Sporting News* "All-league player" by his peers in 1965 and who was part of the Giants inaugural "Ring of Honor" class in 2010, retired from the game at the age of 33.

30

THE
CATCH

David Tyree will forever be remembered as a hero for his 32-yard catch in the fourth quarter of the Giants Super Bowl XLII win. And rightfully so. "The Catch," as it's become known in Super Bowl lore, was one that you had to see to believe, one that left scores of spectators, teammates, and opponents asking, "How did he catch that?"

Tyree, a profoundly spiritual man, credits God for all he's had in life, including one of the most significant contributions ever made on a football field at any level.

Tyree made the catch look easy. In reality, the circumstance leading to that reception and that game were anything but.

* * *

Tyree was born on January 3, 1980, but if you ask him, he'll tell you that his true birth came in early March 2004.

Two days after delivering a motivational speech about making smart choices to members of the Montclair High School football team, Tyree had been out with friends when he was pulled over by a police officer for speeding in Fort Lee, New Jersey.

The investigating officer smelled what he believed to be marijuana coming from the car and questioned the vehicle's occupants. A half-pound of marijuana was found in the car. Also, a background check done on the vehicle uncovered an outstanding traffic warrant that had been issued in Blairstown.

Tyree and his friends were taken into custody and booked into the Bergen County Jail. As Tyree, something of a reckless youth who smoked marijuana and who, in college, often drank until he blacked out, sat in his cell that cold March night, he hit rock bottom.

Tyree, a sixth-round draft pick of the Giants in 2003 and a player known more for his special teams prowess, admitted that before his arrest that night, he had thought he had it made because he was on an NFL roster and had earned accolades as a member of the 2003 All-Rookie team.

What he failed to realize until that night was that what he did in the past didn't necessarily guarantee him anything for tomorrow.

"It was time for me to grow up," he said.

* * *

Special teams players are a dime a dozen in the NFL, often composed of Day 3 draft picks and undrafted free agents.

If one works at it, though, they can make a career on special teams and as a spot player on offense or defense. But if one doesn't work at it or plays fast and loose with his life, it becomes too easy for the team to move on and find someone else.

In looking back, Tyree said he was fortunate that he didn't fall into the latter category, even though he wouldn't have blamed the Giants had they cut their losses with him.

Tyree, now the Giants director of player engagement, believes he was an exception not because there was anything special about him, but because in 2004, the Giants hired Tom Coughlin to be their head coach who in turn gave all the players a clean slate.

"At the moment of my greatest failures, there was an opportunity for redemption and not just spiritual redemption," Tyree said.

"When I think about the direction that this franchise was moving in 2004, and how a person with the character and reputation of Tom Coughlin and how he was willing to give everyone a new, clean slate, I knew the opportunity was right there before me."

Tyree prayed, and reflected on where he was in his life and where he wanted to be. Through prayer, he said, he found the strength he needed to clean up his act.

Having promised Coughlin that he'd make more of an effort to be responsible, by the time the team gathered for its first off-season program under Coughlin, the one-time wild child transformed into to a model citizen.

"I had everything to gain regarding my redemptive process and had an opportunity to be restored right in the same locale that I disappointed," Tyree said.

"So it meant the world to me that I had the opportunity to come back [to the Giants]. I look at my second training camp [in 2004], and it was nothing memorable in my eyes, but I think I did enough to put myself in a position to compete.

"But that they put faith in me to be a man of my word—that meant everything to me, and that was the catalyst to what I hoped would be bigger things to come."

Bigger things, like a Pro Bowl appearance and being named as a first-team All-Pro, both in 2005.

And of course, "The Catch."

* * *

Coughlin was getting very nervous as he watched his team's practice the Friday before Super Bowl XLII.

With Plaxico Burress secretly nursing a knee injury from a fall in the shower earlier that week, there was some grave concern as to whether Burress would be able to play in the Super Bowl.

If he couldn't, Tyree was the next man up, so to get him ready, Tyree took Burress' practice reps.

"Friday is usually your dress-rehearsal day, and the day you're supposed to be at your sharpest in practice," Tyree explained.

"But that Friday was probably the worst practice I ever had in my life. I had a bad case of the drops. You'd think two or three drops—I think I had five or six that day, though depending on who you ask, I dropped everything. Either way, it was an inexcusable practice."

It was also a practice that Tyree learned something about himself that would serve him well later on.

"For me, it wasn't a big deal in my mind because if you have a bad practice, you have a bad practice, and you get over it. The timing of it sucked, but when I left at the end of the day, I was pissed that I had that kind of performance on a Friday."

Tyree credited quarterback Eli Manning for coming to him after the practice with words of encouragement.

"I think that was the signature moment, not just for me, but for Eli as someone who was still showing he could be a leader," Tyree said. "Eli approached me as we were leaving the practice field and said, 'Hey man,

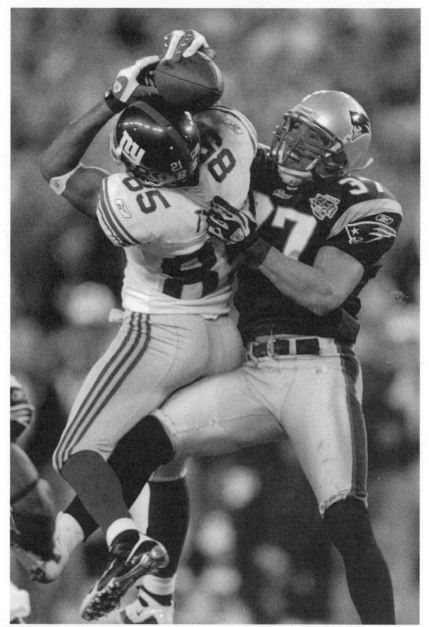

David Tyree pins the ball to his helmet to hang on to Eli Manning's 32-yard pass, better known as "The Catch," in the fourth quarter of Super Bowl XLII. (AP Images / Gene Puskar)

I know you'll be ready. So, don't even worry about it and just shake it off.'"

* * *

Tyree finished the 2007 NFL season with 35 yards on four receptions, with his first two catches that season coming in a Week 13 win over the Bears, and his final two receptions of the regular season coming in the Week 17 loss against the Patriots.

Statistics aside, it hadn't been an easy year for the receiver. He began the season inactive due to a broken wrist suffered in a preseason game.

Then his mother Thelma suffered a fatal heart attack on December 15, 2007, the day before a Week 15 game against Washington. Tyree would miss that game and the next week's game while grieving for his mother, but he did return for the Week 17 regular-season finale against the Patriots and was available throughout the playoff run.

When it was determined that Burress was healthy enough to play in the Super Bowl, any thoughts of an expanded role for Tyree were shelved.

But that didn't mean that Tyree wouldn't play a role in one of the biggest upsets in Super Bowl history.

For as much attention as Tyree's catch receives, it was his 5-yard touchdown reception from Manning to cap a six-play, 80-yard fourth-quarter scoring drive that gave the Giants a 10–7 lead, their first in the game.

The Patriots would take back the lead 14–10 on Tom Brady's 6-yard touchdown pass to receiver Randy Moss. But on the Giants' next drive, history was about to be made.

Thanks to Brandon Jacobs imposing his will on a fourth-and-inches play against Patriots nose tackle Vince Wilfork, a 6'2", 325-pound plugger who, at least on that play, was no match for the 6'4", 265-pound Jacobs, the Giants had a fresh set of downs and 1:28 left to bleed out the clock and score the game-winning points.

On a second-and-5 from the Giants 44-yard line, Manning tried to connect with Tyree on a deep ball along the right sideline, but the pass almost picked off by Patriots cornerback Asante Samuel.

On third down, Manning, who found himself under heavy pressure but who managed to avoid being sacked, fired the ball down the middle of the field.

Tyree, meanwhile, was covered by safety Rodney Harrison. The two men ended up leaping for the ball, with Harrison desperately trying to swat it away.

THE SEQUEL

"Make 'em go to Manningham!"

Such was the strategy of Patriots head coach Bill Belichick, perhaps the most brilliant mind in today's game, when the Giants and Patriots squared off against each other in Super Bowl XLVI.

Belichick's thinking was that if his defense could contain Hakeem Nicks and Victor Cruz, the Giants' top two receivers in 2011, that would force quarterback Eli Manning to throw to "less appealing" receiving options like receiver Mario Manningham and tight end Bear Pascoe.

But not even Belichick could have anticipated a case of déjà vu unfolding in the Super Bowl rematch with the Giants.

By making the Giants go to Manningham, who had 523 yards on 39 receptions and four touchdowns that season, the Giants were put in a position to again upset the heavily favored Patriots.

Manningham's catch came with 3:26 left in the game, the Giants trailing 17–15 and although it wasn't as flashy as Tyree's helmet catch in Super Bowl XLII, Manningham's reception was without a doubt one of the key plays in the game for the Giants.

On the first play of the nine-play scoring drive, Manning threw the ball deep down the left sideline, putting it in a spot where only Manningham, who had two Patriots in pursuit, could get it.

Manningham did a masterful job of not only making the 38-yard catch, but also in making sure he kept both feet in bounds.

Manning then targeted Manningham on the next three pass attempts. The first fell incomplete, but the next two went for a combined 18 yards before Belichick finally realized that maybe it wasn't such a good idea, after all, to "Make 'em go to Manningham" after the receiver gained 56 of his 73 receiving yards on that drive alone.

By then, it was too late for Belichick to adjust, as the Giants continued to march down the field on a drive cumulating in Ahmad Bradshaw's six-yard touchdown run to give his team the 21–17 lead and win.

Ironically, it was Harrison's swatting that set up the defining characteristic of the catch when he momentarily pinned the ball against Tyree's helmet, putting it in a better position to where Tyree could secure it.

Tyree did just that, and then quickly brought his other hand up to secure the ball while Harrison was still tugging at Tyree's right arm to pry the ball loose.

Tyree then quickly used his left hand to keep the ball from being ruled incomplete. Once both men were on the ground, the receiver promptly hoisted the ball in the air to remove any doubt as to whether it was a catch, with Harrison still trying to knock it loose.

It was a valiant effort by Harrison, but the play by Tyree that Manning later said "saved the game" stood as a completion and an extension of what would become the Giants' game-winning drive cumulating in Manning's 13-yard touchdown pass to Burress on a fade for the 17–14 lead and winning score.

* * *

When Tyree tries to put "The Catch" into perspective, he notes that it has played both a macro and micro role in his life.

One the one hand, it's a play that was so spectacular that his helmet was sent to the Pro Football Hall of Fame.

On the other hand, the catch was part of what Tyree set out to do as an athlete dating back to his college years at Syracuse, which was to be great.

He shared a story about a game in college where he decided that he was going to rush the punter on every play, regardless if a return was set. On one of those rushes, Tyree ran into the punter, drawing a penalty.

"So, the media asked me about that play after the game," he remembered, "and I said, 'Well listen. I'm not going out on the field to be an average player. My goal, when I step on the field, is to make a play. I want to be remembered.'

"When I look back at the catch, the reality is, by no means am I a spot on the radar in anybody's conversation. I was perfectly content with my career, and I had modest success in the National Football League.

"But the catch has now put me in a position where I'm a part of the game, and I really can't take credit for that. There have been so many careers that supersede my résumé, and I can fully admit that. But by the grace of God, I have a part in the history of a great game."

31

A GIANT ROMP

"The art of war is simple enough. Find out where your enemy is. Get to him as soon as you can. Strike at him as hard as you can and keep moving on."
—U.S. President Ulysses S. Grant

Such was the message that accompanied a Minnesota Vikings team flag and a Randy Moss jersey emblazoned with the Super Bowl XXXV logo on the sleeve. Both items had been put on full display in the Giants locker room on orders from head coach Jim Fassel in the days leading up to their NFC Conference championship battle with the Vikings.

The Giants, if the critics were to be believed, didn't belong in the 2000 playoff hunt.

Seriously, how could they? Thanks to their 7–9 finish, good for third place in the division the prior year, the Giants were handed a "soft" schedule that they turned into a 12–4 record to gain home-field advantage throughout the playoffs.

But the Giants were far from becoming a one-and-done team in the postseason. In the NFC Divisional round, they eliminated the Philadelphia Eagles, 20–10, a win some critics believed the Giants had been lucky to get.

Those same critics were almost unanimous in their belief that there was no way the Giants were going to have the same kind of luck against a Vikings team whose offense put up 5,961 yards and 397 points that season.

It could be argued that if the critics had had their way, the Vikings should have been crowned the NFC Conference champions without even bothering to play the title game.

These sentiments were not lost on members of the Giants defense.

"There was this big deal made in the papers leading up to the game about how we didn't stand a chance and how Minnesota had the best offense that had been assembled," linebacker Jessie Armstead recalled.

"And you know, we all took it personal."

Armstead said that no one took it more personal than defensive coordinator John Fox, who came up with a strategy to humble the Vikings and shut the mouths of the critics.

Fox's game plan centered around a couple of things. One, he was determined to take away the Vikings' deep passing game, thereby neutralizing Moss and Cris Carter. Two, he was going to send a mostly four-man rush after quarterback Daunte Culpepper to disrupt the shorter passing game.

If the defense could do those two things and the Giants offense get a decent lead, the third domino—neutralizing running back Robert Smith and the Vikings running game—would fall into place.

Giants head coach Jim Fassel holds the George Halas Trophy after the Giants crushed the Minnesota Vikings 41–0 in the 2000 NFC Championship at Giants Stadium. (Copyright New York Football Giants)

The plan was so promising that Armstead, confident of a win, hid a piece of paper under the podium in the postgame interview room before the game, the paper reading "Giants 31, Minnesota Vikings 17." When he took to the podium after the game to address the media, Armstead brought out the paper and held his prediction up for everyone to see.

"The reason I did that because every week you go in the game and you hope to get a shutout, or hopefully go in there and make some big plays and win the game," he said. "Then there are times when you just throw it out there and say, 'This is what is going to be.'"

The Giants certainly made sure that they gave themselves every opportunity to fulfill Armstead's prediction of a win. Fassel had invited eight former Giants from the 1986 and 1990 Super Bowl championship teams—linebackers Harry Carson and Lawrence Taylor, offensive linemen Brad Benson and Bart Oates, receivers Stephen Baker and Phil McConkey, and defensive linemen Jim Burt and George Martin—to attend the Giants final workout before the game.

Taylor, one of the honorary captains for the game, delivered a heartfelt speech on behalf of his former teammates.

"I'm not here to give you guys a pep talk. I'm here to tell you how proud we—myself and my teammates are about you as a team," he said in his comments which later were distributed to the media. "You know what's going on, and you know what's at stake: supremacy and going to the Super Bowl."

Taylor wrapped up his impassioned speech by reminding the players how the 1986 and 1990 Super Bowl teams were never really given a chance by their critics, yet they found a way to use that as motivation to get it done.

"From the bottom of my heart," Taylor said earnestly, "We're proud of you. Whatever it takes, *get it done.*"

* * *

It wasn't going to be easy, but nothing in life worth having ever is.

From an offensive perspective, the Giants were going against a Vikings defense that had issues. That season, Minnesota had allowed 397 points, seventh-most in the league, and were allowing 356.3 yards per game, the fourth-highest average in the league.

Minnesota's pass defense, in particular, had issues. The unit finished 28th that year, allowing 3,913 yards through the air, fourth-most in the league.

"They were grossly overrated defensively," said former running back Tiki Barber, whose 69 rushing yards on 12 carries led both teams' ground games that afternoon.

"Sean Payton was our offensive coordinator at that time, and he came into that meeting before the week before the NFC Championship Game and said, 'We're going to score 50 points on this team.'"

Barber went on to recall how Payton almost took delight in pointing out the various vulnerabilities of the Vikings defense during film sessions.

AN ILL-TIMED ABOUT-FACE

Receiver Amani Toomer thinks back to the Giants' deflating 34–7 loss to the Baltimore Ravens in Super Bowl XXXV, and wonders what might have been had the Giants coaches stuck with what had worked all year.

Toomer acknowledged that the Ravens had an outstanding defense that year. But he also believes that the most significant difference for the Giants, who had rolled over the Vikings 41–0 in the NFC Championship Game, was the coaching staff got too cute with its plans leading up to that game, which created unnecessary distractions for the team.

"We did some innovative things at the time. Before the snap, we had a lot of like different types of motions that not a lot of teams did," Toomer said. "In the NFC title game, we beat the Vikings playing the same way we always played on offense, but then all of a sudden, we felt like we had to change for the Super Bowl.

"So I felt like we lost that Super Bowl because our coaches changed what we did instead of making the Ravens stop what we did well all season. People always ask, 'Oh, you played against the 2000 Ravens—how good were they?' and I'm like, 'I don't really know because we didn't do what we had done the entire season, and we never really found out what would have happened if we would've just run our bread and butter plays.'"

That wasn't the only change the coaching staff made leading up to that game. Toomer opined that the Giants became distracted when head coach Jim Fassel, who had alternated introducing the offense and

"Sean was like, 'All you gotta do is look at the tape. They make mistakes. They're vulnerable. They have liabilities all over the place. It's our job to design it and to devise a game plan to take advantage of it.' So that was one of the most intense film study weeks that I can remember," Barber added.

"What they do isn't very complex," receiver Amani Toomer told reporters before the game. "They have a couple of base coverages they stick to, and they do have some real tendencies."

One of those tendencies, according to Barber, was the number of gambles the Vikings would take, especially in coverage.

"They got themselves out of position, and they gambled a lot," Barber said. "And they would lose people in coverage at times because they were

defense each week, decided to have the defense introduced before the Super Bowl despite having had the unit introduced before the NFC Championship Game.

"I remember us going to the meeting room, and all of us were so upset," Toomer said about having learned of Fassel's decision. "We usually go over like the first 15 plays, and I don't remember any of that at all. I just remember as I was looking around pissed off, like, 'What just happened?' So that's what I mean when I say we were a distracted team. We were worried about who was getting announced than the team we were playing against."

Running back Tiki Barber agreed that the decision threw things off. "Coach Fassel said our defense had been the strongest part of our team and that we were going to introduce them at the start of the Super Bowl," he said. "It was just this letdown—the offense kind of went into a shell a little bit."

And that decision made that much of a difference?

"There was a disappointment," Barber admitted. "It's hard to explain because it ultimately means nothing. You still have to go out, and you have to play the game. I don't want to put [the loss] on the fact that we weren't introduced; football is mostly physical, but there is an emotional, psychological component that gets discounted sometimes."

"Of course, we have to take some accountability," Toomer added. "We did lose the game, but there was just so much unnecessary stuff going on. That's what bothers me about that Super Bowl—we were completely distracted."

peeking into the backfield, looking to be opportunistic—get interceptions, get turnovers, and such because that's how they would go win."

Defensively, the Giants had faced some big offensive lines before, but in the Vikings, they were about to face probably the biggest group of the season, which the Vikings were hoping would be a key to the game.

The Vikings also hoped to run the ball down the Giants' throat.

Minnesota had led the NFC in rushing with 133.1 yards per game and 5.0 yards per play that season. But Smith, the NFC's second-leading rusher, who from Weeks 10 through 14 had rushed for over 100 yards in each game, had started to cool down, rushing for 67, 26, and 37 yards in his final three regular-season games, and only 25 yards in the divisional playoff game the week prior against the Saints.

The Giants, in no mood to play the role of hospitable hosts, cruised to a 34–0 halftime lead.

Defensively, Fox's game plan worked to perfection. The Giants held the Vikings to just one third-down conversion out of eight attempts and dominated the time of possession battle, 42:22 to 17:38. The nine first downs converted by the Vikings matched a team playoff low set back in a Super Bowl loss to the Pittsburgh Steelers in 1975.

New York held the mighty Vikings offense to just 114 net yards, including 54 on the ground. Future Hall of Fame receivers Moss and Carter were nonfactors, the former catching two out of seven pass targets for 18 yards and Carter coming up with three out of seven targets for 24 yards.

The Giants offense, not to be outdone, had itself an afternoon. Quarterback Kerry Collins finished 28 of 39 for 381 yards with five touchdown passes, a postseason franchise record for touchdowns thrown in a single game.

With a date now set to face the AFC champion Baltimore Ravens in Super Bowl XXXV, the joyous Giants made little attempt to hide their ecstasy over how far they had come.

"Today, they'll say we were the worst team to ever with the NFC championship," said team president Wellington Mara after the game. "In two weeks, I hope they'll say we're the worst team ever to win the Super Bowl."

32

THE UNSUNG HEROES OF SUPER BOWL XLVI

I n so many ways, the Giants Super Bowl XLVI over the New England Patriots was identical to Super Bowl XLII.

Besides having the same outcome (a Giants win albeit by a different score), the same MVP (Eli Manning), the same general margin of victory (less than a touchdown), and even a highlight-reel catch (albeit not by David Tyree, who made the helmet catch in 2007), the game was a thriller for Giants fans.

But this victory for the underdog Giants on the Lucas Oil Stadium field had a little bit of a different feel to it, as were it not for the contributions of two of the most unsung heroes in that game, who knows what might have happened?

* * *

Chase Blackburn probably wondered if his NFL career was finished.

Blackburn, a linebacker who signed with the Giants as an undrafted free agent out of Akron in 2005, was initially brought on board for his special teams prowess. But when given a chance, Blackburn's versatility and high football IQ made him invaluable at linebacker.

But after the 2010 season ended, Blackburn was a free agent, and the Giants didn't seem interested in retaining his services.

In 2011, the Giants had kept four rookie linebackers on their roster, two draft picks (Greg Jones and Jacquian Williams), and two undrafted free agents (Spencer Paysinger and Mark Herzlich). They hoped that one or more from that group would step up and become a part of the team's foundation.

What the Giants weren't counting on, however, were injuries at the position.

Michael Boley, who started 13 games for them at inside linebacker, missed two games with a hamstring strain. His replacement, Herzlich, suffered an ankle injury. With Paysinger mainly a special teams player and Jones still feeling his away around the pro game, the Giants made the call to Blackburn, whom they signed on November 29, 2011.

Blackburn, who knew the Giants defense inside-out and who was well respected by the coaching staff, wasted little time contributing.

In his first game back, he picked off Packers quarterback Aaron Rodgers in a 38–35 Giants loss. Blackburn's football intelligence and knowledge of the defense was so intact that he finished second to Boley in the postseason with 25 tackles.

For all the plays Blackburn made during the 2011 season and postseason, there was none more significant than his interception in Super Bowl XLVI.

The pick came on the second play of the fourth quarter, on a pass by quarterback Tom Brady intended for tight end Rob Gronkowski. On the play, Brady was hit by defensive end Jason Pierre-Paul as he threw the ball. Gronkowski tried to outreach Blackburn for the ball but was unable to do so.

If Blackburn, who in that game also contributed six tackles, doesn't make that interception, the Patriots, up 17–15 at the time, might very well have gone on to make it a two-score game.

* * *

Mario Manningham was a third-round draft pick by the Giants in 2008, a 6'0", 185 wiry-looking receiver out of Michigan who was supposed to be able to slice the top off of the defense.

Manningham played four seasons with the Giants, 2011 being his last. (He did attempt a comeback with the Giants in 2014 after rehabbing from a knee injury suffered in 2012, but it didn't work out).

While with the Giants the first time, Manningham's most productive season was in 2010 when he recorded a career-high 944 yards on 60 receptions and nine touchdowns in what would be the only 16-game season he played in his career.

Looking to build on that in 2011, Manningham missed four games that year due to injuries, though between Weeks 8 and 10, he had a receiving touchdown in each of those games.

In the final two games of the Giants regular season, Manningham, who missed the Week 16 game against the Jets, was a nonfactor. Between the injuries and the drop-in-a-bucket production, he was barely considered a threat to take over a game by himself by his postseason opponents.

Their hunch proved correct. Manningham's stats in the Wild Card, Divisional and Conference games totaled eight receptions for 116 yards with three touchdowns—not enough to cause tremendous concern for Patriots head coach Bill Belichick in the Super Bowl.

Instead, Belichick seemed more concerned about containing receivers Hakeem Nicks and Victor Cruz.

Manningham, who finished the Super Bowl catching five out of nine pass targets for 73 yards, would make the Patriots pay for doubting him.

Before Manningham got his chance to shine, the Patriots ended up hurting themselves. With 9:24 left in the game and the Giants having used two of their three timeouts, New England was in control.

But Brady and crew couldn't get the job done, as on a second-and-11, the quarterback tried to connect on a deep ball to sure-handed receiver Wes Welker, who was streaking down the middle of the field with no Giant in sight thanks to what looked like a busted coverage by the Giants' defensive secondary.

Had Welker caught that pass, the Patriots would have had a fresh set of downs and a chance at expanding their 17–15 lead. Instead, the ball fell through Welker's outstretched hands, and, following another deep pass attempt that went incomplete, the Patriots punted the ball back to the Giants.

With 3:46 left on the clock, the Giants wasted no time. Quarterback Eli Manning heaved a deep pass along the sideline to Manningham, who ran a go route.

Manningham not only reached out to secure the ball, but he also maintained possession and got both feet in bounds before safety Patrick Chung pushed him out of bounds, the catch good for 38 yards.

With the Giants now at midfield, Manning began to move the ball down the field. He again targeted Manningham on first-and-10, the pass falling incomplete. Unfazed, Manning went right back to Manningham on his next two pass attempts, completing both and moving the ball 18 yards to the Patriots' 32-yard line.

After the two-minute warning, the Giants, who on the preceding play had another pass completion (Manning to Hakeem Nicks for 14 yards which put them at the 11-yard line,) tried to chew up the clock.

However, three plays later, running back Ahmad Bradshaw, on second-and-6 from the Patriots' 6-yard line, scored to give the Giants a 21–17 lead, leaving less than a minute left in the game.

With 57 seconds left for Brady to work his magic, it was up to the Giants defense to finish the game.

But the Giants defense wasn't having it, as although Brady and the Patriots did convert a fourth-down attempt on that final drive, Brady's final pass attempt, a 51-yard strike intended for tight end Aaron Hernandez in the end zone, was knocked away by safety Kenny Phillips.

Although Manning was named the game's MVP, Blackburn and in particular Manningham, were heroes.

Blackburn finished third on the team with six tackles, along with his big interception and a pass defensed.

Manningham, who had failed to catch his lone pass target in the first half, contributed three of his five game receptions and 56 of his 73 receiving yards on the game-winning drive.

"We just tried to be patient," Manningham said of his big-play contributions after the game. "We knew big plays was [sic] going to come. We just had to take advantage of them."

The Giants did, and, in the end, they were able to hoist the Lombardi trophy for the second time in five years.

33

MICHAEL STRAHAN

Michael Strahan flashed his famous gap-tooth grin as he addressed the reporters assembled before him.

"My career has far exceeded all expectations," he said, at times getting choked up. "I was hoping to get in maybe three years and move back in with my parents. That was my goal. As far as accomplishments, personally, Wow! You hear about games played and sacks and [being mentioned with] Lawrence Taylor and all these guys. To do the things I've done, it just doesn't seem real."

Indeed, the Giants were only too happy to take the entire package—the on-field accomplishments, the leadership, and yes, even the bad days that all players had on occasion—from a player who, much like Taylor in his prime, dominated.

Strahan, a 1994 second-round pick out of Texas Southern (the Giants didn't have a first-round pick that year because they had spent the first-round pick in the 1993 supplemental draft to acquire quarterback Dave Brown) was initially supposed to be a situational pass rusher.

Injuries would limit him to six games as a rookie. Then over the next three seasons, he recorded 4.5 sacks in 1994, 7.5 sacks in 1995, and 5.0 sacks in 1996, numbers that fell within what was expected.

Then came 1997, the year of Strahan's official arrival. That year he recorded the first of two consecutive double-digit sack seasons (14.0 in 1997 and 15.0 in 1998). He began to establish himself as a player against whom offensive coordinators would double—if not triple—team to try to slow him down.

What was it about Strahan that made him such a dominating opponent for scores of offensive tackles who tried—and often failed—to neutralize him?

According to fellow defensive end Osi Umenyiora, the Giants' second-round pick in the 2003 draft who became Strahan's pass-rushing protégé, Strahan wasn't the strongest guy on the field nor the fastest.

Defensive end Michael Strahan sacks Patriots quarterback Tom Brady in Super Bowl XLII. (Copyright New York Football Giants)

But he was by far the best at what he did, a man who seemed to impose his will on others whenever he set his mind to doing so, resulting in pure domination of some of the league's best offensive tackles.

Umenyiora, an impressionable young kid at the time out of Troy, was intrigued and wanted to find out what it was that made Strahan such a superhuman power on the field.

Putting aside some trepidation because, as Umenyiora said, Strahan was the "biggest personality I had ever been around," he reached out to the veteran to pick his brain.

To his surprise and delight, Strahan was more than happy to share his tricks of the trade with Umenyiora, including a couple of valuable intangibles Umenyiora swears were instrumental in him developing his own game as a pass-rusher.

"The first thing he taught me was what you might call 'want-to.' He literally wanted it more than the other people," Umenyiora said.

"I know it sounds like a cliché, but to see someone who was that hungry go out there and because he wants to physically impose his will on somebody, he finds success, that rubbed off on you when you're watching and learning from him.

"The second thing was he would do things that other people weren't doing after practice, like working out and watching film and taking care of his body. After practice, a lot of guys couldn't wait to get in their cars and go home for the day. But there was Stray still working after hours doing the little things that allow you to play in this league for a long period and at a higher level even against the more talented guys you might face on Sunday."

Umenyiora paused for a moment and said, "He's the reason why I became a successful football player. The things he told me to do, I did, and that let me take my game to the next level. I owe him so much, man. He means the world to me."

* * *

The laws of physics suggest that when two heavy masses collide against one another and exert force, the heavier should prevail.

Strahan, who routinely faced offensive tackles who had 30-plus pounds on him, was an anomaly who used his tremendous quickness off the line and his swift hands to get the upper hand against his opponents.

Simply put, Strahan would time his jump so that when the ball was snapped, he often got his hands into his opponent's chest before the tackle could set up in his pass block. This usually meant that Strahan was successful in catching his opponents off-balance, leaving them unable to extend their arms to keep him at bay or to swat away his punch.

Strahan would then use his strength and momentum to push into the opponent's chest, often knocking him to the ground because the opponent was off balance. With the man in front of him out of the way, Strahan was then free to wreak havoc in the opponent's backfield.

That's exactly what he did in the Giants 2000 playoff run. Strahan's 4.5 postseason sacks were second that year, behind Ravens defensive end Michael McCrary's 6.0.

Defensive end Michael Strahan, 1993–2007.
(Giants artifact from the Legacy Club in MetLife Stadium).

In the 2000 divisional playoff game against the Eagles, Strahan went against Jon Runyan, one of his regular divisional battles and probably one of his most fun to watch. Runyan, a 6'7", 330-pounder who mostly lined up at right tackle for the Eagles during the 2000–08 seasons, faced Strahan 15 times over his career. In their first five meetings, Strahan got 8.0 of the 14.5 sacks he'd logged against the Eagles offensive line.

In that divisional playoff game against Runyan and the Eagles, Strahan finished with four tackles, 2.0 sacks, one tackle for loss, and a big forced fumble that came on his second sack of quarterback Donovan McNabb, the ensuing Giants recovery snuffing out the Eagles scoring drive.

In the 2000 NFC title game against the Vikings, Strahan lined up across from Korey Stringer, who outweighed him by over 50 pounds. Regardless, Strahan managed to record two tackles and one sack which came early in the second quarter on second-and-14 on the drive just before the Giants would go up 24–0 in their eventual 41–0 rout of the Vikings.

Although the Ravens got the better of the Giants in Super Bowl XXXV, Strahan still managed to come up with six tackles (five solo) and 1.5 sacks.

* * *

Ask any athlete how he or she would like to wind down a lengthy career, and he or she will probably tell you that they'd like to do so, having won the top prize in their respective sport.

For Strahan, that would have been achieving NFL immortality by winning a Super Bowl championship, something that he had come close to reaching in 2000 only to see his Giants end up as literally no match for the Baltimore Ravens.

But long before the Giants 2007 roster, to borrow one of Strahan's most famous battle cries, "stomped out" the New England Patriots' quest for a perfect season, the defensive end was at a crossroads.

Facing his 15th NFL season, Strahan, who by that point in his career had also been named as the 2001 AP Defensive Player of the Year, voted to seven Pro Bowls and four first-team All-Pros, and to the Pro Bowl seven times as part of a Hall of Fame résumé, was contemplating retirement.

THE SACK KING

In the official NFL gamebook, the play is listed simply as *B. Favre sacked at GB 35 for -7 yards (M. Strahan)*.

But that sack for -7 yards—one of Strahan's 141.5 career sacks recorded over his 15-year Giants career—would not only be a record-setter for the Giants defensive end, but it would also become one of the most hotly debated topics in sports at the time.

The play, which came with 2:46 left in the 2001 regular-season finale on January 5, 2002, a game in which the Green Bay Packers would go on to win 34–25 on the Giants' home turf, took place on the Packers final series.

On first-and-10, Packers head coach Mike Sherman, looking to run out the clock, called for a handoff to running back Ahman Green.

Favre, for reasons only known to him, decided to audible out of the play. There was just one thing different about this audible:

Favre's teammates claim that the quarterback didn't communicate his intentions.

Favre instead ran a naked boot in which he faked the handoff to a running back as he rolled to his right, where Michael Strahan was lined up across the line of scrimmage.

"That was called as a running play," Packers tight end Bubba Franks told reporters after the game.

"I don't know if it was a bad snap or what. I was run blocking. I didn't know it was a pass."

Strahan, who had been kept out of the sack column up until that point in the game and who looked as though he wasn't going to break the NFL single-season record of 22 sacks set 17 years earlier by New York Jets defender Mark Gastineau, quickly came free off his edge and approached Favre, who, upon seeing Strahan coming at him, started to retreat to the ground as Strahan began to wrap the future Hall of Fame quarterback for the record-breaking sack.

"I just react to what happens," Strahan said after the game. "[Favre] was booting out on the same play earlier, and I missed him, as far as containing and keeping him in the pocket.

"This time, he went down, and I hopped on him. What am I supposed to do? Get up and say, 'Brett! Why didn't you throw it?'"

Still, speculation ran wild as to whether Favre, who was a friend of Strahan's, purposely looked to help him break the record.

Both men denied it then and continue to deny to this day that the record-setting sack was a gift.

"That's not the first time I've faked a run without anyone knowing," Favre said. "Sometimes it's the best play out there. I just wish I was a little bit faster."

His explanation did little to quiet the critics, especially when in the days leading up to the game, Favre opined, out of respect for Strahan, that he thought it was just a "matter of time" before the defensive end would break the single-season sack record.

Favre also added fuel to the conspiracy flames when, in an attempt to be funny, he cracked a joke about possibly making it happen in the days leading up to the game.

"I was going to joke with Mike to say: 'On the first play, I'll give you one sack, that way you can relax the rest of the game to let me have a little fun,'" Favre said.

Favre, who also hugged Strahan after the sack, tried to put everything into perspective. "We wanted to win the football game," he said. "If a sack happens great. But when we leave today, we wanted to leave here a winner."

As for Strahan, that he even got himself in a position to break the single-season sack record shouldn't be overlooked.

While double-digit sacks are certainly a feasible accomplishment for a premier pass rusher, getting to 20 or more sacks in a single season is no easy task. Besides Strahan, only 10 other players since 1982—Minnesota's Jared Allen (22.0 in 2011), New York Jets' Mark Gastineau (22.0 in 1984), Kansas City's Justin Houston (22.0 in 2014), Minnesota's Chris Doleman (21.0 in 1989), Philadelphia's Reggie White (21.0 in 1987), Los Angeles' Aaron Donald (20.5 in 2018), Giants' Lawrence Taylor (20.5 in 1986), Houston's J.J. Watt (20.5, twice in 2012 and 2014), Kansas City's Derrick Thomas (20.0 in 1990), and Dallas' DeMarcus Ware (20.0 in 2008)—have recorded at least 20 sacks in a season.

When the Giants reported to the State University of New York at Albany on July 27, 2007, for training camp, they did so without their defensive captain. Whereas Strahan always insisted his absence was due to his uncertainty, his critics believed he simply didn't want to subject himself to the rigors of training camp.

Strahan tried to set the record straight by releasing a heartfelt open letter to Giants fans via his agent, Tony Agnone.

"When an athlete like myself who does what I do for a living starts having doubts, then it's time to take a step back and seriously consider my future," Strahan said in his letter. "Anyone who plays in the NFL with doubts or second-guessing is not only putting themselves at risk but their teammates also. I will never do that."

Strahan even reached out to head coach Tom Coughlin and general manager Jerry Reese to assure them that his absence was strictly about him doing soul searching about whether he was up for a 15th NFL season.

The Giants, who had roster decisions to make if Strahan was indeed going to retire, briefly looked into adding Simeon Rice, who had previously played with the Cardinals and Bucs.

In the end, Strahan, whose 2006 season had been cut short due to a Lisfranc injury, reported to the Giants facility on September 3, 2007. In a show of good faith, the Giants, who had fined him $14,288 for each day of training camp he missed, absolved a good portion of that fine as they welcomed No. 92 back into the fold.

In 16 games that year, Strahan went on to record 57 tackles, 9.0 sacks, and two passes defensed, but he would save his best performance for the four-game postseason, logging 23 tackles, seven quarterback hits (including 2.0 sacks), one pass defensed and two forced fumbles as the Giants rolled to their third Super Bowl championship.

* * *

Sometime after the last piece of confetti from the parade down New York City's famed Canyon of Heroes honoring the Super Bowl XLII heroes fell, Michael Strahan decided there would not be a 16th season.

During his June 2008 retirement press conference, Strahan, who finished with 141.5 career sacks that saw him lead the league twice (in 2001 and 2003) in that category, admitted that he struggled with the decision, especially after those close to him told him he had more left to give.

"The 15 years have taken a toll on me," he said before the packed house gathered to bid his playing career farewell.

"I don't think I could muster it up and do it one more time. Usually, in sports, you go out when they tell you to go out. I have an opportunity to leave when I want to leave.

"And that is the best thing about this. I have been blessed with great health. I think after 15 years, the man upstairs said, 'Michael, I let you stick around for 15 years. I gave you a ring. Now don't be stupid.' So, I'm trying not to be stupid."

Did he have any regrets?

"Not at all. I've been through the good times; I've been through the fires. But it's made me so much better I feel like I can handle anything. I'm able to leave as a champion. I'm able to leave as a New York Giant— 15 years as a New York Giant, the only place I've known, the only uniform I've ever put on. And that's something very special to me."

34

SEPTEMBER 11: UNITED IN GRIEF

No matter what the sport, there are those games that are so heartbreaking to the fans of the losing team that the loss lingers for days, if not weeks after.

But some things are much more important than the outcome of a sporting event.

On the morning of September 11, 2001, terrorists launched one of the deadliest strikes on American soil using hijacked aircraft to target both towers of the World Trade Center in New York and the Pentagon in Washington, DC.

A fourth aircraft believed headed to Washington, D.C., crashed in a Pennsylvania field, killing all on board.

The night before the attacks, the Giants lost to the Denver Broncos 31–20 on *Monday Night Football*.

After the game, the dejected Giants took a charter flight back to Newark Airport, as it was then known, arriving approximately 5:45 AM. Their arrival was believed to be right around the time that passengers, including the four hijackers, were checking in for United Airlines Flight 93, the San Francisco-bound flight that crashed into a field near Shanksville, Pennsylvania after the passengers attempted to overpower the hijackers.

Although the Giants players had that Tuesday off, many had been scheduled to report to Giants Stadium to have injuries treated, while still others came in to lift weights or watch film.

But all that activity took a back seat as word of the attacks that had begun early that morning began to flood the news channels.

"It's an unbelievable tragedy," quarterback Kerry Collins said in a team-issued statement. "It's beyond the scope of rational thought that something like this could happen. The first thing you do is think about the families and the victims affected by this, and your heart goes out to them. I don't think, as human beings, we are able to process this kind of thing."

The Giants honored members of the Port Authority, New York Fire Department, New York Police Department, and Emergency Technicians at their September 30, 2001, home game, the first game to be played at Giants Stadium following the devastation. (Copyright New York Football Giants)

"I live right by the water, so I saw everything from my window," added receiver Amani Toomer. "I looked out and what I saw... was shocking. I was sitting there watching it in disbelief."

Guard Jason Whittle ended up losing a close childhood friend, Randy Drake, who was on location at a job located at 195 Broadway. Drake was struck in the head by falling debris following the second plane's crashing into the World Trade Center.

And Giants head coach Jim Fassel revealed that one of the pilots onboard the American Airlines flight that crashed into the Pentagon, Charles Burlingame, was a classmate of his at Anaheim (California) High School.

As the shock of the attacks began to sink in, the last thing on anyone's mind was football.

* * *

Nearly 38 years earlier, NFL Commissioner Pete Rozelle made a decision in a time of national crisis that would haunt him for years.

On Friday, November 22, 1963, President John F. Kennedy was shot during a trip to Dallas Texas, the news of his assassination bringing the country to a screeching halt.

Rozelle, meanwhile, wrestled with the decision regarding postponing that weekend's games, which would have been played the day before Kennedy's funeral.

Rozelle was so conflicted that he reached out to his good friend Pierre Salinger, Kennedy's press secretary. Salinger urged Rozelle to continue with the games as planned because football was a favorite sport of Kennedy's.

In announcing that the games would go on as scheduled, he said, "Football was Mr. Kennedy's game."

Rozelle's decision was, in a way, backed by precedent. When Japan attacked Pearl Harbor on December 7, 1941, then-president Franklin Roosevelt gave his blessing for the scheduled NFL games to be played.

Still, Rozelle's decision following the Kennedy assassination sparked outrage not just across the nation but within the NFL itself. Owners and players pleaded with him to reconsider while some local politicians even attempted to get court orders to force the league to postpone the games for a week.

And if the Kennedy assassination hadn't created enough stress on the nation, just before the games scheduled to kick off at 1:00 PM eastern commenced, Lee Harvey Oswald, the suspect in the shooting of the president, was shot and killed on live television as he was being transported by law enforcement officials.

The decision to play the games through a national mourning period and a day before Kennedy's funeral would come to be one Rozelle ended up regretting.

But this time, the league, now under the direction of Commissioner Paul Tagliabue, who in 1990 had worked closely with the White House regarding the postseason play going on as the nation became involved in the Gulf War, got it right.

Tagliabue announced that the league's Week 2 schedule, set for September 16–17, 2001, would be postponed, and rescheduled for the weekend of January 6–7, 2002.

During a conference call with the national media to explain his decision, Tagliabue said, "We ultimately concluded that the most appropriate thing was to cancel all the games and take a pause and do what all citizens do in this type of situation, which is to focus on the loss of life and what we can do for others."

Giants co-owner Wellington Mara, one of the owners Tagliabue consulted before reaching a decision, lauded the commissioner in his handling of the league's response to the national tragedy.

"I've always believed that when you get hit, and it hurts, the last thing you want to do is let that guy know that he has hurt you," Mara told reporters two days after the attacks.

"The answer to terrorism is not to fold your tent and go away. In this case, the humanitarian considerations outweigh everything else.

"I think Paul's horn-lock has always been you can get it quick, or you can get it right. He always prefers to get it right, and I think he's gotten it right this time. He got unanimous consent and support from everybody in the league."

The Giants players and coaches agreed.

"It was not the right thing to do; it was the only thing to do," Collins said.

We're like the rest of the country. We have a lot of different feelings going through us, from anger to sorrow for the victims and their

GIANT HEROES

Following the events of September 11, Arizona Cardinals defensive back Pat Tillman decided to leave his playing career behind and enlist in the U.S. Army, a heroic yet tragic choice that led to his untimely death by friendly fire.

Years earlier, with the U.S. embroiled in World War II, the Giants would lose two of their own who had also responded to the call of duty.

The first was Jack Lummus, a rookie two-way end for the Giants who appeared in nine games during the 1941 season. A little more than a month after the Japanese attacked Pearl Harbor on December 7, 1941, Lummus, who would play in that year's NFL Championship Game, enlisted in the Marines Corps Reserves, where he rose through the ranks.

During the Battle of Iwo Jima, which commenced February 19, 1945, Lummus, part of a deployment to capture the island's airfields from the Imperial Japanese Army, was twice knocked down by grenade blasts. Still he continued to lead his men in battle until he stepped on a landmine that cost him both of his legs.

Despite his injuries, Lummus pulled himself up and continued to direct his troops until he was taken for medical treatment. Before succumbing to his wounds, he urged his platoon to carry on without him and just before he died, he said to the attending physician, "I guess the New York Giants have lost the services of a damn good end."

Lummus received a Congressional Medal of Honor posthumously and was inducted in the Giants Ring of honor in 2015.

Al Blozis, a hulking offensive tackle from Garfield, New Jersey selected by the Giants in the fifth round of the 1942 draft, enlisted in the Army and was deployed overseas after playing in the 1944 Championship Game against the Packers.

On February 20, 1945, the *New York Times* reported that Blozis went missing in action. On April 9 of that same year, the paper, citing reports, said that Blozis, who was inducted in the Giants Ring of Honor in 2010, had "died a hero's death" when he had set out alone to search for two of his men who went missing.

In their December 1945 game program, the Giants honored their fallen heroes, saying, "Blozis and Lummus typified the finest tradition of skill and sportsmanship on the gridiron; they were equally proficient in the grim business of war."

families," Fassel added. "What we do is such a highly emotional game. You have to be at a high emotional pitch to go out and perform. If you're not, it's just not the right thing to do. I think all of us—players, coaches, administrators—feel that way. The fans would be the same way. It's just the right thing to do."

With football temporarily paused, the Giants took the opportunity to meet with specially trained grief counselors from the New York Human Services Center.

"This is going to go on for a while," Fassel said of the grief counseling.

* * *

In the days following the 9/11 attacks, the country—including the Giants—began to take baby steps in the healing process.

There were memorial services for those who died. Police, fire, and emergency service personnel worked around the clock, often in dangerous conditions given the release of asbestos in the air and the unstable structures around the areas of Ground Zero, on search and recovery efforts.

The Giants, when they weren't practicing, put their celebrity to good use.

Cornerback Jason Sehorn gathered supplies from Home Depot at the Jacob Javits Center, one of the relief efforts distribution points.

Running backs Tiki Barber and Greg Comella teamed up to deliver toys and supplies for the children of first responders lost during rescue and recovery efforts.

Still, other teammates paid visits to area hospitals, firehouses, and command centers around the city where emergency personnel were working around the clock.

When football finally did return on Sunday, September 23, the Giants headed to Kansas City for a road game. The outpouring of support they received from the Chiefs fans was like nothing they could have ever imagined.

That afternoon, Chiefs head coach Dick Vermeil and team owner Lamar Hunt donned New York fire and police department baseball caps to show their support. So too did the game's officials, who wore the caps before the game in a show of solidarity.

It didn't stop there. Kansas City, Missouri Mayor Kay Barnes, in a moving pre-game ceremony, proclaimed that Sunday as "New York Day."

Even the Chiefs' home crowd, one of the most loyal in sports, put aside any dislike of the visiting team.

Several "We love New York!" banners popped up throughout the crowd. The fans also delivered several standing ovations, the loudest of which occurred after the Giants left the field following pre-game warmups and an equally booming greeting when the Giants returned to the field at the start of the game.

The most touching moment came when cameras caught the crowd dropping donations into a fireman's boot to support relief efforts.

That collection, believed to be the largest single-day outpouring of spontaneous support by a group of fans and a pro sports team, was matched by both the Chiefs and the Hunt family, the amount reportedly exceeding $450,000.

"The way they handled everything and greeted our players was incredible," Fassel said of the Chiefs. "This is a class organization, top to bottom, fans included."

From a football perspective, when the Giants beat the Chiefs, 13–3 to even their 2001 season record to 1–1, a win that took some of the pressure off their 0–1 start.

But given what had happened to the nation, linebacker Micheal Barrow probably said it best when, after the win against the Chiefs, he said, "Pressure is going into a 110-story building when it's about to collapse on you. Pressure is having 2,000-degree temperatures coming down on you.

"This is a game."

35

TIKI BARBER

The Giants ground game of the late 1990s was supposed to have been the "Thunder and Lightning" show.

"Thunder" was 1999 Heisman Trophy winner Ron Dayne, the Giants 5'10", 249-pound first-round pick in the 2000 NFL draft out of the University of Wisconsin.

"Lightning" was 5'10", 205-pound Atiim Kiambu "Tiki" Barber, the Giants' 1997 second-round pick out of the University of Virginia, a player whom the Giants envisioned as the third-down back to Dayne's smashmouth downhill running style.

While the concept was a marketer's dream, the duo soon became a solo act after Barber, a player whom some skeptics had concerns regarding his durability, put those fears to rest.

Barber, would go on to play in 154 games, gaining 10,449 yards on 2,217 carries and 55 rushing touchdowns, and 5,183 receiving yards on 586 receptions for 12 touchdowns before retiring after the 2006 season.

Yet for as electrifying as Barber was on the field, his major vice, at least early on in his career, was ball security. He finished his NFL career with 53 fumbles, 22 of which were lost. Between 2000–04, Barber averaged 8.75 fumbles per season.

After that 2004 season, the first Barber spent with head coach Tom Coughlin, the head coach had a message for the Giants' star player.

"He said to me, 'If you're going to put the ball on the ground, you're not going to play,'" Barber recalled.

Barber, who took pride in his game, sought extra help from Giants running backs coach Jerald Ingram, whom to this day he credits with having help fix his fumbling problem.

Like a teenager assigned to carry around an egg for a parenting class, Barber carried the football high and tight everywhere he went until it became second nature, wrapping it up in sort of a cross-like pattern, with his free hand clasping the wrist of the hand which held the ball.

Not only did the change help Barber cut down on his ball security issues, but he believes that it also helped improve his balance as he attacked the line between the tackles, making him a more powerful runner.

"When I started running with the ball under my chin it forced my arm stride to shorten, which also shortened my leg strides. So I became more powerful because I was taking shorter steps and my balance improved," Barber explained.

Whereas in his first eight seasons he ran for 6,927 yards on 1,533 carries (4.5 yards per carry) and 49 fumbles in the regular season games, in his final two seasons, Barber racked up 3,522 yards on 684 carries (5.1 yards per carry) and cut his fumbles down to four over that period.

* * *

Barber recorded several impressive performances throughout his career, but it was his 203-yard performance on 32 carries in the 2002 regular-season finale against the Philadelphia Eagles that might have been one of his craziest.

Barber recorded three fumbles that afternoon, none more significant than the ball he lost with the Giants three yards away from making it a 7–7 game late in the second quarter.

He would go on to fumble again in the third quarter, this time on his own 41, and then again in the fourth quarter on his own 15.

For most running backs, one fumble in a game that had playoff implications would have been more than enough reason to yank the offender out of the game.

But not for head coach Jim Fassel, who in the postgame interview admitted that people were urging him to pull Barber from the game.

"I told everybody, 'He's staying in. He's the guy that got us here. He's gonna win it for us,'" Fassel said. "You got a player that does it for you all year long; he's going to stay in there."

Fassel wasn't the only one who sought to calm down the running back. Defensive end Michael Strahan, who had been upset when Barber openly backed management during Strahan's contract dispute, had begun to warm up again to his teammate. Strahan told Barber that the defense had his back and would get him the ball back.

Besides his 203 rushing yards, Barber also added eight receptions for 73 yards. And in an almost delicious twist of irony, it was Barber who, in the overtime period, recovered a fumble by quarterback Kerry Collins to keep the drive alive for kicker Matt Bryant, whose 39-yard field goal gave the Giants a 10–7 win that helped put them into the postseason.

Four years later, Barber, in what was his final NFL season, would once again help carry his team to the postseason with another big rushing performance.

Against Washington in the regular-season finale, there had been rumors swirling that head coach Tom Coughlin's job was on the line if the Giants missed the playoffs.

Giants running back Tiki Barber holds the franchise's marks for rushing attempts in a career (2,217), in a season (357 in 2005), rushing yards in a career (10,449), in a season (1,860 in 2005), and a game (234 at Washington on December 30, 2006).
(Copyright New York Football Giants)

Barber, who famously didn't get along with Coughlin, made sure to put any personal feelings aside and delivered the best regular-season rushing performance of his career.

He recorded a regular-season career-high 234 rushing yards on 23 carries and scoring three touchdowns to give the Giants a 34–28 win and a rushing yardage performance that as of the end of the 2019 season still stands as a franchise-best for a single game.

* * *

Because Barber wasn't afraid to speak his mind, it sometimes got him into trouble, as it had with Strahan and Coughlin.

Barber, who didn't like Coughlin's management style—he equated it to being treated like a child—let his frustration boil over after a 26–10 loss to the Jaguars in 2006. After the game, Barber questioned why the Giants, whose strength on offense was its running game, ended up throwing the ball 41 times while rushing it just 14 times. Those comments, he said, resulted in "the mother of all screaming matches" with the head coach.

Barber even got into hot water with the team after he retired when, in the summer of 2007, Barber, trying to launch a broadcasting career, made headlines for characterizing quarterback Eli Manning's leadership style as "comical."

TIKI BARBER'S
GIANTS FRANCHISE RECORDS

Most Rushing Attempts, Career: 2,217
Most Rushing Attempts, Season: 357 (2005)
Most Yards Gained, Career: 10,449
Most Yards Gained, Season: 1,860 (2005)
Most Yards Gained, Game: 234, at Washington, December 30, 2006
Most Games 100+ Yards Rushing, Career: 38 (1997–2006)
Most Games 100+ Yards Rushing, Season: 9 (2004)
Longest Run from Scrimmage: 95 yards, at Oakland, December 31, 2005
Highest Average Gain, Career (500 Attempts): 4.71 (2,217–10,449)
Most All-purpose Yards, Career: 17,359
Most All-purpose Yards, Season: 2,390 (2005)

"My comment was actually more about how loose Eli is," Barber explained. "He's a prankster, but in a quiet sort of way. He likes to have fun, and sometimes that can come off as comical, but not in a bad way."

While some of his harshest critics perceived Barber as a self-centered individual, running back Brandon Jacobs, who arrived in East Rutherford in 2005 as a fourth-round draft pick, believes Barber was often misunderstood.

"Tiki was a great guy, and a great teammate. He was someone who had a right to speak up about what he thought would be better for the team," Jacobs said.

"He didn't mind taking the smoke for everybody else [by speaking up]. I'm very lucky and fortunate to have had a chance to play with him."

When Barber retired, he limited his visits to the team's East Rutherford headquarters to avoid upsetting Coughlin, though he did participate in the team's inaugural Ring of Honor induction ceremony.

Barber even flirted with the idea of returning to the NFL in 2011 when the Giants, who held the contractual rights to Barber's services after he retired, decided to release him.

Although Barber drew interest from Miami, the flirtation ended almost as quickly as it began, leaving the Giants as the only team Barber played for professionally.

At the time of his retirement, he was one of three NFL players to record 10,000 yards rushing and 5,000 receiving yards in his career, joining Marshall Faulk and Marcus Allen.

"I like the saying, 'Always leave them wanting more,'" Barber said, adding, "Leave too early rather than too late."

36

GIANT HEARTACHES

In the fall of 2005, the Giants family lost both of their co-owners, Wellington Mara, to lymphoma on October 25, and Preston Robert Tisch to brain cancer on November 15.

Although the team had a succession plan in place—Ann Mara and Joan Tisch, technically became the team's owners, and their oldest children, John Mara and Steve Tisch would be the leading voices of their respective families regarding decisions and league affairs—the loss of the two men had a profound effect on the Giants franchise.

Mara, whom then–general manager Ernie Accorsi, once called the "moral conscience of the league," touched the lives of every generation of players who walked in the team's front door in some way.

"There was no more dignified person that I've ever come across in my professional life than Mr. Mara," running back Tiki Barber added.

"He carried himself was a quiet confidence, but with an indelible presence. You remember moments you spent with Mr. Mara mainly because he didn't speak that much, and so when he did it was, it was always something profound. He wouldn't say a lot, but you just felt like by being near him, you were absorbing the history of the game."

Mara's funeral, held on a crisp autumn day in New York City, was fit for the "Duke" of football.

Held before a standing-room-only congregation at the historic St.

Patrick's Cathedral, there was nary a dry eye among the assembled crowd. Among those in attendance were league personnel and former Giants coaches Bill Parcells, Bill Belichick, John Fox, and Romeo Crennel, who had made the trip to New York two days before their respective teams' games that weekend to honor their one-time boss.

There were also scores of former players from decades past as well as the entire roster of players, coaches, and administration from the 2005 season, and members of the local and national media in attendance.

"I can't help but think he would have been so embarrassed by this," said John Mara, who delivered the eulogy during the nearly two-hour-long ceremony officiated by Cardinal Edward Egan.

"He would have shaken his head and tried to hide in a corner somewhere."

Perhaps, but there's no doubt that Wellington Mara also would have been beaming with pride that Sunday when before the game, 35 of his grandchildren and great-grandchildren took the field in his honor.

One of his oldest grandchildren, actress/singer Kate Mara, delivered one of the most moving renditions of "The Star-Spangled Banner" before the packed Giants Stadium crowd.

The game itself was no contest—a 36–0 beatdown of the Washington Redskins. In that game, Barber, who had been one of the last players to visit with the Giants patriarch before he died—delivered one of the best games of his career at the time, rushing for 206 yards on 24 carries with one very special touchdown.

"I remember Timmy McDonnell, Wellington's grandson, coming to me and saying at some point, 'Are you going to score a touchdown or are you going to keep getting caught?' I had had a 57-yard run to start the game, and another long run in the third quarter, but I kept getting caught," Barber said.

"In the third quarter, we called a draw on the 4-yard line, and I scored a touchdown. I took the ball, went over to the sideline and gave it to Timmy, and said, 'This is for you and your family and your grandfather. I can't thank you enough for all your family has done for me.'

"I then took myself out of the game, which was a record-setting game for me at that point. I had done what I needed to do to pay my respect to one of the greatest men in the game."

Tisch's memorial service a month later was a little more low-keyed.

Still, it wasn't any less emotional for an organization that had come to love and appreciate his kindness.

The Giants would honor both of their late owners with a special uniform patch bearing both men's initials for the rest of that season. And as the players had been determined to do for Mara, they sought to honor the memory of Tisch with a victory in the next game played.

This time, it was against the 4–5 Eagles, who were coming into Giants Stadium looking to keep their playoff hopes alive against the 6–3 Giants.

The Giants lost both of their beloved team owners, Wellington Mara (left) and Preston Robert Tisch, within a month of each other during the 2005 season.
(Copyright New York Football Giants)

"You know what Mr. Tisch would say if he were standing here right now?" head coach Tom Coughlin told the players in a team meeting? "'Don't spend any time feeling sorry for me. I've had a great life.' He would say to us, 'Get going; get on with the business of preparing for the Philadelphia Eagles.'"

The Giants would do just that with their 27–17 win over the Eagles, a game in which Barber ran for 112 yards on 21 carries and in which receiver Plaxico Burress caught six passes for 113 yards and a touchdown.

In many ways, the Giants' victory following Tisch's passing was a reflection of how he lived his life: simple, yet practical with an eye toward getting the job done at the end of the day.

But the Giants players and coaches weren't just ready to settle for the two wins. They had wanted to honor their fallen patriarchs with a Super Bowl championship. Unfortunately, after finishing 11–5 that season, that quest fell short when they were shut out 23–0 by the Panthers in the NFC Wild Card round.

"THE DUKE" LIVES ON

In 2006, NFL owners approved renaming of the game's official game ball "the Duke" in honor of the late Wellington Mara, who, as a young ball boy for the club, had been given the moniker of "the Duke" by Giants players.

"The Duke," manufactured by Wilson Sporting Goods, initially made its debut in 1941. It got its nickname when Chicago Bears owner and founder George "Papa Bear" Halas, who collaborated with Wellington's father Tim in negotiating the official game ball's manufacturing deal with Wilson, suggested that the official game ball be named "the Duke," after Tim's younger son.

"The Duke" was discontinued after the 1969 season in favor of a new design to commemorate the AFL-NFL merger. But after Mara's passing in 2005, NFL owners, at the league meetings, voted unanimously to bring back "the Duke" for the 2006 season.

Then Commissioner Paul Tagliabue presented the first "Duke" ball to Mara's widow, Ann, and the oldest of his 11 children, son John, the team's current president and chief operating officer.

37

PRESTON ROBERT TISCH

For 65 years, the Giants franchise was nurtured by the Mara family, first by founder Tim who then split the shares of the club evenly between his two sons, Wellington and Jack.

When cancer claimed Jack Mara, his share of the club passed on to his widow Helen and their two children, Tim and Maura, with Tim taking up his father's mantle in the franchise's daily operations.

The business relationship between Wellington Mara and his nephew was tumultuous, so much so that twice, in 1984 and again in 1986, Tim contemplated selling his family's share. However, both times, he concluded that the timing just wasn't right.

That changed in the fall of 1990 when the right time and the right buyer came along in the form of 65-year-old Preston Robert "Bob" Tisch, a 1948 economics graduate of the University of Michigan, who went on to become the head of the Loews Corporation and the U.S. postmaster general under President Ronald Reagan from August 1986 to March 1988.

In Tisch, Wellington Mara would find a business-savvy partner who, in addition to knowing a few things about growing multimillion-dollar businesses, had been looking to enter the exclusive NFL ownership club for many years.

Before the opportunity with the Giants came along, Tisch had explored purchasing the New England Patriots and Philadelphia Eagles. When those deals failed to materialize, he became part of a group interested in taking ownership of an expansion team in Baltimore.

Tisch first learned of the potential Giants sale from Art Modell, a close friend of Wellington Mara's. Before too long, Tisch would meet with the elder Mara to gauge the suitability of acquiring Tim Mara's half of the franchise.

Unlike some business deals which can take months if not years to come together, the parameters of the Giants' deal quickly fell into place. The Tisch family never disclosed the sale price due to a confidentiality agreement with the Mara family to protect the value of the franchise, but multiple reports put the sale price in the neighborhood of $75 million.

The sale would be officially finalized just after the team won its second Super Bowl championship in early 1991, but there was one more hurdle to clear before it could become official.

In addition to getting the majority approval from the league owners on the transaction—21 of the 28 owners at the time had to approve the deal—the Tisch family, who back then owned a minority interest in CBS, one of the networks with television rights to NFL games, had to address concerns regarding a potential conflict of interest.

With Tisch's brother, Laurence serving as the chairman of the television network, Bob Tisch took the necessary steps to confirm that he was not involved with CBS and that the sale of the team would be to him as an individual rather than to a business entity owned by his family.

When the deal closed, a new divide among responsibilities was established, with Tisch stating that "Wellington will continue to be responsible for the day-to-day football operations, and I'll handle the financial aspects. I will take an active part in that part of the operation."

The one exception was player contracts, which both Tisch and Mara agreed to let their general manager, George Young at that time, continue to have the final say.

John Mara, who these days works in concert with Steve Tisch, Bob's oldest son, said the franchise couldn't have asked for a better partner.

"Bob helped us run our business much more efficiently because he was so successful in the various business he has been involved with," Mara said. "He brought a different approach to us because we were such a mom-and-pop operation when he came in.

"To a certain extent, we still are because we're a relatively small company, but our business practices became so much more sophisticated when he joined us."

Mara also praised the late business mogul for knowing what he didn't know, and in trusting those who did to advise him on those decisions.

"He did not interfere with what was happening on the field. He certainly took part in the selection of a general manager and the selection of the head coach, but he didn't try to interfere with personnel decisions because he knew that was not his strength," Mara said.

Besides business being a strength, Tisch was a tireless philanthropist who, often anonymously or without fanfare, gave back to his community.

He was also an accessible and friendly man who took an interest in not only those who worked for him but those with whom he came in contact.

"Bob was as much of a friend as he was a boss," former head coach Tom Coughlin recalled for Tisch's 2010 Giants Ring of Honor tribute video.

"Bob's interest was sincere—he'd come into your office and ask you how your family was, and he would visit with us in training camp and had his most fun when he was there with the players."

Hall of Fame defensive end Michael Strahan fondly recalled Tisch's kindness being on full display during his rookie season when the billionaire owner went out of his way to help the defensive end, who was on crutches due to a foot injury.

"We're at Fairleigh Dickinson University for training camp, and we had to move between the upper field and the lower fields," Strahan said in Tisch's Ring of Honor tribute video.

"I'm trying to hobble to get between both. He saw that, and every day after that, he put me in a cart with him and took me to and from practice, so I didn't have to get on my crutches."

Running back Tiki Barber, who was close with Wellington Mara, also developed a bond with Tisch.

"I don't know if there was an adult that I was closer to than Bob Tisch," Barber said. "I live in the city, and he was at the Regency, which was about 15 or 20 blocks away from my apartment, and we spent a lot of time together. I considered him a mentor.

"He mastered the art of being everywhere but being nowhere.

He would pop into events and be there for 20 or 30 or 40 minutes or whatever he needed to be to see everybody. Whether it was the CEO of some company or just the regular employees, he treated people with this amazing deference."

When Tisch was diagnosed with brain cancer in 2004, Barber remembered how even as the cancer treatments drained him of his stamina, Tisch refused to give in.

"My son, A.J., was a two-year-old at the time, and I remember him chasing around this Giants-logo pool ball on the floor with Mr. Tisch," Barber recalled.

"It was just this moment that I'll never forget. Despite the veneer that we all knew Mr. Tisch to be—this philanthropist and extraordinary businessman—he was gentle with people who he was close with him, and I considered it a blessing to be one of them."

Tisch lost his battle with brain cancer on November 15, 2005, less than a month after the Giants lost Wellington Mara to lymphoma.

The double whammy of losing both owners to cancer served as an inspiration to the coaches and players, who knew of their bosses' health struggles long before they were made public.

"Coach Coughlin would say to us at the beginning of that season, 'We have to be the team of record for Bob and Wellington.'" Barber recalled. "I took that to heart, and it's not a coincidence that I had my best season with 2,390 scrimmage yards that year."

Nor is it a coincidence that the Giants, who the year before finished 6–10, finished that 2005 season with an 11–5 mark, their second-best record during Coughlin's 12-year tenure.

Unfortunately, the Giants, who had hoped to win a Super Bowl to complete their tribute to the franchise's late owners, fell embarrassingly short of that goal when the Carolina Panthers came into Giants Stadium and shut out the Giants 23–0 shutout in the NFC Wild Card round.

Since then, the Giants have, of course, added two more Super Bowl championships to the franchise's history.

And speaking of the franchise, thanks in part to Tisch's business acumen, the team has also grown in value, bringing the franchise's value to an estimated $3.9 billion, which puts it third behind the Dallas Cowboys ($5.5 billion) and New England Patriots ($4.1 billion), according to *Forbes Sports Money 2019 NFL Valuations* released in September 2019.

38

ELI'S GUYS

David Diehl, Chris Snee, Shaun O'Hara, Rich Seubert, and Kareem McKenzie.

That was the Giants starting offensive line for the 2007–10 seasons. They weren't glamorous. They didn't have a catchy nickname like "The Suburbanites," the offensive linemen from the 1986 championship season.

There wasn't a first-round pick among them, and, depending on which one of them you ask, they'll also tell you there wasn't a good-looking one in the bunch.

But all of that didn't matter, because they took their collective job of protecting quarterback Eli Manning and opening holes for the running backs seriously, believing if one failed, they all failed.

To understand why these five men meshed so well on and off the field, It's important to know a little about their origins.

Seubert, an undrafted free agent who signed with the club in 2001 out of Western Illinois, was the very definition of a tough hombre.

"We used to call him 'Rich the Bitch,' not only because it rhymed, but it also fits him because he loved to bitch," O'Hara said.

"That was his therapy and his way of getting through things. [Offensive line coach Pat Flaherty] always used to joke and say, 'I never worried when he's bitching; I'm worried when he stops.'"

Seubert, who probably would have fit in perfectly on offensive lines of past generations that played when leather helmets without facemasks were the norm, grew up in Wisconsin and took tremendous pride in his blue-collar workmanship.

"Rich was a grinder, and to this day, I don't think he got enough credit about how good of a player he was," O'Hara said.

Not to mention tough. In October 2003, Seubert suffered a broken tibia, fibula, and ankle when Eagles defender N.D. Kalu stepped on the back of his right leg.

With his career in jeopardy, Seubert, never a man of many words, endured multiple surgeries and endless hours of rehab to make it back onto the playing field, at first in a limited role in 2005, before earning a starting job as the team's left guard in 2007.

Diehl, a gregarious Chicago native who prided himself on his accountability, was the Swiss Army knife of the group. Before settling in at left tackle for the 2007 championship season, the Giants' 2003 fifth-round draft pick became the first Giant to start all 16 games in his rookie season since tight end Mark Bavaro in 1985.

Offensive linemen Kareem McKenzie (67), Chris Snee (76), Shaun O'Hara (60), Rich Seubert (69), and David Diehl (66) break the huddle during training camp in Albany, New York. (AP Images / Mike Groll)

By the time his career ended after 11 years, Diehl, who was as business-like as they came and wasn't much for the pranks that took place among his fellow line mates, had played at every position on the offensive line except center.

O'Hara, who, like Diehl, has an outgoing personality, was one of the more mischievous guys of the group.

Born in Chicago, but a product of Rutgers University and before that Hillsborough (New Jersey) High School, O'Hara went undrafted in 2000 and, instead of signing with the Giants, who had an interest in him, he signed with the Cleveland Browns.

O'Hara played both guard and center, starting 38 out of the 54 games for the Browns before signing with the Giants in 2004 as an unrestricted free agent.

Snee followed O'Hara in the door in 2004. The youngest of the group, Snee, was the Giants' second-round pick that year out of Boston College, a prospect who, in the beginning, was better known for being new head coach Tom Coughlin's son-in-law.

A somewhat introverted personality whom his fellow linemen dubbed a "grumpy troll" because, as O'Hara explained, Snee complained about being sore all the time, Snee would go on to anchor the right guard spot until injuries forced him to retire after his 2013 season was cut short due to injuries.

McKenzie was the quietest and most reflective of the group. Originally a third-round pick of the Jets in 2001 out of Penn State, the 6'6", 328-pound McKenzie was born in Willingboro, New Jersey, where he also attended high school.

He signed with the Giants as an unrestricted free agent, joining the offensive line as their right tackle in 2005 after spending the first four seasons of his pro career with the Jets.

Snee, Seubert, Diehl, O'Hara, and McKenzie—five guys from different backgrounds and with different temperaments who were thrust together as a starting unit beginning with the 2007 season—became the driving force behind the Giants' skill position players being able to work their magic.

* * *

The words of former Washington quarterback turned ESPN analyst Joe Theismann, who during a 2004 preseason broadcast called them the worst offensive line in the league, caused Giants offensive linemen to stew for years after.

"We made that a rallying cry for us, that 'Oh hey, we're the worst line in the NFL. All right, we're off to prove that we're not, and we're never going to let them say that about us ever again.'" O'Hara said.

"We didn't have a lot of high draft picks," O'Hara added. "We had some guys that felt like they had something to prove. That's why that group was so much fun to work with because we pushed each other. We never let anybody take a day off, and we never let anybody take the easy way out.

"And if they tried to, we were going to give them hell. [The media], I'm sure, saw plenty of practical jokes and pranks, and you know, ball busting going on with that group. I think that's really what made that group close, and that's what made us good."

What also made that line so good was Flaherty.

"You're never going to have a good offensive line without a really good offensive line coach," O'Hara said.

"Pat Flaherty was tremendously important and critical in the growth of our room and our identity. I still don't think he gets enough credit for how great of a job he did during his time with the Giants."

O'Hara revealed that Flaherty, who served as the Giants' offensive line coach from 2004 to 2015, was also the Giants run game coordinator.

Flaherty's direction, along with the contributions made by running backs Tiki Barber through 2006 and then later Brandon Jacobs, Derrick Ward, and Ahmad Bradshaw, certainly made an impact.

In 2003, the Giants' rushing game finished 28th out of 32 teams, averaging 97.4 yards per game. Once Coughlin and Flaherty, along with running backs coach Jerald Ingram, arrived in 2004, the Giants would average over 119 yards per game in all but one season between 2004–10.

In 2007, the Giants running game finished as the fourth-best rushing offense (134.2 yards per game) in 2007; a year later, they ranked first in the league in rushing (157.4 yards per game).

"Flats was our bell cow for the run game," O'Hara said. "He was our advocate and was always pushing for what runs to be in the game plan.

He knew that that was really where we needed to create our identity and how we were going to become physical and impose our will.

"I think he did a great job of letting us create an identity, and that workmanlike attitude and mentality and mindset goes with that."

* * *

There's a classic line from the 1980 movie *The Shining*, that "All work and no play makes Jack a dull boy."

You'd get no argument about that from the members of the Giants offensive linemen, who were notorious for their pranks.

None will come right out and admit their naughtiness, though ask them about each other, and well, that's a different story.

"Rich use to love to stir the pot," O'Hara said. "He was one of the biggest instigators I've ever met in my life. He would always try to start something and blame somebody else, and he loved getting under people's skin, specifically Snee. He and Snee would get after each other pretty good."

Seubert, however, said it was O'Hara who was the pot-stirrer. "Figures he would blame me," O'Hara said, trying to keep his voice from cracking into a chuckle when told of Seubert's allegations.

MEN OF THE PEOPLE

Eli Manning wasn't the only Giant to benefit from the quintet of David Diehl, Rich Seubert, Shaun O'Hara, Chris Snee, and Kareem McKenzie.

The Giants' running game also benefited from the offensive line's prowess, especially in 2008, when Brandon Jacobs (1,089) and Derek Ward (1,025) became only the fifth duo at the time to rush for 1,000 yards in the same season.

Ward put the Giants in the record books set the record by rushing for 77 yards on 15 carries in a Week 17 road game against the Minnesota Vikings as the Giants finished that season with the league's best rushing offense (157.4 yards per game).

Jacobs and Ward are joined by Larry Csonka and Mercury Morris (1972 Dolphins), Franco Harris and Rocky Bleier (1976 Steelers), Kevin Mack and Earnest Byer (1985 Browns), Warrick Dunn and Michael Vick (2006 Falcons). DeAngelo Williams and Jonathan Stewart (2009 Panthers) later became the sixth duo to accomplish that feat.

Diehl and McKenzie would sit by and take in the show, but both usually tried to steer clear of engaging in pranks. Diehl, O'Hara said, didn't mix it up too much because he didn't like to worry about how others might retaliate against him.

And McKenzie?

"Kareem was that guy that you would get nervous about pulling a prank on because you never knew how he was going to retaliate. When he did, he would do so with a vengeance," O'Hara said.

So, what about those pranks?

Snee, O'Hara, and Seubert claim that most of the pranks they pulled on one another weren't PG-13, but they all agreed that no matter how harsh the pranks, it was all done in fun and out of love for one another as brothers.

"The pranks were frequent but fun," said Snee, who described himself as the "quiet assassin" of the group.

"The game is so serious, and it's professional, but at the same time, you gotta be able to let your guard down a little bit and truly enjoy the guys are out there with you in the trenches. We were all very comfortable with one another, and that was obvious by what we did to each other. But yeah, there was plenty of stuff going on."

And not just against each other. Eli's guys occasionally took aim at the man they protected on Sundays, well, because he was their guy.

O'Hara famously pranked the young quarterback during a Saturday morning walkthrough early in Manning's career when he cut a hole in the crotch area of his practice pants and went commando.

When Manning went to place his hands under O'Hara's backside for the snap, instead of getting a handful of pigskin, he got a handful of a different kind of skin.

Manning, a prankster in his own right, retaliated—yes, even against the guys whose job it was to protect him.

One of his tamer retaliations was to dip his offensive linemen's dress shoes in purple paint before the team was scheduled to leave for a road game.

Manning would also change up his cadence during the Saturday walk- through to leave his offensive linemen with their proverbial pants down. Coughlin, who didn't like to waste practice snaps and who grew less tolerant of mistakes made later in the week, would become irate and bark at the guilty parties to get their heads out of their backsides.

"I think that's why we were so close, and that's what I think kept our locker room together," Seubert said of the pranks. "We worked hard, but we also had fun."

And success.

39

CRUUUUUUZZZZ

Even if one has been blessed with all the athletic talent in the world, there still is no substitution for hard work.

Such was the lesson receiver Victor Cruz, the Giants very own "Cinderella" story, learned as a youth growing up in Patterson, New Jersey.

Cruz, a 6'0", 204-pound receiver who transformed from an undrafted free agent hopeful into a globally recognized superstar, almost didn't realize his dreams thanks to his own doing—or, more specifically, lack of doing.

He struggled academically throughout high school because he didn't take his studies seriously. Although he managed to get his grades high enough to be admitted into the University of Massachusetts, his academic struggles continued.

With Cruz, who also lost his father Michael Walker, a firefighter and one of Cruz's biggest boosters, in need of an epiphany to get his own life back on the right path, it took a close encounter to open his eyes.

Not long after his father's passing, Cruz had been out at a local night club with friends to unwind when a brawl and gun fire broke out between two rival gangs.

Cruz, who wisely headed for the exits at the first sign of trouble, was unhurt but shaken. That experience that night served as the epiphany he needed, making him realize that everything he always wanted was right there in front of him if he just worked for it.

"I decided I was going to ace my final exams, get back into school, and achieve all my goals," Cruz wrote in his book *Out of the Blue*.

"No more excuses. No more pitying myself. No more sleepless nights spent staring at the ceiling wondering how I had pissed it all away. No one was going to do it for me. No one was going to give me anything. I'd have to scrape and crawl and earn every grade, every yard, and every dollar."

The death of his father also served as a catalyst in his maturation. In a February 4, 2012 interview with the *New York Times*, Cruz said, "I had to be the man of the family. It was up to me not to waste the opportunities I had been given. I had to study and work. There was still light at the end of the tunnel for me, and while it might have been dim, I had to run to it with everything in me."

It would take three years after he was first admitted into UMass before Cruz finally recorded his first reception for the Minutemen, that coming on November 10, 2007.

By the time Cruz completed his college career at UMass, he finished fourth in school history in career receptions (131) and fifth in receiving yards (1,958).

As Cruz continued to build his football résumé, he also worked toward completing his degree in African American studies, becoming the first person on his mother's side of the family to earn a college degree.

Despite his sudden surge on the football field, he would go undrafted.

* * *

When NFL teams announce their undrafted free-agent signings every spring, even the most ardent of college football fans will sometimes ask, "Who?" when an unfamiliar name is mentioned.

Well, for those who asked "Who?" when Victor Cruz was signed as an undrafted free agent, they'd soon get their answer.

Cruz finished as the Giants' preseason receiving leader in 2010, catching 15 passes for 297 yards and four touchdowns. But it was his three-touchdown performance against the New York Jets, then coached by the boisterous Rex Ryan, which put the young receiver (who before getting his familiar No. 80 jersey wore No. 3) on the map.

Ryan, whose Jets that year were the stars of the HBO football documentary *Hard Knocks*, was so enthralled by Cruz's speed and elusiveness in that game, that when he went to greet Tom Coughlin at midfield to shake hands after the game, Ryan couldn't help himself.

"I don't know who No. 3 is," Ryan was captured on tape telling Coughlin, "but holy shit!"

Ryan's public gushing about Cruz might have very well cost himself a chance to sign the receiver when, after the game, he told reporters,

Paterson, New Jersey, native Victor Cruz went from being an undrafted rookie free agent to one of the team's most popular players during a career that saw the Giants win their fourth Super Bowl (XLVI). (Copyright New York Football Giants)

"I hope they cut him. I know one team that would be ready to sign him, and that'd be us."

If the Giants were planning to waive Cruz with the hopes of sliding him onto their practice squad, any such plan was scrapped thanks to Ryan. Instead, the Giants added Cruz to the 53-man roster where he would be protected from being poached.

Despite making the 53-man roster, Cruz's rookie season was cut short due to a hamstring injury he suffered while running sprints.

The following year, the NFL lockout turned the league upside down as far as its off-season schedule. With the players barred from accessing their team facilities, coaches, and resources, Giants quarterback Eli

B.C. (BEFORE CRUZ)

Before Victor Cruz became one of the biggest homegrown success stories among Giants receivers, there was Amani Toomer.

Unlike Cruz, an undrafted free agent, Toomer, was a second-round pick in the 1996 draft. But like Cruz, Toomer had had an inauspicious start to his Giants career due to a knee injury his rookie season followed by limited chances to contribute to the passing game in his next two seasons.

Toward the end of the 1998 season, Toomer began to see an increased role on offense. He caught a 37-yard touchdown pass from quarterback Kent Graham with 48 seconds left in a 20–16 come- from-behind victory over the previously undefeated Denver Broncos in Week 14.

From 1999 to 2003, Toomer recorded consecutive 1,000-yard receiving campaigns, the best of which came in 2002 when he set Giants' single-season records at that time in receptions (82) and receiving yards (1,343).

Toomer's final season with the Giants came in 2008. He did flirt with joining the Kansas City Chiefs in 2009, but less than one week into camp, he had a change of heart and asked for his release, which was granted.

Toomer, who retired as a Giant, currently owns the franchise records for the most career pass receptions (668), the most consecutive games with a reception (98), the most career receiving yards gained (9,497), and the most career receiving touchdowns (54).

Manning decided to organize workouts at a high school field in Hoboken, New Jersey for any of his teammates who wanted to work out.

Cruz was just one of several players who regularly took part in those voluntary workouts, but in having done so, the receiver was about to reward the Giants' faith in him once the lockout ended.

When the lockout ended in July 2011 and free agency and contract negotiations were allowed to begin, Giants receiver Steve Smith, primarily the Giants' slot receiver, signed with the Eagles.

Meanwhile, the Giants, who had discovered during Smith's late-season absence in 2010 that neither Hakeem Nicks or Mario Manningham was a natural fit for the slot, decided to give Cruz a chance to make the position his.

He did just that. In 2011, Cruz recorded 82 receptions for a franchise single-season record 1,536 receiving yards, and nine touchdowns.

According to Pro Football Focus, an advanced analytics web site, 64 of those receptions, 1,208 of those yards, and seven of those touchdowns that season came from the slot.

Cruz, who by this time had adopted the Salsa as his signature touchdown celebration in honor of his late *abuela* who had taught him the dance when he was younger, had become a fan favorite. Every time he caught the ball, he was greeted by chants of "Cruuuuuuzzzz!"

And for as much as the fans loved Cruz, he too loved the fans, spending as much time as he could to accommodate autograph and picture requests.

It was his play that endeared him most to the Giants faithful. Cruz gave Giants fans many exciting moments in his first full NFL season, but he might have saved his best for the end of the 2011 season.

In the second quarter of a Christmas Eve game against the Jets, Cruz caught a franchise record-setting 99-yard touchdown reception, beating defensive backs Antonio Cromartie and Kyle Wilson to give the Giants a 10–7 lead.

The Giants would never relinquish that lead, going on to a 29–14 victory that eased the previous week's sting of an embarrassing 23–10 home loss to Washington.

The win over the Jets, many believe, might very well have been the catalyst that put the Giants back on track for a playoff berth that season.

The following week, Cruz delivered a 74-yard touchdown reception against the Cowboys to put the Giants on the scoreboard first. The Giants would never look back, beating their division rivals to earn a Wild Card berth, which they rode to their fourth Super Bowl Championship.

After his breakout season, Cruz's star continued to soar. In 2012, he recorded his second straight 1,000-yard season and was voted to his first Pro Bowl. The following year, he just barely missed recording his third-straight 1,000-yard season by two yards, an opportunity missed in part because a minor knee injury caused him to miss the final two games of that season.

On July 8, 2013, Cruz's rags-to-riches story went to the next level when he signed a five-year, $45.879 million contract extension. In 2014, he then realized a career-long dream when his teammates voted him a team captain.

But like all good Cinderella stories, eventually, the clock strikes midnight. For Cruz, his midnight came in the harshest and most ill-timed fashion six weeks into the 2014 season.

That year, the Giants had started that season 3–2 and were looking to record a big win against the Eagles in an October 12, 2014, primetime game at Lincoln Financial Field.

Unfortunately, the Eagles dominated the Giants, taking a 20–0 halftime lead on their way to a 27–0 shutout.

With the Giants forced to pass to play catchup, Manning tried to connect with Cruz on a three-yard touchdown pass on a fourth-and-goal.

Unfortunately, Cruz's right leg buckled underneath him as he tried to come down with the pass. He immediately grabbed his right knee in obvious pain.

As teammates stood by trying to offer words of encouragement to the fallen receiver, trainers and doctors rushed to his side to help Cruz onto the back of a cart where he was taken across the field to the opposite tunnel and back into the locker room for further evaluation.

The Giants, already sucking wind thanks to the beating the Eagles were administering, lost whatever life they had left when Cruz, his head in his hands as he sobbed uncontrollably, was driven past their sideline to the locker room.

Cruz was diagnosed with a season-ending torn patellar tendon and was kept overnight at a hospital in Philadelphia.

"Incredibly huge loss," head coach Tom Coughlin said after the game. "I was standing there with him, but it was not a good situation. It was not a good scene."

Once the shock subsided, Cruz, who overcame the odds in his quest to get to the NFL, had his eye on returning for the 2015 season.

He attacked his post-surgery rehab with the same vigor as he had shown in overcoming the odds to make it to the NFL.

In retrospect, Cruz had maybe pushed himself a little too hard. During the 2015 training camp, he developed what was reported to be dehydration, but what was later revealed by Cruz in an interview with *The Newark Star-Ledger* at that season's Super Bowl to be a torn fascia in his left calf.

Initially, Cruz hoped that rest would cure what ailed him. But when he experienced another setback in trying to get back on the field, his comeback from the devastating knee injury that he later surmised might have been at fault for his calf issue, would have to wait another year.

Cruz refused to give up. He spent his second go-round on injured reserve being more patient with himself and paying closer attention to what his body was telling him.

His patience paid off. By 2016, Cruz was ready to return to the game he loved, determined to show people that he was as good as new.

But again, it just wasn't meant to be.

There were questions about how his injury affected him physically, if he was the same player he had been prior to the injury. In addition, with the Giants having selected Sterling Shepard in the second round of the 2016 draft to be their future slot receiver, the team moved Cruz to the outside, a plan that didn't quite yield the desired results.

According to Pro Football Focus, Cruz played a career-high 753 snaps split wide versus a career-low 55 snaps in the slot position in the 2016 season. He caught just 39 passes for 586 yards and one touchdown that year.

Besides his production decline, Cruz was facing other challenges. For one, he didn't participate on special teams, and because of that combined with his production decline, his 2017 salary cap number was set to rise to $9.4 million, of which $7.5 million was his base salary, made it hard to justify carrying him.

In February 2017, the final clang of the clock striking midnight sounded on the Giants' modern-day Cinderella story when they announced they were releasing Cruz.

In the team-issued statement, Cruz described his time with the Giants as an "amazing journey."

"I pretty much grew up in front of the eyes of this entire organization," he said. "The Giants fan base, the community, my hometown, my family. I grew up there. It's very much a family atmosphere, and it's very much like leaving your family.... I did some great things there."

But he wasn't done doing great things, at least not in his mind.

Months later, Cruz got another chance to take his NFL career off life support when the Chicago Bears signed him to a one-year deal.

By then, however, Cruz's body had had enough. He not only suffered a knee injury in Chicago's preseason finale, but he also had a rather nondescript showing in which he caught six passes for 37 yards with a touchdown in four preseason games.

Even after being cut by the Bears, Cruz still had hopes of playing again, which he revealed during a May 2018 charity event appearance. When no teams came calling, Cruz, who had already become a globally recognized philanthropist and "brand" across multiple arenas, retired from football to join ESPN as an analyst.

"I'm excited to close down and open a new chapter and join the media world at ESPN," Cruz said, announcing his retirement in a video for Uninterrupted.

"I'm excited for the future; I'm excited for the next chapter, and I'm excited for you all to be a part of this with me."

Although Cruz did get a Super Bowl ring, his exit from the game wasn't the ride off into the sunset that he likely envisioned for himself.

But for Cruz, it was closure on a fairytale career that initially looked as though it would never get going.

40

THE SNEAKERS GAME

O n December 9, 1934, the New York Giants, locked in a bitter cold battle in the with the Chicago Bears for that year's NFL championship, made a drastic change to keep their chances of glory from slipping away.

They changed their footwear from cleats to basketball shoes at halftime to gain better traction on the icy turf of the Polo Grounds in what famously became known as the "Sneakers Game."

* * *

The Giants, having finished their tenth season in existence with an 8–5 record, weren't supposed to have, well, a snowball's chance in hell on that cold, wintery day against the Bears.

Not only were the Bears the defending NFL champions, they entered the 1934 Championship Game with an 18-game winning streak (including postseason dating back to the end of the 1933 season) that included a 13–0 season record 1934.

The Giants had the mammoth task of having to dethrone the George Halas and Bronko Nagurski led Bears, but they would also have to do so on a field which, thanks to a steady frozen rain from the night before, had turned the Polo Grounds into a something closely resembling an ice rink.

While the grounds crew tried to figure out how to remove the frozen tarp from the grass without bringing up chunks of the turf before kick-off, Giants head coach Steve Owen was worried about how his team would stop the 6'2", 226-pound Nagurski, who in the 1934 regular season posted a career-high 586 rushing yards on 123 carries (4.8 yards per carry), with a career-best seven rushing touchdowns.

Despite his attempts at trying to appear in control and having some secret plan to slow down the future Hall of Famer, Owen himself had wondered if there was a legitimate way to lessen Nagurski's impact.

He was so obsessed about it that at one point before the game, he was overheard by one of his players mumbling about how the hell the Giants were going to stop Nagurski, a player who had proven himself capable of operating on any type of field.

Imagine Owen's surprise when, during one of his mumblings, another voice other than his own delivered a suggestion.

"Basketball shoes," a player said.

Owen, already in a foul mood, snapped to attention and asked the player—team captain Ray Flaherty—to repeat himself.

"Basketball shoes," Flaherty said.

Flaherty went on to explain to his head coach how he, during his college years at Gonzaga, experienced similar playing conditions in a game against Montana, and how basketball shoes had made a noticeable difference in allowing the players to gain traction on the icy terrain.

Owen was skeptical at first, but perhaps out of desperation and because he couldn't think of a better idea, he was willing to try Flaherty's idea.

Owen asked his friend, Abe Cohen, a tailor who helped the Giants sideline, to find basketball shoes.

Cohen, who had been friendly with Chick Meehan, a member of the Manhattan College athletic staff he had first come to know when Meehan was with New York University, paid a visit to Manhattan College's gym where he rounded up several pairs of basketball sneakers.

While Cohen was rounding up the shoes, the Giants had arrived at the Polo Grounds for the game. When they took the field for warmups shortly before noon, they soon realized just how bad the turf was.

With temperatures holding steady in the single digits at kickoff and no sign of Cohen, the Giants had no choice but to begin the game, all the while hoping that Nagurski wouldn't embarrass them in front of the 39,000-plus fans who braved the artic-like conditions.

At halftime, the Bears held a 10–3 lead, the Giants' lone points coming on a 38-yard field goal by Ken Strong.

Despite the slim Bears lead, the score that didn't begin to reflect the punishment Chicago and Nagurski, who gave his team a 7–3 lead to start the second quarter on a 1-yard touchdown run, were inflicting on the Giants.

At halftime, hope was beginning to dwindle. The Giants began to exit the locker room to return to the playing field for the second half when suddenly, Cohen burst through the door with the kryptonite to the combat the Bears' Superman.

No sooner did Cohen drop the basketball shoes on the locker room floor than did a scramble ensue among the Giants players trying to find the right size and get them onto their feet so they could begin the second half on time.

When the players returned to the sideline, Halas noticed how funny the Giants were moving. When told that the Giants had changed into basketball shoes, Halas smirked and said, "Good. Step on their feet."

At first, the sneakers didn't make a difference for the Giants, who were trying to get used to the difference in the traction between the sneakers and the spiked cleats they wore in the first half.

Once they became used to the shoes, it was a whole new ballgame.

Not only was Nagurski no match for them—he was thrown for losses for as little as five yards and as much as 15 yards in the game—the Giants offense put on a scoring clinic.

New York racked up 27 unanswered points in the fourth-quarter, including two touchdowns by Ken Strong, one by Ed Danowski, and one by Ike Frankian.

On the other side of the ball, the Giants defense held the Bears vaunted running game, which came into the contest averaging six yards per carry, to just 89 rushing yards, 68 of those by Nagurski on 24 carries, 2.83-yards-per-attempt.

The sneakers—and by extension Abe Cohen—weren't the only heroes for the Giants that day. Danowski made people forget about quarterback Harry Newman, the Giants' leading rusher and passer that season who had to miss the game after suffering a back injury in a November 18 loss to the Bears.

Danowski completed six out of 11 pass attempts for 83 yards, one touchdown, and two interceptions while rushing for 59 yards on 20 carries for a touchdown that afternoon.

As for the borrowed sneakers, they were returned to Manhattan College despite their game-worn condition.

Upon receipt of the shoes, Manhattan College head basketball coach Neil Cohalan (later the first head coach of the NBA's New York Knicks) took note of their condition and said, "I'm glad our shoes did the Giants some good. Now the question is, did the Giants do our shoes any good?"

41

A GAME
OF REVENGE

The 1990 NFC Championship Game between the Giants and San Francisco 49ers had all the makings to be epic. And with several future Hall of Famers set to take the field that day, the game—a 15–13 Giants win—did not disappoint.

At stake for the 49ers was a chance to become the first team in NFL history to three-peat as Super Bowl champions. For the Giants, whose 1990 season had been begun with adversity, it was a chance to show the world their resiliency.

The Giants' adversity began that summer in training camp. Two of their defensive stars—defensive lineman Leonard Marshall and linebacker Lawrence Taylor—staged holdouts over contract disputes.

The problems then continued into the season. Quarterback Phil Simms, who led the Giants to an 11–3 record that included winning their first 10 games of the season, was done for the year after breaking his foot against the Buffalo Bills in a Week 15 loss.

Adding to the questions skeptics had about the Giants, more than half of the players from their 1986 championship season team were no longer on the roster, leaving some question as to how much the team's chemistry had been affected.

If all that wasn't enough to question whether the Giants were equipped to make another run at a championship title, the 49ers had beaten the Giants 7–3 in Week 13 at Candlestick Park.

For every adverse situation, the Giants found a solution.

Taylor and Marshall each received new contracts.

Jeff Hostetler, the backup quarterback, seized his opportunity to lead the Giants on a two-game winning streak to close out the 1990 regular-season campaign, the streak continuing into the postseason and leading to the team's second Lombardi Trophy.

And the new faces that had replaced the over three dozen departed Giants from the 1986 squad brought their A-games right through the final whistle of Super Bowl XXV.

* * *

After making short work of the Chicago Bears in the division playoffs—the Giants pounded the Bears 31–3—up next on their road to Super Bowl XXV was a rematch with the 49ers at Candlestick Park for the NFC title game set for January 20, 1991.

That weekend, the 49ers were favored to roll over the Giants, this despite their quarterback, Joe Montana, having missed two days of practice with the flu.

Not that it mattered to the Giants, who were on a mission. As had been the case in their 1986 championship run when the 1985 playoff loss to the Bears left them with a bitter taste in their mouths, this time, the Giants were still smarting from a 19–13 divisional playoff loss to the Los Angeles Rams at home to end their 1989 postseason run.

"I wanted to kind of put a little more into that 1990 season because I had a nasty taste in my mouth," defensive tackle Leonard Marshall said. "Every day that went by leading up to that season, I kept seeing (Rams receiver) Flipper Anderson catch that touchdown pass and run down the field and up the ramp in the stadium tunnel with the ball in that 1989 playoff game, and I remember thinking about how shitty I felt.

"I know we did everything we could have done and that the play was a great one. But speaking for myself, when I was holding out that next summer, I was at home watching game film and thinking about things that I could do to improve when I got back to the team to make sure that wouldn't happen again," Marshall added.

That wasn't the only fuel stimulating the Giants fire. There was also the regular-season win by the 49ers on *Monday Night Football*, a game in which Simms famously got into a screaming match with 49ers defensive back Ronnie Lott.

"All of us left that game with the same bitter taste that we had in our mouth against Chicago [in 1985]," Marshall said. "After that game, [the 49ers] acted like they thought they had won the Super Bowl, and we didn't like it one bit."

With that kind of ire brewing inside of them, it's no wonder that Marshall and his defensive teammates came through in a big way.

The 49ers, who between their running and passing offenses had scored 40 touchdowns that season, were held to one touchdown by the

Giants, that coming on a third-quarter 61-yard strike from Montana to receiver John Taylor to give them a 13–6 lead.

But then the tides turned against the 49ers when on a third-and-10 in the fourth quarter, Marshall, the Giants team leader in sacks that day, delivered a bone-crushing hit that caused the quarterback to lose the ball.

That hit not only knocked Montana (who suffered a broken right hand) out of the game, it helped set up a key Giants scoring drive punctuated by a little razzle-dazzle.

Facing fourth-and-2 on their 46-yard line, linebacker Gary Reasons, who after the game told reporters that head coach Bill Parcells had given

Pepper Johnson (52) comes to celebrate and Steve Young (8) walks off the field after Lawrence Taylor recovered a 49ers fumble in the fourth quarter of the NFC Championship Game on January 20, 1991. (AP Images / Rich Pedroncelli)

him as the punt team's signal-caller, autonomy to call for a fake if the opportunity was there, did just that.

Reasons spotted a gaping hole on the right side of the formation, took the snap and ran 30 yards to the 49ers' 24-yard line in what he would later describe as "the longest run" he had since high school.

"Bill is aggressive about it," Reasons told reporters after the game. "If I like what I see at the line of scrimmage, I can call [the fake punt]. If not, I don't."

Were it not for punt returner John Taylor making the tackle, Reasons might very well have scored.

Three plays later, kicker Matt Bahr, who had been cut by the Browns in the preseason only to land with the Giants in Week 3 after Raul Allegre suffered a groin injury, hit a 38-yard field goal to cut the 49ers' lead to 13–12.

THE OTHER HIT

Much has been made of the historic hit by Giants defensive lineman Leonard Marshall that knocked Joe Montana out of the game, given its bone-crushing nature and the impact it had on the 49ers' quest to "three-peat." But there was another hit against a quarterback in that game that almost proved to be just as catastrophic.

That hit was suffered by Giants quarterback Jeff Hostetler. Hostetler to a hit to his knee by 49ers defensive tackle Jim Burt, his one-time Giants teammate, on a 13-yard pass completion to Mark Ingram.

On the next play, Matt Cavanaugh entered the game to finish out that drive, running three plays.

Hostetler, meanwhile, returned to the game on the next series despite having suffered a hyperextended knee that left his teammates holding their breaths.

"With the angle of that hit, I thought he was gone," center Bart Oates said after the game. "I was petrified."

Hostetler was too at first.

"At first, I thought it was bad," he said. "Then, I got better quickly. The pain subsided a little bit. If it had been unstable, it probably would have kept me out of the game. As long as it was stable, I was going to go back in."

With one more game to go, no one expected anything less from the gritty Hostetler.

With Montana out of the game, backup Steve Young was now in charge of the offense.

But if there was one thing that Young, like Montana, couldn't overcome that day and on that final drive, it was the lack of a running game that, in that year's postseason, had averaged 42.5 yards per game, dead last among the 12 playoff participants.

The 49ers began that final drive on their 20-yard line, but after advancing the ball to the Giants' 40-yard line, running back Roger Craig was hit and stripped of the ball by Giants defensive lineman Erik Howard, the loose ball recovered by Lawrence Taylor.

The Giants, who that season saw their running game finish eighth in the then 28-team league, would run the ball on four of their five ensuing plays, including a third-and-1 converted by Ottis Anderson's two-yard gain.

With the clock down to four seconds, the Giants took their final time out to give kicker Matt Bahr and the field goal unit time to get onto the field for the potential game-winning kick.

Bahr, it turned out, had sprained his neck on a tackle in the previous week's win over the Chicago Bears, an injury that created some concern for the Giants earlier in the week before the title game as to whether he might be available to play.

Thankfully for the Giants, Bahr shook off his injury and was indeed ready to go. The 49ers, however, called their second time out hoping to "ice" Bahr, who at the top of the fourth quarter had missed a 37-yard field goal attempt wide left.

The tactic didn't work; in fact, Bahr, who kicked a postseason record five field goals in that game (including the game-winner), would later say that the extra time gave him more of an opportunity to pick out where he wanted Hostetler, his holder, to place the ball for the 42-yard attempt.

On Bahr's game-winning kick, the ball started to drift to the left, just as his earlier miss had, But this time, the kick cleared the uprights as time expired, putting an end to the 49ers' quest for a three-peat as Super Bowl champions.

42

THE WILDERNESS YEARS

As the NFL continued to solidify its footing in the American sports scene's landscape, the New York Giants, with their winning ways, innovative coaches, and household names, remained one of the sparkling jewels in the league's crown.

But for all the glory the Giants enjoyed, eventually that all crumbled and led to a nearly two-decade period known as the Wilderness Years.

There is still some debate as to exactly when the Giants dry spell commenced, but many football historians point to the 1964 season as the start.

That year, the Giants finished 2–10–2 in what was the start of a nearly two-decade long playoff drought.

Although they would finish 7–7 in 1965, the following year, they slid so far back in the standings that they would finish the 1966 season with an embarrassing 1–12–1 mark while also allowing a franchise-record 501 points on defense.

The quality of the Giants roster also began to deteriorate as the players began to age and the drafts, which had in years past yielded sustainable talent, began to turn up empty.

Personnel issues aside, the Giants had other problems during that bleak period in team history. For one, they managed just two winning seasons (against 12 losing ones and three in which they reached the .500 mark).

They also were left without a permanent home when team president Wellington Mara reached an agreement with the New Jersey Sports and Exposition Authority to move the franchise from Yankee Stadium to the new Giants Stadium facility in East Rutherford, New Jersey, only to learn that construction issues would delay the scheduled opening of the facility.

If that all wasn't bad enough, Jack Mara, Wellington's brother, and business partner lost his battle with cancer on June 29, 1965.

As Jack's only surviving son, Tim Mara represented his mother and sister in the business dealings of the franchise. But whereas Wellington and Jack had shared a productive relationship, the same couldn't be said of Wellington and Tim.

The final kick in the gut was that as the Giants' ship was sinking, the Jets, their cross-town rivals, became the toast of the town thanks to two playoff seasons, including the Super Bowl championship season in 1968 and their 1969 divisional playoff appearance (a loss), and their glamorous quarterback, Joe Namath.

The Giants, desperate to get back on track, engineered a blockbuster trade with the Minnesota Vikings to acquire quarterback Fran Tarkenton before the 1967 season, sending Minnesota their first and second-round draft picks that year, their first-rounder in 1968 and their second-rounder in 1969.

The Giants also made a head coaching change after the 1968 season, replacing Allie Sherman, who after starting out with three winning seasons, managed to win only 24 games in his final five years, with former fullback Alex Webster.

But Webster's tenure saw the Giants mostly go up and down from year to year, though in 1970 after an 0–3 start, they did finish 9–5, just barely missing a chance at the playoffs.

The success was short-lived. In 1971, running back Ron Johnson, who in 1970 became the first Giant to rush for 1,000 yards during a regular-season (1,027 yards), suffered a knee injury. And Tarkenton had lost whatever magic he had, finishing 226 out of 386 pass attempts (58.5 percent) for just 2,567 yards while throwing 11 touchdowns to 21 interceptions in a 4–10 season.

After the 1971 season, the Giants traded Tarkenton back to the Vikings, for quarterback Norm Snead, who would serve as the Giants quarterback for the 1972–73 seasons and part of the 1974 campaign before being traded to the 49ers.

The Giants did have a few bright spots during their wilderness years, among them four-time Pro Bowl punter Dave Jennings; tight end Bob Tucker; two-time Pro Bowl defensive back Carl "Spider" Lockhart; five-time Pro Bowl linebacker Brad Van Pelt, and, of course future defensive staples such as defensive end George Martin, future Hall of Fame linebacker Harry Carson, and receiver Homer Jones, the "inventor" of the touchdown spike celebration and whose 22.6 average gain (based on a minimum 200 career receptions) is still an NFL record as of 2019.

Although by October 1976 the Giants had been able to settle in Giants Stadium, their new state-of-the-art facility, and had started to rebuild the talent with additions such as quarterback Phil Simms (1979) and linebacker Lawrence Taylor (1981), the playoff drought didn't end until 1981.

That year, the Giants finished 9–7. Thanks to the overtime heroics of kicker Joe Danelo, who nailed a 35-yard game-winning field goal in the regular-season finale against the Cowboys, the Giants were headed back to the postseason for the first time since 1963.

The Giants' 27–21 win over the Eagles in the 1981 Wild Card round marked their first postseason victory since the 1956 Championship game win over the Chicago Bears.

Unfortunately, the Giants' euphoria ended the following week when the 49ers beat them 38–24 in the divisional round.

43

MANNING'S STREAK ENDS

"**G**eno Smith to Start at QB on Sunday."

When those eight words, the subject line of an e-mail announcement sent by the Giants public relations department on November 28, 2017, just after 3:30 pm, hit the airwaves, people thought the team's e-mail account had either been hacked or that some unfortunate set of circumstances had befallen longtime starting quarterback Eli Manning, the holder of 222 consecutive NFL games (including postseason) started.

It turned out to be neither.

The Giants, who the year before had strung together an impressive 11–5 record to earn their first playoff berth since 2011, saw their 2017 season fall upon hard times in which they lost their first five games, falling one game shy of matching their 0–6 start from 2013.

They would go on to win just one game in their first nine, that being a 23–10 road win over the Denver Broncos on October 15 before logging an upset win in overtime over the Chiefs in Week 11 and a Week 17 win on their way to a 3–13 season, their worst mark since they went 3–12–1 in 1983.

There are many reasons for the Giants' collapse in 2017, starting with injuries. That season, the Giants seemed to be averaging placing a player on injured reserve at a rate of one per week.

Perhaps partially desperate to find a spark, head coach Ben McAdoo put the wheels in motion that would lead to Manning's benching.

In retrospect, McAdoo, a man who had coached the mobile Aaron Rodgers with the Packers, couldn't help himself when it came to talking about Manning. During a press conference at the combine earlier that year, McAdoo seemed to save his harshest critiques for Manning.

"We all know that turning the ball over 27 times [the total of interceptions and fumbles Manning had in 2016] isn't acceptable," McAdoo said.

MAN(NING) OF STEEL

Eli Manning has a lot to be proud of in his career—two Super Bowl championships, the franchise records, the riches his athletic talents have brought him, and, of course, his perfect attendance since 2004 in which he never missed a game due to illness or injury.

But there was one instance where the Giants iron man nearly missed a start—and oh, what a big one it would have been for him to miss had things not worked out.

On January 20, 2012, the Giants were scheduled to play the 49ers for the NFC Conference title in San Francisco. That week, Manning came down with a nasty case of the flu, which left him too sick to do much of anything.

With Manning trying his best to kick the bug, his backup, David Carr took all the snaps in practice.

Carr, now an NFL analyst, told the story about how Manning came out to go through warmups, the part of the practice that was open to the media, only to retreat to the trainer's room once the team escorted the press back to the press room because he was too sick to continue.

Carr, who always did what his team needed him to do, didn't think much of it, figuring that Manning would get a practice in on Friday and be ready for the game Sunday.

"No, we roll into Friday, and he's still sick," Carr said. in a segment airing on NFL's Total Access during the 2018 conference championship games.

"He can't practice. He's literally in the training room getting IVs all day—had the flu for four straight days.

"I practiced on Friday with the team. So now Eli hasn't had any practice time; I've taken all the reps for the NFC Championship Game. He shows up on Saturday, looks fine, goes through the walk-through, goes to the game, and everything is normal—no one knew that he hadn't practiced during the week."

Manning and the Giants would defeat the 49ers 20–17 in overtime thanks to the 31-yard game-winning field goal by kicker Lawrence Tynes to set up a Super Bowl rematch with the New England Patriots a couple of weeks later in Indianapolis.

Manning finished 32 of 58 for 316 yards and two touchdowns in that game. He had also been hit 12 times, six of those being sacks.

Ironically, Giants defensive end Justin Tuck approached Carr on the sideline of that game after noting how the iron man was getting beaten to a pulp by the 49ers defense.

"You're going to have to play this game," Carr recounted Tuck telling him. "Good thing I practiced for three days," Carr quipped.

"We're fortunate to have the wins that we had, turning the ball over the way we turned the ball over.... We can't have it come out. Sixteen interceptions, 11 fumbles—way too many fumbles."

* * *

When McAdoo came to the Giants as their offensive coordinator in 2014, Manning threw for three straight 4,000-yard seasons and completed 62.9 percent of his pass attempts, while seeing his average pass attempts exceed 605 per season.

Following Tom Coughlin's resignation, McAdoo was named the new head coach and decided to retain the play-calling duties. But after the Giants offensive line saw its sack total grow from 21 in 2016 to 31 in 2017, McAdoo appeared to give the unit a pass.

"I think [the offensive line] is an easy blame," he said. "The offensive line, they need to play better; I agree with that. [But] I think Eli needs to do a better job of playing with fast feet, and I think he needs to sit on that back foot in the pocket.

"We're seeing a lot of man coverage, so the receivers—it's gonna take a little time for them to get open, so everything may not be rhythmical.

"So [Eli] has gotta play with fast feet; he's gotta sit on his back foot and be ready to hitch into a throw. Things aren't always clean in this league, but you watch film of the end zones throughout the league, and you're seeing a lot of dirty pockets."

If Manning was bothered by McAdoo's criticism, he never let on, and would continue to state after every game, regardless of its outcome, he had to play better.

But when the losses began to pile up during that tumultuous 2017 season, McAdoo met with general manager Jerry Reese to broach the topic about playing backup quarterbacks Geno Smith and rookie Davis Webb.

Having received buy-in from Reese, McAdoo met with Manning in his office on a Monday and told the quarterback that he wanted to get a look at Smith and Webb. Aware of Manning's consecutive games started streak, the head coach offered Manning a chance to keep his streak alive by proposing that Manning start and play half the game before giving way to the next quarterback.

The idea of playing up until a certain point in the game—a preseason arrangement, Manning would later say—didn't sit well with the veteran.

That next day, he not only officially rejected McAdoo's proposal, but Manning also requested that the Giants immediately put out a press release announcing the coach's decision to go in a different direction at quarterback for that weekend's game at Oakland.

"Coach McAdoo told me I could continue to start while Geno and Davis are given an opportunity to play," Manning said in the statement. "My feeling is that if you are going to play the other guys, play them.

"Starting to keep the streak going and knowing you won't finish the game and have a chance to win it is pointless to me, and it tarnishes the streak. Like I always have, I will be ready to play if and when I am needed. I will help Geno and Davis prepare to play as well as they possibly can."

McAdoo, who would sooner disclose his social security number than reveal personnel plans, suddenly had a five-alarm fire that week that overshadowed the team's upcoming game.

"I have a lot of confidence in Eli as a player, as a quarterback," he insisted during his regular Wednesday press conference the day after the announcement rocked the NFL.

"But at this point, it's my responsibility for the organization to make sure we take a look at Geno and, at some point, take a look at Davis, and give them the opportunity to show what they can do heading into next year.

"I think a lot of Hall of Fame quarterbacks who have done a lot for a lot of teams haven't been able to choose the way that they get to move on," he added. "I'm not saying that we're moving on [from Manning], but at some point, you have to make hard, tough decisions for the best of the franchise. And, that's what I have to do here."

Manning, to his credit, handled the incident like a professional.

Standing at his locker that Wednesday and, at times, fighting back the tears, he explained why he declined to keep his starting streak alive.

"It's not a preseason game where you're going to play the start to the half," he said. "What's the next week? A quarter? A series? That's not fair to me, that's not fair to Geno—that's not how you play. You play to win.

"I'll be a good teammate. I don't like it, but it's part of football," he added.

As the outrage from outside the building grew, team president and chief operating officer John Mara made a rare in-season visit to the Giants media workroom to conduct an informal, on-the-record press conference.

"I normally don't speak to the coach directly about which players are playing and which players are not playing," Mara said.

"I mentioned to [Reese] a week or two ago, 'Don't you think it's time that we start to get a look at these other quarterbacks at some point during the games?' He agreed and said he had already had a conversation with Ben about that."

Mara, who admitted that there might have been a better way to handle the situation, chose his words very carefully when asked about how the proposal had been presented to Manning.

"It was presented the way that Ben thought it ought to be presented," he said. "Could we have done it differently? I guess you could argue we could have, yes."

McAdoo, whose remaining press conferences that week continued to be dominated with questions about his decision, was asked that next day [Thursday] if he thought the way the idea was conveyed to Mara was the same way it was to Manning.

"I was honest," he said. "I was upfront with Eli, and I don't have any regrets with the way it was handled."

In the end, McAdoo's attempt to light a spark under the team fizzled as the Raiders topped the Giants 24–17. Smith finished the game 21 of 24 for 212 yards and a touchdown (89.3 rating). Still, the problems that had plagued the Giants all year long—the lack of a running game, the inability to win the starting field position battle, the injury-related absence of their top receivers, and the struggles on defense—were too much to overcome.

Not long after the Giants returned from Oakland, McAdoo became the first head coach since Bill Arnsparger in 1976 to be fired in-season. While Reese became the team's first general manager to be fired.

At a more formal press conference held in the team's auditorium, Mara, in his opening statement after the announcement of the dismissals, denied that the Manning situation was behind the decisions, praised McAdoo and Reese for their contributions.

But while Mara made sure to praise and thank Reese and McAdoo for their contributions, he also made it known that not everyone was on the same page when it came to how Manning's situation had been handled.

"I mean, we were, and we weren't," he said. "Ben came up with the plan. I initially signed off on the plan. My hope had been to talk to [McAdoo] to try to have a little more flexibility with it, and not have a hard, fast time when [Manning] was going to come out of the game.

"By then, Eli rightfully had rejected the notion of only starting and playing the half and coming out. We issued a statement, and it was just too late at that point."

After McAdoo was terminated, defensive coordinator Steve Spagnuolo was named the interim head coach. One of Spagnuolo's first orders of business was to reinstate Manning as the starting quarterback for the rest of the season.

"I'm excited. Excited about the opportunity to play this week, get back on the field with teammates and go play against the Dallas Cowboys," Manning said after the announcement had been made.

As for McAdoo, Manning again took the high road.

"I feel for Coach McAdoo. He's been a great coach for me, a great friend. I don't think this is his fault, but obviously, just where the team is. The Giants had to make a decision, and that's what happens when you're 2–10."

44

ON THE MOVE

Imagine being in existence for 46 years and yet never really having a place to call your own.

Such was the circumstances the Giants found themselves in since their inception when they would share their home fields—the Polo Grounds from 1925 to 1955 (with baseball's Giants, Yankees, and Mets) and Yankee Stadium from 1956 to 1973 (with baseball's Yankees).

So when William H. Cahill, then the governor of New Jersey, offered to give the Giants a home of their own within the state's planned Meadowlands Sports Complex in East Rutherford, New Jersey, it was an offer that Giants team president Wellington Mara couldn't refuse.

Who could blame him? The proposed new stadium would bear the team's name and was part of a lease that would mandate the Giants paying an annual rental of 15 percent of their gross ticket sales, the same rental fee they were paying for the use of Yankee Stadium.

Under the proposed multiyear Meadowlands lease, the Giants would also get 50 percent of the concession sales plus a share of the parking revenue.

With the Giants' lease at Yankee Stadium set to expire after the 1974 season, a year before the targeted opening date of the new stadium, the timing seemed perfect for the Giants to make the move.

Plus, as far as Mara was concerned, the new stadium, which could seat over 77,000 in three different tiers and which would be stylized after the Giants' red and blue color scheme, would offer an improved gameday experience for the team's loyal season-ticket holders.

"If you have a seat at Yankee Stadium, you will have a better one in Giant Stadium," he said. "And the 10,000 to 15,000 of you who don't have seats in Yankee Stadium will have one in Giant Stadium."

On August 26, 1971, Mara, with Governor Cahill and New Jersey Sports and Exposition Authority (NJSEA) chair Sonny Werblin in attendance, inked a 30-year lease for the Giants to move their executive and football operations to the stadium that was set to be built in the midst of a swampland area along New Jersey's Route 3.

What should have been a joyous occasion quickly turned sour. The city of New York, remember, had already lost two Major League Baseball teams, the Giants and the Dodgers, who relocated to San Francisco and Los Angeles, respectively.

The city also lost several large corporations that had funded its structure through its tax dollars. So when the Giants rejected New York City mayor John V. Lindsay's offer to keep them in New York, he and the rest of the New York politicians weren't happy.

Mara and Cahill tried to soften the blow for the people of New York. At a news conference at Central Park South's Essex House, Mara said, "New York is not losing a team but is gaining a sports complex."

Mara also insisted that there were no plans to change the team's official name from the New York Football Giants, which they are still known as to this day, to the New Jersey Giants, as some New Jersey politicians in past years have desired to see.

Cahill, meanwhile, tried to reassure New York–based fans that their beloved Giants were "just as close to Manhattan as they ever have been."

They might as well have stood there singing the chorus of the 1969 Steam classic, *Na Na Na Na Hey Hey-hey Goodbye*, because no matter what was said, there was just no softening what some viewed as the ultimate betrayal of a team that was turning its back on the city that had helped the franchise grow into a flourishing and beloved business icon.

As a result, city politicians began exploring the possibility of evicting the Giants before their Yankee Stadium lease expired in 1974.

Mara, for his part, had every intention of honoring the remaining years on his team's lease with the city and had expected that the city would allow for the same. However, once Mayor Lindsay's administration acquired the title to Yankee Stadium, which was to eventually undergo a two-year, $24 million renovation, all bets were off.

"The city has this power [of eviction] once it acquires the stadium," Lindsay said at a news conference in discussing the fate of the football Giants as tenants. "Whether or not we'll do it, we don't know."

It didn't take too long for Lindsay to figure it out. On October 1, 1973, a day after the Yankees lost their regular-season finale 8–5 to the Detroit Tigers, the decision was made to bring the bulldozers in—the mechanical kind, not the big men that manned the pit for the Giants—to begin work on the renovation project.

Left without a home, the Giants now had to scramble to come up with a plan until their new home was ready.

Their first choice was the Yale Bowl, located in New Haven, Connecticut. However, that choice was initially ruled out due to concerns over the distance Giants fans would have to travel and, for those who couldn't make the drive, the existing television blackout rules.

The Giants then contacted Princeton University to inquire about using their stadium, but those discussions didn't get very far.

Meanwhile, NFL commissioner Pete Rozelle, who, on an experimental basis, had agreed to lift the blackout rule for Super Bowl VII the year prior if the game sold out 10 or more days in advance of kickoff (which it did), collaborated with politicians about implementing a similar solution for the Giants.

The result was the passing of Public Law (PL) 93–107, an amendment to the Communications Act of 1934. PL 93–107 allowed for the televised broadcast of a sporting event in the home team's local market if all tickets were sold out at least 72 hours before the event's scheduled start time.

With the blackout issue resolved but Giants Stadium's completion delayed, the next obstacle to overcome was finding a venue for the Giants' home games. The Giants would finish the 1973 season and play the 1974 campaign at the Yale Bowl.

In 1975, the Giants worked out a deal to play their home games at Shea Stadium, home of baseball's New York Mets and the NFL's New York Jets.

As Shea Stadium's third tenant, the Giants often took a back seat to the Mets and Jets as far as scheduling priorities. Still, Shea Stadium's facilities were at least deemed more in line to handle a professional football game, plus the location was more favorable for the Giants season- ticket holders.

Meanwhile, back in New Jersey, construction managers were scrambling to finish Giants Stadium in time for the start of the 1976 season.

NEW YORK GIANTS

Unfortunately, they encountered more delays, which forced them to work literally around the clock and well into the fall of 1976 to ready the building.

In 1976, the Giants, who hoped to settle into their new home by Kickoff Weekend, faced being homeless for part of the season.

That prompted the NFL schedule makers to send the Giants on four straight road games to start the 1976 season while the state-of-the-art stadium was completed.

On October 10, 1976, Giants Stadium officially opened its doors for football. The Giants, who started that season 0–4, lost their first game in their new home to the Dallas Cowboys 24–14. The Giants' first win in their new building came on November 14, 1976, a 12–9 victory over the Washington Redskins.

Ironically, the Jets moved into red-and-blue themed Giants Stadium after their lease with Shea Stadium expired in 1983.

Giants Stadium officially closed its doors after the 2009 NFL season and was demolished during a six-month, $10 million project that ran from February to July 2010. It has since been replaced by the New Meadowlands Stadium—MetLife Stadium—an 82,500-seat venue shared by the Giants and Jets.

45

THE FIRST TIME

There's an old belief that you always remember your firsts in life—your first kiss, your first love, your first date, and yes, even your first heartbreak.

When it comes to the 1927 New York Football Giants season, their first-ever championship title, well, that might be the exception.

But why? Why do most football historians barely bat an eye when it comes to the Giants' impressive 11–1–1 record and their first-ever franchise championship?

There are many possible reasons, starting with the obvious, which is the 1927 season occurred over 90 years ago at a time when most modern-era football historians weren't even born. Also most of the men who were part of that season have since passed on.

There was also the fact that the Giants, like the NFL, were still in the infancy stage, the Giants just three years into its existence, the NFL five. As with all new sports entities, there was a degree of uncertainty as to whether the Giants and the NFL for that matter would have staying power over the long-haul, a concern backed by the low number of fans who initially attended the games.

Perhaps the biggest reason though, was that the Giants were still trying to find their footing in the New York sports landscape where baseball's New York Yankees, established in 1901, were the darlings of the tri-state area that year thanks to their impressive 110–44 record, and their eventual World Series sweep of the Pittsburgh Pirates.

Whatever the reason—and it might very well have been a combination of all of the above—Tim Mara's scrappy football Giants did some good things in that 1927 season.

According to the website Pro Football Reference, the 1927 Giants outscored opponents 197–20 in 13 games played, unofficially boasting the NFL's top-ranked defense and second-best scoring offense (behind the Cleveland Browns).

If that wasn't impressive enough, 10 of the Giants' 11 wins were shutouts, with the two exceptions coming against the Chicago Cardinals (28–7) on November 20, and then a week later against the Chicago Bears (13–7) on December 4.

As for star power, well, the Giants didn't exactly lack in that department. Under first-year head coach Earl Potteiger, the football Giants fielded future Hall of Fame players such as tackles Cal Hubbard, then in his rookie season and the only man to be voted to both the Football and Baseball Halls of Fame (the later for his work as a baseball umpire); and Steve Owen, a captain on that team who, following his career as a player, became the franchise's head coach from 1930 to 1953.

A game ball from the Giants' 1927 season, their first-ever championship season. The team went 11–1–1 that year under head coach Earl Potteiger. (Giants artifact from the Legacy Club in MetLife Stadium)

Other members of that team who would be enshrined in the Hall of Fame as members of other teams included tackle Wilber "Pete" Henry, who at 250 pounds was thought to be the biggest player of his time; and halfback Joe Guyon, who caught a touchdown pass that gave the Giants the win over the Chicago Bears to give the Giants a 9–1–1 record that led to that season's championship.

Another possible reason the Giants first-ever championship season flew under the radar might have been how the championships back then were decided. Unlike the new 14-team playoff format that cumulates in the spectacle known as the Super Bowl, there was no postseason playoffs until the 1933 season to decide the annual champion.

Instead, the league championship was to be awarded to the team with the best won-loss record, a somewhat controversial method given that there would season-ending ties and no consistent structure to break those ties.

Fortunately, the 1927 Giants didn't have to worry about that thanks to their 11–1–1 record, the best of the 12-team league at the time.

* * *

Whatever the reason for the football Giants having to compete for their share of the New York sports market's kudos, there's no denying their firepower during their first-ever championship season.

They began the campaign with an 8–0 shutout of the Providence Steam Rollers on September 25, the only points in the game scored in the second quarter by the visiting Giants.

In their second game, the Giants, also the road team, ended up in a scoreless tie with the Cleveland Bulldogs only to improve to 2–0–1 the following week with a 19–0 thumping of the Pottsville Maroons, against whom they took a 3–0 lead in the second quarter before piling it on with 16 points over the second half.

The Giants suffered their only loss of that season in a rematch with the Bulldogs, who shut them out 6–0 in front of the Giants home crowd at the Polo Grounds.

From that point on in the season, it was all Giants, as they would score no less than 13 points in their remaining games while allowing opponents to score just 14 total points. That streak began with a 13–0 road win against the Frankfort Yellow Jackets in which the Giants did all their scoring in the second half to improve to 3-1-1.

The next week, October 23, the Giants hosted the Yellow Jackets at the Polo Grounds, stomping all over their opponent 27-0 in front of 15,000 people.

On October 30, also at the Polo Grounds, the Giants scored eight points each in the first and fourth quarters to top the Maroons 16-0. They followed that up with a 21-0 home-game shutout against the Duluth Eskimos, a game in which the Giants scored in every quarter except the third.

The following week, the Giants rolled over the Steam Rollers 25-0. They would then give up their first points to an opponent that season since October 16, when the Chicago Cardinals managed to score seven points in a 28-7 Giants win.

New York also handled the Chicago Bears the following week, 13-7, allowing what would be the last points yielded to an opponent that season.

On December 4, the Giants got touchdowns in the first and third quarters to top football's New York Yankees 14-0. In the season finale, the Giants repeated their shutout against the Yankees, this time capping a 13-0 road win by doing all their scoring in the second half of the game.

Individually, the Giants scoring leaders included fullback Jack McBride, who scored 57 points (six touchdowns, two field goals, and 15 extra points), and tailback Hinkey Haines and wingback Mule Wilson, each of whom scored 36 points (six touchdowns).

Overall, the Giants' 1927 record was their best mark in the 13-game season format. And although their first championship might not have come with all the fanfare and spoils that one finds in the modern era, it's still pretty special.

46

THE GAME THAT PUT THE NFL ON THE MAP

Very rarely does a start-up business take off to new heights in its first year.

The Giants, who, despite having a winning season record in five out of their first six years of existence (the 1927 season bring their first championship), were still struggling to build a following due to questions concerning the game's quality being on par with college football.

And why should anyone at the time have believed in the quality of the NFL when college teams like Notre Dame had established a dynasty under legendary coach Knute Rockne?

The Giants, in their quest to find an audience, actually did so through their participation in a charity game held shortly after the 1929 Stock Market Crash, a game that many football historians believe helped put the NFL on the map.

The charity game concept started to take shape when New York mayor Jimmy Walker established his Official Committee for the Relief of the Unemployed and the Needy.

Wanting to stage a fundraising event that would draw a sizeable crowd, Walker reached out to Giants owner Tim Mara to see if he'd be willing to have his team play for charity.

Mara, who had grown up in hard times and who was a compassionate man, was more than willing to oblige. "You name the team, and we'll play them," he is said to have told Walker.

Initially, a small committee consisting of Mara, Walker, and a group of local sportswriters contemplated pairing the Giants with another NFL franchise.

The concern, however, was whether such a matchup would draw.

After more discussion, a sportswriter came up with the idea of matching the Giants against Notre Dame.

While there was some intrigue over the potential opponent, there was also some trepidation, specifically the Giants' potential embarrassment if they were to lose to a college team.

Such an occurrence, it was feared, would set the struggling NFL back in its quest to gain traction among football fans and would validate the widespread belief that college football was indeed of a higher quality.

Willing to take that chance, Mara gave the go-ahead to get the ball rolling. Sportswriter Dan Daniel, named by Walker as the chairman of the committee tasked to organize the game, reached out to Rockne, holder of a career 105–12–5 head coaching record at Notre Dame, to see if the Fighting Irish would be interested in being the Giants opponent for a game scheduled December 14, 1930.

Rockne loved the concept and agreed to the game but had concerns about having the Irish play back-to-back games on different coasts despite the week in between.

Instead of bringing his current roster in for the matchup, he proposed assembling a team of Notre Dame All-Stars from the past.

"I'll even coach 'em!" Rockne was said to have declared.

With both sides having agreed to that plan, Rockne reunited the famed "Four Horsemen"—left halfback Jim Crowley, fullback Elmer Layden, right halfback Don Miller, and quarterback Harry Stuhldreher—for the game. He also managed to recruit five of the "Seven Mules," the Horsemen's offensive line, and put together a roster that was the very definition of a "dream team."

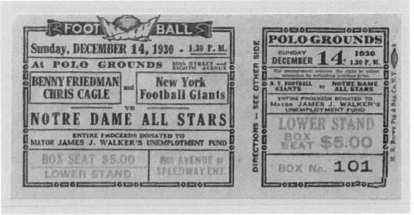

A game ticket from the Giants-Notre Dame All-Stars event that helped stimulate interest in the National Football League. (Artifact shown is from the Pro Football Hall of Fame)

If there were any concerns about the quality of football Rockne would get from his former players, many of whom were several years removed from playing the game, those were quickly put to rest.

"At first, I thought these fellows might not be able to put up a good game after several years' layoff," Rockne told reporters after concluding four days of practice before the charity game.

"But when I got to South Bend, I found them a little older but was pleasantly surprised to see the way they handled the ball. This is not going to be merely a spectacle but a real game."

Ticket sales for the game at the Polo Grounds started to boom, with field seats going as much as $100 each.

When his Fighting Irish hit the field on game day, and he saw just how big the Giants players were, Rockne was said to have been taken back. Still, he didn't let his confidence waver, telling his team that the Giants were "heavy, but slow" and urging his players to score quickly to gain the upper hand.

"Go out there, score two or three touchdowns on passes in the first quarter," Rockne told his players, "And then defend—and don't get hurt."

Playing in front of an estimated 50,000 fans on a frigid winter day, the Fighting Irish, giants of college football, were no match for the NFL Giants of New York.

The Giants took a 2–0 lead on the opening drive after dropping Stuhldreher in the end zone for a safety.

By halftime, the Giants were up 15–0, getting touchdowns from quarterback Benny Friedman in the second quarter.

Rockne, who bumped into Giants team president Harry March as the teams returned to their respective locker rooms at halftime, was dumbfounded over the Giants' dominance.

"I came here to help a charity," Rockne was said to have told March. "You are making us look bad. Slow up, will you? I don't want to go home and be laughed at. Lay off next half."

The Giants accommodated by sitting Friedman and some other starters in the second half, but even that wasn't enough.

New York iced the game on a 22-yard touchdown reception by Glenn Campbell from quarterback Hap Moran in the third quarter to wrap up a 22–0 win.

The score, though, only told part of the story of the Giants domination. Notre Dame never made it into Giants territory and managed just one first down the entire game.

The win not only put an end the misconception that the quality of pro football wasn't on par with that of the college game, but it also generated more than $115,000 for Mayor Walker's Committee for the Relief of the Unemployed and the Needy, making the charity the real winner of the day.

47

ODELL

In the 90-plus-year history of the New York Giants franchise, the team has had numerous talents, and personalities.

But not since the days of the legendary linebacker Lawrence Taylor (1981–93) have the Giants had that combination of an "all-world" talent and a larger-than-life personality until receiver Odell Beckham Jr walked through the doors as the Giants' first-round pick in the 2014 draft.

"He brings a lot to the table for us," then-general manager Jerry Reese said after the Beckham pick. "He's a dynamic receiver, dynamic punt returner, and a dynamic kickoff returner. You are getting a guy that can score touchdowns in three different ways for you. There's no way we would pass him up."

Perhaps Reese wanted to make sure that the Giants' West Coast-orientated offense being installed by new offensive coordinator Ben McAdoo got off to a good start and that Beckham, out of LSU, would be a perfect fit for the scheme.

Unfortunately, Beckham immediately missed parts of the spring and summer with a hamstring strain that was so bad that it cost him the first four weeks of the regular season.

When Beckham did return, it wasn't very long until the team's fan base, craving some excitement following two seasons with no playoffs, fell in love.

By Week 9 of the 2014 campaign, Beckham had recorded his first 100- yard receiving performance, catching eight balls for 156 yards. He would follow that up with a 108-yard receiving performance.

Then it all broke wide open for Beckham on a single play.

"The Catch," as it became known—not to be confused with David Tyree's helmet catch in Super Bowl XLII, Mario Manningham's acrobatic catch along the sideline in Super Bowl XLVI, or even Hakeem Nicks' "Hail Mary" touchdown reception in the 2011 NFC Division playoff game against the Packers—ended all grumbling about Beckham being the latest in a long line of recent Giants first-round draft picks destined for the proverbial "one-and- done" contract.

That single reception in a 31–28 home loss to the Cowboys during that November 23 *Sunday Night Football* broadcast literally put the Giants—and Beckham in particular—on the map.

Almost instantly, Beckham transformed from being just another football player into a globally recognizable brand—a player who would later sign the richest shoe deal in sports history with Nike, and whose every move on and off the field was scrutinized on a level on par with that of a Hollywood A-lister.

Beckham, for his part, seemed to enjoy the growing attention, at least in the beginning. He became something of a fashion icon; his unique pregame footwear always a hit among those who watched him delight the pregame crowds with his one-handed catches.

A passionate sort who sometimes let his emotions overrule common sense, it was Beckham's unparalleled intensity for the game that would ultimately prove to be his undoing in New York.

Whereas Beckham should have been revered for his football accomplishments, his (mostly) unreported charitable endeavors, and his genuine affection for the fans, that very same passion, which drove him to the unpredictable and the spontaneous, often overshadowed the good.

Beckham's more troublesome incidents are well-documented—the December 2014 brawl against the Rams which his alleged pre-game behavior was said to have provoked, the December 2015 run-in with Carolina Panthers cornerback Josh Norman that led to a one-game suspension, the distraction caused by his decision to spend an off-day partying in Miami before the Giants 2016 Wild Card game against the Packers, and his angry outburst following his forgettable performance in the Wild Card game in which he put a hole in the wall outside of the visitor's locker room at Lambeau Field.

As Beckham continued making headlines for the wrong reasons, team president John Mara was becoming more and more concerned with Beckham's behavior, so much so that after the receiver simulated a urinating dog following a touchdown reception in a losing effort against the Eagles in 2017, an unhappy Mara sat Beckham down for a heart-to-heart conversation.

PLAXICO

Long before Odell Beckham Jr created headaches for the Giants, another wildly talented receiver by the name of Plaxico Burress created a great deal of consternation.

Burress, who provided franchise quarterback Eli Manning with a legitimate No. 1 receiving threat, delivered two 1,000-yard seasons (2005 and 2007) and two seasons in which he scored double-digit touchdowns (2006 and 2007) in addition to catching the game-winning touchdown in Super Bowl XLII.

Along the way, Burress' transgressions began to detract from his football accomplishments. He was reportedly fined thousands of dollars for violating team rules throughout his Giants tenure. Early in the 2008 season, he was suspended by head coach Tom Coughlin for one game after missing a practice after failing to notify the team he was unable to attend.

Burress' biggest misstep would come later that year when he accidentally shot himself in the leg in a Manhattan nightclub. Burress' gun, which was unregistered in the State of New York, became a big focus of the story when then-New York City mayor Michael Bloomberg vowed to have Burress prosecuted to the fullest extent of the law on an illegal weapons possession charge.

The Giants, who had gone 11–1 in their defense of their 2007 Super Bowl championship, were able to win that weekend's game at Washington to advance to 12–1 without Burress.

As details of the accident continued to come out, the Giants had reached the end of their rope with Burress.

The receiver was fined and suspended for the remaining four games of that season, the Giants going 1–3 over that period.

And although the Giants had done enough before that to earn a playoff berth, they were one-and-done against the Eagles in the divisional round.

Burress would go on to serve 22 months of a two-year jail sentence. After his release from prison and in subsequent media appearances, a more mature and reflective Burress, who resumed his career with the Jets and then Steelers, realized what his immaturity had cost him.

In an open letter written to the 2017 NFL draft class published by The Players' Tribune, Burress said, "I'm living proof that it doesn't matter who you are or what you've done. You could have it all—you could be living the dream— and then one stupid decision can change everything.

"If you take one thing away from reading this," his letter continued, "I think it should be that you're not as special as you think you are. You're not more important than anybody else just because you play in the NFL."

Still, there was hope Beckham would mature, especially after he rehabbed from a devastating season-ending broken ankle suffered five games into the 2017 season. In his first public comments after that injury, Beckham claimed he had a newfound appreciation for being able to play a game he loved.

Throughout his struggles with the "Fame Monster," it is important to remember that Beckham's greatest redeemable qualities were that he was well-liked by his teammates and was genuinely a good person who never got in trouble with the law.

So when head coach Pat Shurmur and general manager Dave Gettleman were hired in 2018, Beckham, whose previous locker room antics were starting to wear thin and of whom Reese once said needed "to grow up," was given a clean slate.

That clean slate was important to Beckham, who at the time was entering the option year of his rookie deal and who was seeking a new contract that would make him the highest-paid player at his position.

Shurmur, intent on making the relationship work with Beckham, put a lot of focus and effort into building a two-way communication channel, even going so far as to personally visit with the mercurial receiver in Los Angeles where Beckham trained in the off-season.

The plan to build a relationship with Beckham seemed to work, at least in the beginning. Beckham, never much of a fan of the NFL off-season program which placed limitations on what players could do, was more of a frequent presence that year at the Giants' program even though he wasn't cleared physically to engage in football activities.

And Beckham even seemed willing to prove himself and wait a little while longer for his big payday.

Behind the scenes, there was some reluctance within the organization to give Beckham a new deal so soon. For starters, all they had to judge on as far as the effectiveness of Beckham's rehab were a handful of training camp practices that had minimal to no contact.

There was also an early year incident in which Beckham appeared in a blink-and-you'll-miss-it controversial video allegedly shot in a Paris hotel room in which some of the participants appeared to be engaged in questionable activities.

That video created even more headaches for Mara who, when he was asked by reporters about it blurted out that he was "tired" of answering questions about Beckham's off-field behavior.

Beckham did what he could football-wise in the spring and during training camp, though he did not play in preseason games. And with team hoping that Shurmur had built enough of a relationship with Beckham to where if something happened, the coach could douse any potential firestorms, the Giants signed Beckham to a five-year contract extension worth up to $95 million, with approximately $65 million in guaranteed money.

Not long after inking his new deal, Beckham met the press, proudly wearing a Giants polo shirt for the cameras and pointing to the Giants logo as he spoke about his gratitude and how he wanted to be a Giant.

The honeymoon, though, would be short-lived.

After the Giants began the 2018 season with a 1–4 start, Beckham, without the knowledge of the Giants public relations staff, gave an explosive interview to ESPN, who had arranged for rap star (and Beckham friend) Lil Wayne to be present.

During that wide-ranging interview, Beckham spoke candidly, dropping bombshell after bombshell that likely made the team's brass cringe.

For instance, he wouldn't rule out quarterback Eli Manning as being a cause of the Giants offensive struggles. He also voiced unhappiness with his role in the offense, opining that he was being held back.

Perhaps the most damning statement made by Beckham, who just a few weeks earlier had been given his contract extension, was when he avoided answering a question about whether he was happy in New York.

Shurmur, Gettleman, and Mara were all said to be livid with Beckham's lapse in judgment. Shurmur was, in fact, so upset with Beckham that according to a FOX Sports report, the head coach not only fined the receiver, he also demanded Beckham stand before his teammates to "make things right."

Mara, whose patience with Beckham had become paper-thin by this point, told reporters later that month at the league meetings, "I wish he would create headlines by his play on the field as opposed to what he says and does off the field. I think he needs to do a little more playing and a little less talking."

As the Giants limped to their fifth losing season in the last six years—this one a 5–11 campaign—they did so without Beckham in the final four games due to the receiver having suffered a quad contusion.

But even that took on added drama.

After Beckham at one point opined that the team could make a run and somehow salvage a playoff berth despite their sluggish start, his extended absence from the lineup wasn't viewed favorably.

Not that it mattered from the Giants' perspective. After seeing the offense function just fine without Beckham—they scored 92 of their 362 points that season (25.4 percent)—a generational talent who at one time probably would have been untradeable regardless of the offer, suddenly seemed no longer worth the headaches he was causing.

On March 13, 2019, the Giants in a blockbuster trade that also included sending edge rusher Olivier Vernon to the Browns for guard Kevin Seitler, also traded Beckham to the Cleveland for safety Jabrill Peppers, and the Browns' first- (No. 17 overall) and third-round (No. 95 overall) draft picks that became defensive lineman Dexter Lawrence II and edge rusher Oshane Ximines respectively.

Although the Giants initially claimed not to be actively shopping Beckham, Gettleman later admitted that he reached out to Brandon Beane, the Bills general manager, and his one-time colleague in Carolina to gauge Beane's interest in Beckham after the Bills had been unable to acquire then-Steelers receiver Antonio Brown.

Gettleman also confirmed that the Giants had discussions with the 49ers about Beckham, but in the end, the deal died on the vine when the 49ers refused to include the No. 2 overall pick in the 2019 draft and insisted that the Giants throw in their No. 6 pick as part of the package.

Gettleman, who earlier in the year insisted the team "didn't sign Beckham to trade him," told reporters that the decision to move Beckham was "purely a football business decision."

He further justified the move by pointing out that the Browns' offer represented exceptional value beyond what the Giants might have gotten had they franchised Beckham, and another team had signed him away.

Although he insisted it was all about value, Gettleman at times hinted that there were more layers to the decision.

"Obviously, there's a lot of stuff that factors in, but at the end of the day, for us to move Odell, the other team was going to have to knock it out of the park," he said. "You look at everything, but at the end of the day, it's really about football. We've got positions to address. This was about us having the ability to address multiple positions."

48

A CHAMPIONSHIP SHOWING

On January 25, 1987, the New York Giants beat the Denver Broncos 39–20 in Super Bowl XXI, winning the first-ever Super Bowl in team history and ending a postseason drought in which they hadn't won a championship title since 1956.

While that Super Bowl is forever etched in Giants lore, it was the NFC Championship title game on Sunday, January 11, 1987 at Giants Stadium against the Washington Redskins that convinced skeptics that the Giants were indeed a contender for Super Bowl immortality.

The Giants, 2–0 against Washington that season, had won the NFC East title despite Washington finishing with an identical 12–4 record (this thanks to the Giants holding the head-to-head tiebreaker).

With New York set to face Washington for only the second time in their postseason history, there was still some doubt that New York could get over this final hurdle to get to its first Super Bowl because no team had ever beaten Washington three times in one season.

Another concern that made critics doubt the Giants was that Washington, who hadn't posted a losing season since they finished 6–8 in 1970, had posted double-digit wins every year since 1983.

Impressive? Yes.

Intimidating?

As defensive tackle Leonard Marshall recalled years later, "Hell no!"

* * *

For all the critical calls made in that game by both sides, perhaps none was more significant than the coin toss. Hours before kickoff, Giants head coach Bill Parcells walked onto the field and tossed a piece of paper into the air to gauge the strengths of the wind.

Right then, he decided that if the Giants won the coin toss, they would kick off and take the wind.

When it came time for the coin toss, the Giants sent one team captain—middle linebacker Harry Carson—to midfield to meet Washington's six captains.

Washington, as the visitor, called heads. When the silver coin landed on the turf, it was tails. Carson informed referee Pat Haggerty of Parcells' instructions, which meant that Washington would have to face the wind in the first and third quarters.

The coin toss was so critical that after the game, Washington head coach Joe Gibbs admitted it was one of the deciding factors in the game.

Also, Washington quarterback Jay Schroeder, who at the time set a playoff record with 50 pass attempts, struggled to throw the ball, and punter Steve Cox had two punts shortened by the 20-plus mph winds.

"THAT WAS OUR TICKER-TAPE PARADE"

For decades, the City of New York has thrown ticker-tape parades honoring heroes from all walks of life, all corners of industry and entertainment, and all parts of the country.

But in 1986, New York City Mayor Edward Koch declared that if the Giants were to become the tri-state area's first Super Bowl Champions since the Jets made good on quarterback Joe Namath's January 1969 guarantee to upset the Baltimore Colts in Super Bowl III, there would be no ticker-tape parade down the Canyon of Heroes.

Koch, thought to be still bitter over the Giants move from the Big Apple to the Meadowlands in 1976, was said to have considered the Giants as a "foreign team" and hence not worth the estimated $500,000 expense that came with hosting a ticker-tape parade down the Canyon of Heroes.

"Let them have a parade in Moonachie," Koch said, referring to the small borough just to the north of the Meadowlands Sports Complex.

In the end, Koch backtracked when American Express offered to pick up the tab for the city to honor the Giants if they won the Super Bowl.

However, the Giants rejected Koch's offer after witnessing what happened as the NFC Championship Game against Washington wound down.

With about three and a half minutes left in the game, the Giants fans, many who would go on to stay until the game clock read zero, began tearing up any paper they could find. With the wind continuing to swirl

The first of Cox's two wind-affected punts came after Washington went three-and-out on the opening drive. He hit the ball 23 yards out of bounds, giving the Giants first-and-10 on the Washington 47-yard line.

Although the Giants had the wind at their back, they relied mostly on the legs of running back Joe Morris, who picked up 17 yards on three carries, including a first-down conversion, to set up a 47-yard field goal by kicker Raul Allegre for a 3–0 lead.

On Washington's ensuing possession, they again went three-and-out, but this drive was especially painful when Schroeder failed to hit receiver Gary Clark, Washington's regular-season receiving yardage leader, on a deep ball over the middle that had he caught, would have put the ball at the Giants' 35-yard line.

---

around the stadium, they created a shower of confetti that filled the sky and filtered down to the field where the jubilant Giants were celebrating their first Super Bowl berth.

For many of the players, that single moment remains one they will never forget.

"That Championship Game was almost as satisfying as the Super Bowl because that was our ticker-tape parade," said receiver Phil McConkey, who contributed five punt returns for 27 yards in that game.

"The memory of the NFC Championship Game will forever be in my mind," kicker Raul Allegre added. "When we won, and everybody tore up their programs, and the confetti started raining down—that was very special to be a part of."

Defensive lineman Leonard Marshall agreed. "There was confetti everywhere, and the people were going nuts because the Giants were going to the Super Bowl. That was a powerful moment for me because I had never won a championship in college, so I wanted to soak all that in as long as I could."

The Giants, having had a taste of what a true Big Blue celebration might be like, issued a statement after the NFC Championship Game to settle the matter regarding where their celebration would be held if they were to win Super Bowl XXI.

"The only logical place for a Giants celebration is here at Giants Stadium in the New Jersey Sports Complex," the statement read, ending the two-state argument over who was better suited to host the eventual world champions.

Cox's second punt of the game wasn't much better than his first. This one went 27 yards and stayed in bounds, where Phil McConkey downed it at the Washington 38-yard line.

The Giants began to chip away at the yards but nearly saw the drive stall when a holding penalty was called on center Bart Oates to turn a third-and-10 into a third-and-20.

Quarterback Phil Simms, working from the shotgun, found receiver Lionel Manuel for 25 yards, giving the Giants first-and-10 from the Washington 11-yard line.

But the Giants, despite the fresh set of downs, would have illegal motion called against fullback Maurice Carthon which turned a third-and-5 from the 6-yard line into a third-and-10 from the 11.

No matter as Simms found Manuel in the middle of the end zone for a 10–0 lead in the first quarter.

"We knew we had to get some points on the board," Simms told reporters after the game, adding that the conditions were the windiest he had ever seen at Giants Stadium. "We made a few plays in tough situations, and that was the difference."

Although there would be no more scoring that quarter, the wind continued to mess with Washington. Schroeder tried to hit Clark again on a deep sideline pass coming on third-and-short, a pass that had it been completed, would have moved the ball from Washington's 37 to, at minimum, the Giants' 30-yard line.

This time, despite the ball being on the money, Clark, who had beaten Giants cornerback Elvis Patterson by a good five yards, dropped the pass, and Cox's third punt into the wind traveled only 24 yards.

"We lost the game in the first quarter with field position," Schroeder said after the game. "What we needed to do was get a couple of first downs to get out of our end, and we didn't do that."

Schroeder admitted that the windy conditions were a factor, saying, "The ball got up in the air and took off. It got blown away."

In the second quarter with the wind now against them, the Giants threw the ball just three times, relying on their running game to move the chains. Morris ran the ball seven times for 34 yards, including a 1-yard touchdown with 8:04 elapsed in the second quarter in what would be the final points either side would score that day.

Although Washington now had the wind at their backs in the second quarter, it didn't matter as the Giants defense—and in particular, linebacker Carl Banks—took over.

On Washington's four possessions in that quarter, they went three-and-out on three.

The closest Washington came to scoring came with about 10 minutes left in the second quarter when kicker Jess Atkinson attempted a 52-yard field goal. However, the snap from long snapper Jeff Bostic short-hopped its way to Schroeder, the holder, and Banks, who finished with nine tackles and was a nuisance to Schroeder practically all day, recovered the loose ball at the Washington 49-yard line.

When the clock read all zeros, the Giants' 17–0 win, which some considered payback for a 28–0 drubbing Washington had administered to the Giants in the 1943 divisional playoffs, accomplished something no other team had done before them.

They beat Washington three times in a single season.

"We weren't cocky, and we weren't arrogant," defensive end George Martin, who had two solo tackles and one of the four sacks on Schroeder, said.

"We were just good."

49

TOM COUGHLIN RESIGNS

With the Giants at a crossroad following yet another losing season in 2015, the circumstances staring John Mara in the face were eating away at him.

Mara, like his father Wellington, always hoped that when the time came to part with longtime employees, it would occur under the very best of circumstances.

Unfortunately, the happy ending Mara wanted for one of his most cherished and most significant contributors in his decades-long tenure as team president was not to be.

Head coach Tom Coughlin and quarterback Eli Manning, winners of two Super Bowl championships, could have built a dynasty in New York.

Unfortunately, what Coughlin and Manning didn't have was a sustained lifeline of quality personnel to ensure continuity after Super Bowl XLVI.

The drafts, in particular, were a problem. While some draft picks such as running back David Wilson and defensive back Chad Jones didn't pan out due to injuries, the Giants saw an alarming number of high-risk high- reward gambles by then-general manager Jerry Reese flop.

As the roster's depth began to take a hit, the Giants' quality of play began to decrease. And while Coughlin continued to fight, his skeptics began to wonder if perhaps he had lost his mojo.

After the Giants finished their fourth straight season out of the playoffs, and their third in a row without a winning record, something had to give.

That something was Coughlin's resignation.

"It was not contentious," Mara would later say of the meeting he and Steve Tisch had with Coughlin. "All good things come to an end at some point in time."

Yet when Mara took to the podium to address the media, he, at times, sounded conflicted.

"I asked him would he consider staying on in some capacity," Mara said in his opening remarks less than 24 hours after the announcement of Coughlin's resignation.

"I don't want to let all that knowledge walk out the door.... Let's face it; he brings a unique perspective. He knows our team as well as anybody. He knows the league as well as anybody. There may be some capacity in which he could help us.

"This is not a situation where we wanted to see him walk out the door.

We want him to stay involved because of everything he has brought to this organization, everything he could still possibly do at some point in the future."

Those comments seemed to contradict Mara's earlier sentiments about all good things eventually coming to an end.

Years later, when asked about the decision, Mara still sounded conflicted, admitting that Coughlin's decision to resign was still difficult.

"There comes a point in time where all good things come to an end," Mara said, repeating his words spoken at Coughlin's farewell press conference. "Steve [Tisch] and I felt like we were not progressing at that point, and the players needed to hear a different voice."

The move by Coughlin to walk away raised a few eyebrows.

This, after all, was a tough, gritty head coach who didn't know the meaning of the word "quit."

So why, after enduring four years of missing the playoffs, would Coughlin walk away at that point rather than help the organization out of its mire?

All signs pointed to the direction the roster was taking.

Kevin Gilbride, who worked as Coughlin's offensive coordinator, spoke about how, in later years, there was frustration over the lack of progress in replenishing some of the talent, most notably pointing to the offensive line when the Super Bowl winning group of 2007–10 had started to age.

With no quality replacements in the pipeline, quarterback Eli Manning's play began to suffer. Once a gunslinger who would wait patiently for opportunities to develop down the field, Manning morphed into a shell-shocked version of himself as he often had to run for his life behind patchwork offensive lines.

And with that, one of Manning's biggest flaw—his inability to extend plays with his mobility like Aaron Rodgers of Green Bay was known for—was exposed, creating growing frustration among a fan base over the man they once adored.

In a 2018 radio interview with Amani Toomer and Dan Schwartz for the *Going' Deep* podcast, Gilbride, in trying to defend the growing criticism of Manning at the time, provided a glimpse into what appeared to be a difference of opinion between the front office and the coaching staff regarding personnel.

"Back in 2009, I started to argue that the line was getting old and 2010 we were getting beat up, we were still winning because we were still good enough," Gilbride said. "In 2011 even when we won the Super Bowl, there were multiple guys getting hurt and banged up, and by 2012 we went 9–7, but we were hanging on by dear life.

"When 2013 happened, there were six different starters at running back, three different at right guard, four different at center, three at left guard. That stuff's been going on for a while now."

Gilbride, who had been on Coughlin's original Giants coaching staff assembled in 2004, voluntarily retired amidst rumors that the Giants were looking to get rid of him after the offense had finished 28th overall (307.5 yards per game).

Before Gilbride announced his retirement, Coughlin, according to a New York Daily News report, was prepared to dig his heels in against the "suggestion" that he move on from Gilbride.

Coughlin himself, in an interview with WFAN radio not long after the 2013 season ended, vehemently defended Gilbride as a coach, further lending credence to the notion that moving on from Gilbride was not an idea he endorsed.

"To think that there's any one individual that is responsible for the circumstances that we found ourselves in, that's crazy," he said.

"Kevin Gilbride is an excellent football coach. He is an excellent teacher and communicator. His players do respond to him. He works very, very hard at his trade."

Coughlin, who interviewed one-time Giants assistant coach Mike Sullivan and Green Bay assistant coach Ben McAdoo to replace Gilbride, ultimately went with McAdoo, touted as an up-and-coming offensive mind.

The hire, though, was curious for several reasons. First, unlike Sullivan, who had experience as an NFL offensive coordinator, McAdoo did not.

But more importantly was the fact that McAdoo came from a West Coast offensive system, a system that was a stark change of direction for what Coughlin had run throughout his career.

"ELI, IT'S NOT YOU"

Football players aren't supposed to cry in public. But Eli Manning, a normally stoic quarterback who at times left people wondering if he was human given how well he hid his emotions, didn't care who saw his tears as he watched the only NFL head coach he ever had say goodbye.

Manning sat in the second row of the Quest Diagnostics Training Center auditorium, his eyes fixated on the man who helped shape his career as a potential Hall of Fame quarterback as Tom Coughlin was delivering his farewell address to a gathering of staff, media, and players.

Manning, who, with Coughlin, won two Super Bowls in the 12 years they worked together, has always been the first player to point the finger at himself when things haven't gone well. So it was no surprise that hours before it became official that the Giants and Coughlin were officially divorcing, Manning gave an impassioned plea on Coughlin's behalf.

"I think he's done a great job, and he definitely has not failed," Manning said. "I feel that we as players failed him by not playing to the level that we could."

As he spoke, Manning struggled to hold back his tears as he recalled the team's earlier—and final—meeting with Coughlin.

"It was [emotional]," he said, catching his quivering lip. "The meeting today was tough."

Not surprisingly, Manning insisted that he wanted Coughlin back for a 13th season, reiterating that the Giants' failures were on the players and not Coughlin.

"We didn't get the job done," insisted Manning.

He was asked if he approached ownership to lobby for Coughlin's return.

"The Maras and Tisches know how I feel about Coach Coughlin and the respect I have for him," Manning said. "He's a great coach to play for. I learned so much from him from an early age when I got here 'til right now."

Coughlin would also make one more significant change to his coaching staff after the 2014 season when he replaced defensive coordinator Perry Fewell with fan-favorite (and the architect of the 2007 Super Bowl championship defense) Steve Spagnuolo.

Despite these changes, the results stayed the same.

Regardless of his words, on January 4, 2016, the Giants announced that Coughlin, whose 12 seasons made him the second longest-tenured head coach in franchise history behind Steve Owen (22 years) was resigning.

During the head coach's farewell press conference—an unprecedented move by the team for an outgoing head coach that wasn't retiring—Manning could no longer hold back his emotions.

Sitting with members of the Coughlin family and some teammates past and present who had played for Coughlin, Manning's lower lip began to quiver as he fought back the tears when Coughlin delivered a personal message to the franchise quarterback of whom he considered another son.

"He thinks he's the reason," Coughlin said of Manning, referring to the team's four-year playoff drought that saw the team's record regress each season. "He's not the reason."

Coughlin then looked directly at Manning, his voice becoming more emphatic. "Eli, it's not you, it's not you—it's us," Coughlin said. "When we win, you guys win. When we lose, I lose. That's the way it is."

If those words weren't enough to open Manning's floodgates, Coughlin, who watched Manning grow from a wide-eyed rookie into a two-time Super Bowl MVP, then threw a vote of confidence to his now former quarterback, who was potentially facing the prospect of having to learn his third offense in four seasons.

"He can handle it all," Coughlin said. "He's done it before, and he'll handle it again. He's extremely bright. He's extremely competitive. He's what you want a son to be.

"He's going to be right in here in about two days starting to work on next year, just like he always does," Coughlin continued. "That's never going to change. God bless him for it."

Sure enough, Manning would waste little time in getting back to work after a short break, even though for the first time in his pro career, he would do so without Coughlin there to oversee things.

As the Giants' record continued to go backward, Coughlin had had enough. He met with Mara and Tisch less than 24 hours after the Giants finished a 6–10 season. Then on January 5, 2016, the team announced that the then 69-year-old Coughlin, after 12 seasons, was stepping down as head coach.

"I met with John Mara and Steve Tisch this afternoon, and I informed them that it is in the best interest of the organization that I step down as head coach," Coughlin said in a team-issued statement. "I strongly believe the time is right for my family and me and, as I said, the Giants organization."

When Coughlin walked out the door, he had delivered to the franchise a 110–93 record (including postseason)and two Super Bowl championships.

The Giants gave Coughlin a farewell press conference, fitting for a man who had not only delivered two Super Bowl championships but who joined Steve Owen as the only other head coach in franchise history to record 100 regular-season wins.

"That was a very difficult day for me personally, because I like and admire Tom so much," said Mara.

"He's exactly the type of person you want representing your organization because he has such high character and is such a good man. But you have to make tough decisions in this business, and that was probably one of the top two or three toughest ones that we ever made."

50

GOODBYE TO AN OLD FRIEND

When demolition crews pulled down the last remaining sections of the original Giants Stadium grandstand on the afternoon of June 28, 2010, the warm, inviting, and one-time state-of-the-art facility named for its first and longest tenant was no more.

No longer considered to be a competitive revenue generator despite a multi-million-dollar renovation to add luxury suites and club seats, the old Giants Stadium hosted its final football game on January 3, 2010, a 37–0 Jets win over the Cincinnati Bengals.

The rubble of the old Giants Stadium might be long gone, but if there was one thing the demolition and cleanup crews couldn't remove, it was the countless memories of the men who at some point in their professional football careers, called the building home.

Cornerback Mark Collins (1986–93), recalled the first time he set foot in Giants Stadium when he and his fellow rookies showed up for their first minicamp.

"When I first got drafted, and I came to the stadium and walked down the ramp into the tunnel, there was a big Giants helmet to the left, and I remember thinking to myself, 'Man, I'm here, I'm with the NFL!'" Collins said.

"And the stadium was huge—I had never seen a stadium that big before. Of course, coming from Cal State Fullerton, we never had a stadium like that. Our home games were at Anaheim Stadium, but that was a baseball field. But yeah, [Giants Stadium] was a fantastic building.

"And the thing is at that the old Giants Stadium, I think they were louder there then they are now for some reason. It just seemed more personable."

Linebacker Jessie Armstead (1993–01) and defensive end Osi Umenyiora (2003–12), agreed that there was nothing like the energy generated by the fans on game day.

"When you came into that stadium, the fans brought out the best out in you," Armstead said. "I feel like we were connected to the fans and that, regardless if we won or lost a game, we did it together."

"When we started doing the whole balling thing in '07, it was a little sick," Umenyiora remembered. "We've had some great games there, but that 12-sack game we had against Philadelphia [on September 30, 2007, with six sacks recorded by Umenyiora]—that crowd was just unbelievable. I'd never heard or seen anything like the way they were that day."

Defensive back Beasley Reece (1977–83) was a member of the Dallas Cowboys the year Giants Stadium opened and was there for the first-ever game played there.

Reece, now the CEO of the NFL Alumni Association, remembered being impressed by the newness of the building that would later become his home stadium the following season.

"It was a special day because they had a lot of celebrations going on because it was the first game for that stadium," he said, his voice growing excited as he recalled the memory.

"Everything was pristine—a state-of-the-art building for its time. I remember how we marveled at the space, and the freshness of the locker room and the lockers and the showers were spotless, and the fans were just amazing how excited they were to find their new seats and cheer on the G-men."

One memory that Reece still carries with him—reluctantly—from that game is that he became the first player to draw a penalty on the Giants Stadium field.

"Yeah, that was me," he admitted sheepishly. "I was a wide receiver back then and early in the game, [the officials] said—and I dispute it to this day—that I pushed off a cornerback to get free in a pass route. And so, I was the first player to have a flag thrown against him in that stadium; I'm the answer to a trivia question."

While there are many memorable moments the Giants were able to share with their fans in that building, for many players, it was the behind the scenes moments that stand out most when they think of the old building.

Linebacker Carl Banks (1984–92) used to marvel over how team patriarch Wellington Mara, even as he got on in years, would always come out to watch practice, even in the blustery cold weather.

"When we were out working on the Giants Stadium field," Banks recalled, "Mr. Mara was doing his laps around the field. He'd have on either a London Fog or Burberry coat and a fedora, and he never missed his laps."

For other players such as defensive end George Martin (1975–88), who in Week 12 of the 1986 season came up with a pick-six of Broncos quarterback John Elway's tipped pass that Martin ran down the sideline just in front of his team's bench, all the while trying to lateral the ball back to a pursuing Lawrence Taylor, his favorite memory of the old Giants Stadium was captured in a photograph that he still has proudly on display in his home.

"My fondest memory is of my father, who has since passed on, being in the corner of the stadium at back of the end zone up in the stands with myself in uniform and my son George in his arms—the three G's," Martin recalled.

"To see those three generations in that picture—my dad lived long enough to see his son become a professional athlete and to see his grandson—is something I'll never, ever forget."

Receiver Phil McConkey (1983–85, 1986–88) still bears the scars from what he said was one of his fondest memory of the old Giants Stadium.

"The first time I walked into Giants Stadium for a tryout, I remember being in a helmet, shorts on that AstroTurf. And I remember diving for balls with my elbows and knees exposed, and how I was a bloody mess for three days.

"The stadium was empty, but you've got the coaches out there, and you have a professional football helmet on, and I had to do everything I could to impress them because it was immensely important to me."

Kicker Raul Allegre (1986–91), who works as a Spanish-language commentator for ESPN, put his feelings about the old building into a column he wrote for the network's website a few years ago in which he bid farewell to the building he called "my old friend."

"I'm not a very good writer, but that's one of the best things that I've ever written," Allegre said.

The last of the team's equipment is loaded on a cart for removal from the Giants Stadium locker room the team had called home from midway through the 1976 season until 2009. (Copyright New York Football Giants)

In 2009, the building's final season, Allegre brought his son with him to show him where he used to work decades earlier.

"I showed him all the shortcuts and all the places that I used to go, and how we got from one point to another and the old locker room," Allegre said. "It was pretty special."

Team president John Mara said he had so many special memories of the old building, but the one that stood out the most came after the

Giants' 13–10 overtime win against the Cowboys in the 1981 regular-season finale to finish 9–7 and their first playoff berth since 1963.

"I was walking down with my father to the locker room after that game. The press box elevator was broken, so we had to walk down through the concourses to get to the locker room," Mara recalled. "Now that trip a few years ago would have been perilous because we had been poor for so long. To see how people were coming up to my father to tell him how happy they were and how revered my father was and how much people were talking about how they loved the team, that will always be one of the special memories I have of Giants Stadium."

Receiver Amani Toomer (1996–08) said his fondest memory was the sight before the 2000 NFC title game against the Minnesota Vikings.

A BUILDING FOR THE PEOPLE

Throughout its lifetime, Giants Stadium was much more than just the home of the Football Giants and, later on, the Jets. The building also hosted band competitions, college football, soccer, concerts, and other special events during its years.

Soccer legend Pele played the final game of his career on October 1, 1977, playing the first half of the match for the Santos FC, the Brazilian *futbol* club for whom he had achieved legendary status, and the rain-soaked second half for the New York Cosmos.

On October 5, 1995, Pope John Paul II presided over a special Catholic Mass attended by a then-record crowd of nearly 83,000 people.

And on September 25, 2005, a football game that was supposed to be played at the Superdome in New Orleans between the Giants and New Orleans Saints was moved to Giants Stadium after Hurricane Katrina displaced thousands of Bayou residents who sought shelter at the Superdome, the Saints' home field.

"I'll never forget like coming out and seeing all the towels waving, and then seeing L.T. (Lawrence Taylor) and all of the old Giants, and I was just like, 'Wow, this is great!' Like that was one of the best experiences I had playing at Giants Stadium."

Offensive lineman Rich Seubert (2001–10), who experienced the highs of seeing his wife and sons smiling down upon him from the family section when he'd run out to the field, and the lows of being carted off after suffering a spiral fracture of his leg in 2003, said that the old building matched the personality of the teams he played on.

"Downstairs where the locker room and meeting rooms were, it was gloomy, and there were no windows, so you'd be sitting in meetings, and you had no clue what it was like outside. You just were focused on what you were doing."

"The old Giants Stadium is kind of the way I was brought up and probably how most of the guys might say they were raised," he added.

"It wasn't anything special, but it got the job done."

[Postscript: Giant Honors]

Throughout their 95-year (and counting) history, the Giants have seen some extraordinary athletes (and even more extraordinary men) proudly represent the franchise since its founding.

As of 2020, the Giants have 22 players, coaches, and executives in the Pro Football Hall of Fame, with 10 additional men who spent a part of their respective lives with the team having been enshrined as members of other franchises.

In 2010, the Giants, as part of their move to the new Meadowlands Stadium (later renamed MetLife Stadium), established the Ring of Honor with a 30-man class that, in addition to players, included coaches and administrators. That number of honorees has since grown to 42 thanks to three more classes inducted, the most recent of which was in 2016.

The Giants have also retired 11 jersey numbers honoring 12 men (Ward Cuff and Y.A. Tittle both wore No. 14, with Tittle having requested and received that number even though it had already been retired years earlier).

Team president John Mara, in January 2020, announced that the club will add No. 10 (Eli Manning) and No. 92 (Michael Strahan) to the club's list of retired jersey numbers.

Here is the list of Giants who have been inducted into the Pro Football Hall of Fame as Giants (through 2020) and/or the team's Ring of Honor (through 2019).

Ernie Accorsi, General Manager (ROH 2016): Accorsi succeeded George Young as the team's general manager in 1998, holding the post through the 2006 season. During his tenure as the Giants general manager, the franchise won two division titles, four postseason berths and advanced to Super Bowl XXXV. Accorsi was also at the organization's helm for its most significant trade in history, that being the acquisition of quarterback Eli Manning from the San Diego Chargers.

Jessie Armstead, Linebacker (ROH 2010): A five-time Pro Bowl linebacker, Armstead, the last of the Giants' eighth-round picks in franchise history (the following year the NFL went to a seven-round format) recorded 100-plus tackles in his first five seasons in the league. In addition to his prowess on defense, Armstead was also a special-teams ace during his first three years with the team.

Morris (Red) Badgro, End (HOF, 1981): Badgro played six seasons at end for the Giants, leading the franchise to victory in the NFL's inaugural Championship Game. Badgro also scored the first touchdown in the league's Championship Game history on a 29-yard pass from Harry Newman in the second quarter and would tie for the NFL receiving title in 1934 with 16 receptions for 206 yards and one touchdown.

Carl Banks, Linebacker (ROH 2011): The third overall selection in the 1984 draft and, as of 2020, the last linebacker chosen by the Giants in the first round, Banks, currently a member of the team's broadcasting crew, was instrumental in the team's victories in Super Bowl XXI and XXV and was named to the NFL's 1980s All-Decade Team. In November 2019, Banks was named as one of the 25 semifinalists for the Pro Football Hall of Fame's Class of 2020, but didn't make the final cut.

Tiki Barber, Running Back (ROH 2010): A Giants' second-round pick in 1997, Barber's 10-year career ended with him as the franchise record- holder for career rushing attempts (2,217), season rushing attempts (357 in 2005); and rushing yards in both a career and season (10,449 and 1,860 in 2005 respectively). Barber also recorded a franchise-best 38 games rushing with 100 or more yards, and his 17,359 all-purpose yards (including postseason) still stands as the franchise's top mark.

Mark Bavaro, Tight End (ROH 2011): One of the greatest tight ends in team history, Bavaro was instrumental in the team's two Super Bowl championships (XXI and XXV). In the 1986 season leading up to the Giants' first-ever Super Bowl championship (XXI), Bavaro led the team with 66 receptions for 1,001 yards, becoming the only tight end in franchise history (through the 2019 season) to record 1,000 yards receiving in a season.

Al Blozis, Tackle (ROH 2010): Blozis played for the Giants for three seasons, his last game coming in the 1944 championship against the Green Bay Packers. Blozis then enlisted in the Army to help support military operations during World War II. He was deployed overseas to France and was tragically killed in France just six weeks later. Blozis' No. 32 jersey was retired in 1945.

Roosevelt "Rosey" Brown, Tackle (ROH 2010, HOF 1975): Brown, a 27th round draft pick who played for the Giants from 1953 to 1965, is regarded as one of the greatest "sleeper" picks of all time. A dominating, athletic offensive tackle who started for 13 straight seasons, Brown was named to the Pro Bowl nine times and was chosen all-NFL eight consecutive years. Because of his, well, "giant" size, Brown not only was a dominating force as a mobile offensive lineman, he also served as a defensive lineman in goal-line situations.

Harry Carson, Linebacker (ROH 2010, HOF 2006): Carson played his entire 13-year career for the Giants. He was voted to nine Pro Bowls, and during his prime, he was widely regarded as the best run-stopping linebacker in the league, leading a run defense that, between 1981–87, allowed opponents an average of 3.59 yards per rushing attempt. Over that period, Carson recorded 856 tackles, 627 of which were solo efforts.

Charlie Conerly, Quarterback (ROH 2010): Conerly played his entire Hall of Fame–worthy career (1948–61) with the Giants, whom he helped to win the 1956 Championship Game. Individually, Conerly, voted to two Pro Bowls (1950 and 1956), earned the NFL Rookie of the Year honors in 1948 and the Newspaper Enterprise Association's Most Valuable Player Award in 1959. Conerly's No. 42 was retired in 1962.

Tom Coughlin, Head Coach (ROH 2016): Initially the receivers coach on Bill Parcells' 1990 Super Bowl–winning staff, Coughlin left the Giants in 1991 for assignments at Boston College and the expansion Jacksonville Jaguars before returning "home" in 2004. At the team's helm for 12 seasons, Coughlin's 102 regular-season victories are second-most in franchise history behind Steve Owen's 151. Coughlin also coached the franchise's last two Super Bowl championship teams in the 2007 and 2011 seasons and led the Giants to three NFC East titles and five playoff berths.

Frank Gifford, Halfback/Fullback (ROH 2010, HOF 1977): Gifford was known as one of the most versatile backs in NFL history. He played for the Giants from 1952 to 1960 and from 1962 to '64, taking a short-term retirement in 1961 after suffering an injury. A first-round draft pick, Gifford became the first player in NFL history to be named to the Pro Bowl as a defensive back (in 1953) and in the following year as an offensive back. An eight-time Pro Bowler, Gifford was also a four-time first-team All-Pro honoree and was named the NFL Player of the Year in 1956 and a member of the Pro Football Hall of Fame's all-1950s Team. Gifford's No. 16 jersey was retired in 2000.

Pete Gogolak, Kicker (ROH 2010): Gogolak, who introduced the soccer-style kicking technique to the NFL, joined the Giants in 1966, becoming the first prominent player to leave the American Football League for the NFL. He finished his Giants career in 1974 as the Giants' highest-scoring player in franchise history (646 points) and the team record holder for field goals (126) and extra points (268) made.

Mel Hein, Center (ROH 2010, HOF 1963): Hein was named All- NFL for eight consecutive seasons and was the Most Valuable Player in 1938. An iron man who never missed a game at any level, Hein played in a then-record 15 seasons with the Giants, a mark later matched by quarterback Phil Simms and defensive end Michael Strahan, and then broken in 2019 by quarterback Eli Manning (16 seasons). Hein's No. 7 was retired in 1963.

Jim Lee Howell, Head Coach (ROH 2010): The Giants head coach from 1954 to 1960 led the franchise to three NFL Championship Games, including a 1956 triumph of the Chicago Bears. Howell finished his coaching career with a 55–29–4 record (including postseason), and would later move from the sideline to the front office as director of player personnel until he retired in 1981.

Cal Hubbard, Tackle (HOF 1963): Hubbard played for the Giants in 1927–28 and again in 1936. A charter member of the Pro Football Hall of Fame, Hubbard was named All-NFL from 1927 to 1933. As a member of the Giants, Hubbard contributed on defense and was instrumental in contributing to a defensive unit that allowed just 20 points in 1927 as the Giants won their first-ever NFL championship.

Sam Huff, Linebacker (ROH 2010, HOF 1982): A third-round draft pick in 1956, Huff delighted Giants fans with his play against the league's top running backs at the time, including Jim Brown of Cleveland, Rick Casares of Chicago, and Alan Ameche of Baltimore. Huff, who played in five Pro Bowls, was named the NFL's Outstanding Lineman in 1959 and was one of the pillars of a defense that helped steer the Giants toward championship title games in 1956, 1958, 1959, 1961, 1962, and 1963.

Dave Jennings, Punter (ROH 2011): A bright spot during the "Wilderness Years," Jennings, the Giants punter from 1974 to 1984, still holds the franchise records for most punts, career (931) and career yards (38,792). Jennings, who had a career-best 44.8-yard average in 1980, was also voted to four Pro Bowls.

John Johnson, Trainer (ROH 2015): Johnson served 60 years as the team's athletic trainer, having joined the franchise in 1948 and serving through his retirement in 2007.

Tom Landry, Defensive Back/Coach (HOF 1990): Landry was a Giants defensive back from 1950 to '55 and as an assistant coach from 1954 to '59. As a player, he was an integral part of the 1956 Giants championship team, a star-studded team that not only would produce several Hall of Fame players but also one of history's greatest coaching staffs, including offensive assistant Vince Lombardi and head coach Jim Lee Howell. Landry would later go on to become head coach of the Dallas Cowboys.

Alphonse (Tuffy) Leemans, Halfback/Fullback (ROH 2010, HOF 1978): Leemans played for the Giants in 1936–43 after having been personally scouted by Wellington Mara. A second-round pick in the league's inaugural NFL draft, Leemans led NFL rushers as a rookie in 1936 with 830 yards on 206 attempts. A two-time All-NFL selection, Leemans also recorded 442 receiving yards and threw 16 touchdown passes in his career. His No. 4 jersey was retired in 1940.

Vince Lombardi, Coach (HOF 1971): Although he would be best known for his work as head coach of the Green Bay Packers (1959–67), Lombardi began making a name for himself as an assistant coach in charge of the Giants' offense during the 1954–58 seasons. Lombardi's offense contributed to the team's NFL championship victory, a 47–7 drubbing of the Chicago Bears on December 30, 1956.

Jack Lummus, End (ROH 2015): Lummus, a two-way end, only appeared in nine games for the Giants during the 1941 season. Shortly after the Giants lost to the Chicago Bears in the NFL Championship Game, Lummus, enlisted in the U.S. Marines Corps Reserves to serve his country in combat during World War II. He was killed during the Battle of Iwo Jima when he accidentally stepped on a land mine and later succumbed to his injuries.

Dick Lynch, Defensive Back (ROH 2010): Acquired via trade from the Washington Redskins after the 1958 season, Lynch appeared in 97 regular-season games as a Giant and four NFL Championship Games. As a Giant, Lynch intercepted 37 regular-season passes and twice led the NFL in interceptions in 1961 and 1963. He also recorded seven career touchdowns, four coming on interceptions and three on fumble recoveries. After his playing career ended, Lynch became a Giants radio analyst, enjoying a 40-year career in the role. The last game he called was the Giants win over the New England Patriots in Super Bowl XLII.

Jack Mara, Co-owner (ROH 2010): Team founder Tim Mara's older son, Jack Mara served as the team's president for 31 years where was primarily responsible for the franchise's business operations. Mara was the driving force behind the team's move from the Polo Grounds to Yankee Stadium before the 1956 season. He negotiated a deal with New York Yankees co-owner and team president Dan Topping to ensure the Giants had a place to play long after the Polo Grounds deteriorated.

Tim Mara, Founder (ROH 2010, HOF 1963—Charter Enshrinee): The franchise founder who, for a reported $500 investment, introduced professional football to the city of New York, Mara survived competition from rival leagues and financial losses to build the Giants franchise and the NFL into solid entities.

Wellington Mara, Team Co-owner (ROH 2010, HOF 1997): The longtime patriarch and son of founder Tim Mara, Mara, who was one of the most influential team owners not just in the NFL but in all sports. Nicknamed "the Duke," Mara was part of a franchise that made 26 postseason appearances, including 18 divisional championships and six NFL championships, including Super Bowls XXI and XXV.

George Martin, Defensive Tackle (ROH 2010): Martin was initially an 11th-round draft pick who defied the odds to carve out an impressive 14-year career as a Giant. By the end of his career, he became just one of five Giants to appear in 200 games, joining quarterback Eli Manning, defensive end Michael Strahan, tight end Howard Cross, and long snapper Zak DeOssie for that distinction. Martin's six career touchdowns scored on defense was, at the time, an NFL record (since broken by Miami's Jason Taylor). Martin also caught a touchdown pass when he lined up at tight end in a game played in 1980 and recorded a huge 78-yard interception for a touchdown during a 1986 game against Denver the Giants won 19–16.

Joe Morrison, Back/End (ROH 2010): During his Giants career that spanned the 1959–72 seasons, Morrison played six different positions: fullback, halfback, flanker, tight end, split end, and defensive back. He finished his Giants career with 2,472 rushing yards and 18 touchdowns and caught 395 balls, the third-highest mark in franchise history, for 4,993 yards and 47 touchdowns. His No. 40 jersey was retired in 1972.

Steve Owen, Tackle/Head Coach (ROH 2010, HOF 1966): Owen began as a tackle for the Giants, where he was named as a four-time All-NFL tackle from 1926 to 1931. After sharing the head coaching duties with Benny Friedman in 1930, Owen became the franchise's full-time and lone head coach in 1931, a position he'd hold until 1953. He'd finish his regular-season coaching tenure 153–100–17 (the wins a franchise record) and would also win eight division and two NFL titles.

Bill Parcells, Head Coach (ROH 2010, HOF 2013): Parcells was named the head coach following the resignation of Ray Perkins after the 1982 season, and would go on to coach the franchise's first-ever Super Bowl championship team. Parcells would guide the Giants to a second world championship in 1990 before resigning due to health issues, but not before he recorded a 77–49–1 regular-season record, the third-most regular-season wins in team history, and a franchise-record eight postseason wins.

Andy Robustelli, Defensive End (ROH 2010, HOF 1971): Robustelli was acquired via trade with the Rams in 1956 and was a driving force in the franchise's championship title quest that season. After his playing career ended following the 1964 season, Robustelli had played in eight championship title games and seven Pro Bowls and had been named to the All-NFL team seven times, including five as a Giant. Robustelli missed only one game in his 14-year career and would eventually serve as a member of the Giants' front office as its director of operations.

Phil Simms, Quarterback (ROH 2010): The very first Giants draft choice of the George Young era, Simms' 513 passing yards on October

13, 1985, against the Cincinnati Bengals still stands as a franchise mark as of the end of the 2019 season. Simms, who finished his 15-year career 101–68 (.598) including postseason, is probably best remembered for his near-perfect outing in Super Bowl XXI when he completed 22 of 25 pass attempts (including all 10 of his second-half pass attempts) for 268 yards and three touchdowns. His No. 11 jersey was retired in 1995.

Chris Snee, Guard (ROH 2015): A second-round draft pick in 2004 (the same class which brought franchise quarterback Eli Manning), Snee immediately stepped into the lineup at right guard, a position he held for ten seasons. A four-time Pro Bowler and two-time Super Bowl champion, Snee started 101 consecutive regular-season games (plus seven in the postseason) from 2005 to 2011 before being forced from the lineup due to a concussion.

Michael Strahan, Defensive End (ROH 2010, HOF 2014): Strahan was a dominating force both against the run as well as on the pass rush. Besides being the picture of durability—he played in 136 straight games beginning in the 1996 season before tearing a pectoral muscle—Strahan's hustle earned him the respect of opponents across the league. He was chosen as the NFL Defensive Player of the Year in 2001 and was named the Giants' Most Valuable Player twice (in 1998 and 2001). Strahan currently holds the club's career sack record with 141.5 (Lawrence Taylor had 142 sacks, but the 9.5 sacks he accumulated in his rookie season weren't counted since sacks didn't become an official NFL statistic until 1982.) Strahan also remains the owner of the NFL single-season sack record set in 2001 when, in the final game of the regular season, he recorded his record-breaking 22.5 sack against the Packers.

Ken Strong, Halfback (ROH 2010, HOF 1967): Strong is one of the original "Swiss Army knives"—a player who did it all during his NFL career (blocking, running, passing, kicking, defense, and punting) with the Giants. He retired as the Giants' career scoring leader at the time with 324 points on 13 touchdowns, 35 field goals, and 141 extra points. He scored 17 points against the Chicago Bears in the 1934 NFL Championship Game—the "Sneakers Game." Strong's Giants career spanned 1933–35, 1939, and 1944–47. His No. 50 jersey was retired in 1947.

Lawrence Taylor, Linebacker (ROH 2010, HOF 1999): By the time Taylor, the Giants' first-round pick in 1981, retired after a 13-year career, he finished second in franchise history with 132.5 sacks, a total that doesn't include the 9.5 he had in his rookie season, before sacks were counted as an official NFL statistic (which would have put him as the franchise's sack leader). Taylor, the NFL Rookie of the Year winner in 1981, was selected to a record 10 consecutive Pro Bowls from 1981 to 1990 and was a unanimous selection for the NFL's All-1980s team and the NFL's Most Valuable Player in 1986. His No. 56 jersey was retired in 1994.

Preston Robert "Bob" Tisch, Co-owner (ROH 2010): The Giants co-owner who in 1991 acquired the 50 percent of the club previously held by Tim Mara, son of the late Jack Mara. Tisch was also a well-known philanthropist within the community who was beloved for his modest mannerisms and ability to connect with people with varied interests and backgrounds.

Y.A. Tittle, Quarterback (ROH 2010, HOF 1971): In the franchise's history of all-time great trades, the move to acquire 35-year-old Tittle from the San Francisco 49ers in exchange for guard Lou Cordileone ranks up there with the best of them. All Tittle did after coming east was lead the Giants to an Eastern Division Championship in 1961 before going on to set two passing records, 33 touchdown passes in a season (since broken) and an astonishing seven touchdown passes thrown in one game, the only quarterback in franchise history to accomplish that mark as of the 2019 season. Tittle, who shared jersey No. 14 with another Giants great (Ward Cuff) after Wellington Mara granted the quarterback's request for that number, saw his (and Cuff's) jersey, initially retired in 1946, retired again in 1965.

Amani Toomer, Receiver (ROH 2010): A second-round draft pick in 1996, Toomer spent his entire career with the Giants where he would go on to etch his name at the top of franchise records such as most pass receptions, career (668); most consecutive games with at least one pass reception (98, 1998–04); most receiving yards gained in a career (9,497); and most career receiving touchdowns in a career (54).

Justin Tuck, Defensive End (ROH 2016): Tuck was a third-round pick out of Notre Dame in 2005 who went on to become a two-time Pro Bowl defensive end and a defensive team captain. Appearing in 127 regular-season games, Tuck was instrumental in the Giants victories coming in Super Bowls XLII and XLVI, in which he sacked Patriots quarterback Tom Brady at least once in both games.

Emlen Tunnell, Defensive Back (ROH 2010, HOF 1967): Despite going undrafted, Tunnell turned into one of the all-time great Giants stories for his perseverance that began with him finding a way to the team's headquarters to request a tryout from team owner Tim Mara. Tunnell, the first African American player to sign with the Giants, rewarded Mara's faith in him by setting a franchise record for interceptions (74) and punt returns (261). Tunnell was such a high-class athlete that in 1952, his interception and kickoff return yards (923) bested the NFL's rushing leader at the time. Named to four first-team All-Pro teams and nine Pro Bowls, Tunnell, who bore the moniker "offense on defense," was one of the greatest players of his generation.

Osi Umenyiora, Defensive End (ROH 2015): Another critical defensive staple in the Giants' last two Super Bowl championship seasons (2007 and 2011), Umenyiora played in 10 seasons for the Giants, appearing in two Pro Bowls. In 2007, the year the Giants defense recorded a league-best 53 sacks, Umenyiora led the Giants with 13.

Brad Van Pelt, Linebacker (ROH 2011): Part of the famous "Crunch Bunch" linebacker crew of the early 1980s (which also featured Harry Carson, Brian Kelly, and Lawrence Taylor), Van Pelt was a five-time Pro Bowler from 1976 to 1980. His 143 games played as a Giant spanned four home stadiums and five head coaches.

Alex Webster, Running Back (ROH 2011): Webster spent his entire 10-year career in a Giants uniform. Currently fourth on the franchise's career list in rushing yards (4,638) and carries (1,196), Webster was the second-leading rusher and scorer and the third-leading receiver for the 1956 championship Giants, and a two-time Pro Bowl selection. Webster also served as the team's head coach from 1969 to 1973.

Arnold Weinmeister, Defensive Tackle (HOF 1984): Weinmeister played for the Giants during the 1950–53 seasons, proving to be ahead of his time by showing an uncanny ability to quickly read and diagnose plays and then proceeding to disrupt them. Weinmeister initially began his pro football career with the New York Yankees of the American Football Conference, where he played both sides of the ball. When he joined the Giants following the 1950 merger, he primarily played defense.

George Young, General Manager (ROH 2010, HOF 2020):
Hired as the team's first general manager to have full authority over
football personnel decisions, Young's arrival helped put an end to
the "Wilderness Years" as the Giants would go on to qualify for eight
playoff berths during his tenure. Young was instrumental in building two
Super Bowl–winning teams (1986 and 1990) as part of an impressive
165–145–2 record (including postseason) and was named NFL Executive
of the Year five times (1984, 1986, 1990, 1993, and 1997).

[Acknowledgments]

Thank you to my parents, my father, Al, who sadly passed away before this book was finished but who, despite his debilitating dementia, always wore his Giants jacket with pride, and my mom, Myrna, who fed my love of reading and writing when I was growing up with endless trips to the local library and bookstore.

Thank you to my brother, Michael, for taking that memorable journey around the state of Florida as we fought Mother Nature to get to Super Bowl XXV. You claimed you were a Jets fan, but we both know the truth.

Thank you to my husband, Lee, who not only was my rock when I was battling cancer, but who has also supported my career as a freelance writer. It's not easy not knowing whether you're going to be renewed from year to year, but when you have a supportive spouse behind you, it sure makes things a lot less scary.

To my beloved "fur baby," Molly, adopting and caring for you has easily been one of the best decisions I have ever made in my life. Thank you for coming to come to "supervise" me while I worked on this book, even if I didn't have any cookies for you during all your visits.

Thanks to the late Dr. Howard Livingston, the founder of *Inside Football* who took a chance on an untested and relatively unknown female writer who dreamed of one day covering Super Bowls, drafts, and NFL games. You taught me how to do the job the right way and are the reason why I've hung around as long as I have.

Thank you to Paul Dottino for picking up where Doc Livingston left off. Your passion for the game, your assistance, and your friendship have meant the world to me.

Much appreciation to Vinny DiTrani, the longtime Giants beat writer from *The Record*, who is now retired. Vinny is without question, *the* dean of the beat and the team historian. His insights and guidance were key in helping me better understand the impact of some of the chapters covering those events that preceded my time.

Thank you to my sister from another mother, Gail Bahr. Your friendship has meant the world to me. There's not a day that goes by when I don't think of you and those wonderful adventures we used to have when the Giants held training camp in Albany. I miss you terribly each day, but I feel you looking down on me from Heaven watching out for my every move.

Thank you to the Giants public relations team—Pat Hanlon, Corry Rush, Jen Conley, and Dion Dargin—and to Doug Murphy, the Giants director of creative services. Your cooperation and assistance with granting me access to your team archives, arranging interviews, and assisting me with photos and viewing artifacts for this project are deeply appreciated.

Thank you to all the players, coaches, front office folks, and league personnel for your help and your friendship over the years. I've learned so much about the game, about player personnel, scouting, and the salary cap through conversations and I have to say such knowledge has been a game changer in how I look at the game.

To the players who contributed to this book, thank you for not only the pleasure of watching you perform your craft every Sunday but for taking time from your lives to speak with me. It's been an honor to watch many of you grow into husbands, fathers, and coaches.

Thank you to Ernie Accorsi, for agreeing to write the foreword to this book and for all those times over President's Day weekend you'd allow me in your office to talk football.

To my readers—thank you for giving a writer named "Patricia" the benefit of the doubt for over 20 years. I still pinch myself when I hear from people not named "Traina" who willingly read my work and I promise to continue bringing you my best.

And finally, thank you to whoever lost that page from the old Carteret (New Jersey) Pop Warner football playbook which I found on the ground during my first-grade gym class. I was convinced it was a treasure map, but although my dad debunked that myth, it actually did turn out to be a treasure map because it led me to a rewarding career as a football writer that I wouldn't trade for any number of first-round draft picks.

[Bibliography]

Interview Subjects

Ernie Accorsi: Assistant General Manager, 1994–97, General Manager, 1998–2006

Raul Allegre: New York Giants, 1986–1991

Jessie Armstead: New York Giants, 1993–2001

Carl Banks: New York Giants, 1984–1992

Tiki Barber: New York Giants, 1997–2006

Harry Carson: New York Giants, 1976–1988, Pro Football Hall of Fame Inductee, 2006

Mark Collins: New York Giants, 1986–1993

Jeff Feagles: New York Giants, 2003–09

Brandon Jacobs: New York Giants, 2005–2011, 2013

Chris Mara: Senior Vice President of Player Personnel, New York Giants, 2011–present

John Mara: President and CEO, New York Giants, 1991–present

George Martin: New York Giants, 1975–1988

Leonard Marshall: New York Giants, 1983–1992

Phil McConkey: New York Giants, 1984–88

Shaun O'Hara: New York Giants, 2004–2010

Beasley Reece: New York Giants, 1977–1983

Rich Seubert: New York Giants, 2001–2010

Chris Snee: New York Giants, 2004–2013

Amani Toomer: New York Giants, 1996–2008

Lawrence Tynes: New York Giants, 2007–2012

David Tyree: New York Giants, 2003–08

Osi Umenyiora: New York Giants, 2003–2012

Books

Carson, Harry. *Captain for Life: My Story as a Hall of Fame Linebacker,* St. Martin's Press (2011).

Cruz, Victor. (with Peter Schrager). *Out of the Blue,* Celebra (2013).

DeVito, Carlo. *Wellington: The Maras, the Giants, and the City of New York,* Triumph Books (2006).

Giants 2019 Information Guide. New York Football Giants (2019).

Gifford, Frank (with Peter Richmond). *The Glory Game: How the 1958 NFL Championship Changed Football Forever.* HarperCollins Publishers (2009).

Gottehrer, Barry. *The Giants of New York. The History of Professional Football's Most Fabulous Dynasty.* G. P. Putnam's Sons (1963).

Huff, Sam, with Leonard Shapiro. *Tough Stuff: The Man in the Middle.* St. Martin's Press (1988).

Landry, Tom, with Gregg Lewis. *Tom Landry: An Autobiography.* Zanderson Publishing House, (1990).

Lewis, Michael. *The Blind Side: Evolution of a Game.* W. W. Norton & Company, (2007).

National Football League. *2019 Official National Football League 100th Season Record & Fact Book.* National Football League (2019).

O'Connor, Ian. *Belichick: The Making of the Greatest Football Coach of All Time.* Mariner Books, (2018).

Owen, Steve. *My Kind of Football,* D. McKay; 1st Edition (1952).

Palladino, Ernie. *Lombardi and Landry: How Two of Pro Football's Greatest Coaches Launched Their Legends and Changed the Game Forever.* Skyhorse Publishers (2011).

Strahan, Michael (with Jay Glazer). *Inside the Helmet: Life as a Sunday Afternoon Warrior.* Gotham Books (2007).

Taylor, Lawrence and David Faulkner. *LT: Living on the Edge.* Times Books (1987).

Tittle, Y.A. (with Kristine Setting Clark). *Nothing Comes Easy.* Triumph Books (2009)

Tunnell, Emlen (with William Gleason). *Footsteps of a Giant.* Doubleday (1966).

Whittingham, Richard. *Giants, in their own words.* Contemporary Books (1992).

Videos
30 for 30: The Two Bills, ESPN Films (2018)
America's Game: 2007 New York Giants Super Bowl XLII Championship,
NFL Films (2008)
Bill Parcells: Reflections on a Life in Football, NFL Films (2010)
NFL Total Access, January 2019
The Violent World of Sam Huff, The Twentieth Century (TV Series, 1960)
Top 10 Giants of All Time, NFL Network

Newspapers and Periodicals
New York Daily News
Smithsonian Magazine
Sports Illustrated
The Bergen Record
The Coffin Corner
The New York Times
The Post-Standard
The Star-Ledger

Films, Websites, etc.
Associated Press
Biography.com
ESPN.com
Giants.com
MentalFloss.com
Newspapers.com
NFL.com
ProFootballFocus.com
ProFootballHOF.com
ProFootballReference.com
ProFootballResearchers.org
SB Nation Buffalo Rumblings
The Players' Tribune
The Rich Eisen Show (2016)
Toomer, Amani and Dan Schwartz. *Going' Deep* podcast (2018)

University of Notre Dame – Department of Athletics
U.S. Coast Guard
U.S. Inflation Calculator
YouTube.com

[About the Author]

Patricia Traina has covered the New York Football Giants for over 20 seasons. She majored in English literature and minored in creative writing at Rutgers University, and completed a master's degree in corporate communications and public relations at Fairleigh Dickinson University.

In 2015, after more than 15 years as a contributing writer, she became one of the principle partners of *Inside Football*, an analytical, by-subscription only newsletter covering the Xs and Os of the Football Giants.

Patricia has covered three Giants Super Bowls and is a regular at Giants games, practices, and press conferences.

In addition to *Inside Football*, her work has appeared in Bleacher Report, The Athletic–New York City, SB Nation, Forbes, *Lindys Pro Football Preview*, and the Sports Xchange wire service. Patricia is currently the senior writer/managing editor of GiantsCountry.com, an SI.com sports channel, and is the host and producer of the *LockedOn Giants* podcast.

A cancer survivor, Patricia lives in New Jersey with her husband, Lee, and their rescue dog, Molly. She can be found on Twitter @Patricia_Traina.